walking
through
different
worlds

annoying people for good

*Inscribe for Dianna
with warm Ukrainian regards*

אויר פֿר מ

Philip Goldenberg has stimulated, encouraged, advised, supported, entertained and (just occasionally) infuriated me over the nearly three decades that I have known him. This book will do the same for you.

Philip has had an exceptionally diverse life, and thrown himself into every facet of it with much force and little tact. His candour can leave me gasping if we are talking over a drink, and it is astonishing and enjoyable to find it on the printed page. Still, as Philip is a very good lawyer, he must know what he is doing!

There are chapters on the law, business, national and local politics, Judaism, faith and antisemitism and the organisations in which he has played his part – from the CBI to the Liberal Democrats, from the RSA to Woking People of Faith. At different times Philip has made an impact on reform of company and pension law, the design of coalition governments, the running of companies, councils, charities and cemeteries, the departure of chairmen and chief executives, and the burial of the dead.

In the discussion of faith, I found an inner tolerance that readers might not necessarily associate with Philip's assertive and opinionated exterior. In the chapters on politics there is a healthy mixture of the determination to make things better and the combative partisanship in which political animals revel. I couldn't find a single cosmetic sentence: he calls a pig a pig, and doesn't bother with any lipstick!

Through the storytelling, the one-liners, the witty letters to the INDEPENDENT and the erudition emerges a patchwork history of the last five decades. and a reflective wisdom about what makes for good leadership, good politics, good governance and right living.

Mark Goyder, Founder Director, Tomorrow's Company

walking through *different* worlds

annoying people for good

PHILIP GOLDENBERG

The Book Guild Ltd

First published in Great Britain in 2019 by
The Book Guild Ltd
9 Priory Business Park
Wistow Road, Kibworth
Leicestershire, LE8 0RX
Freephone: 0800 999 2982
www.bookguild.co.uk
Email: info@bookguild.co.uk
Twitter: @bookguild

Typeset in 12pt Sabon MT

Printed and bound in the UK by TJ International, Padstow, Cornwall

ISBN 978 1912881 567

British Library Cataloguing in Publication Data.
A catalogue record for this book is available from the British Library.

"From quiet homes and first beginning,
Out to the undiscovered ends,
There's nothing worth the wear of winning,
But laughter and the love of friends."

Hilaire Belloc, who was more famous his for humorous writings than as a Liberal MP, but who may have written some of the former while engaged in the more boring aspects of the latter.

This book is dedicated to my wife, Lynda, who has inexplicably put up with me for over 30 years, and to my surviving children Pippa, Ben and Josh; and is also written in loving memory of our eldest son Jonathan[1], who was born with the dreadful genetic condition of **Tuberous Sclerosis Complex** (TSC) and died in 2009, aged 23.

---

1   When he was aged three, I wrote a long piece about him, which was published in a local paper – not least to use my public position to help to de-stigmatise mental-health issues – and I followed it with a piece in *SCAN* (the magazine of the Tuberous Sclerosis Association [TSA]) six years later. These pieces appear after the preface.

HOUSE OF COMMONS
LONDON SW1A 0AA
15 April 1986

To Lynda,

Thank you for your letter of 8 April. I hope your celebration for Philip goes well.

I am not sure I have an anecdote, but I am happy to say:

"I like calling on Philip for help and advice. He is one of those rare lawyers who can explain a financial or technical issue to you, and leave you clearer at the end of his explanation than you were at the beginning.

My only concern is that the conception of his child during the party assembly in Dundee may have occurred during my speech, in which case I can think of few more pleasurable acts of disloyalty to his leader!"

I was 39 when I married Lynda. For my 40th birthday the following year, she garnered contributions to a "This is Your Life So Far" collection. More in hope than expectation, she wrote to David Steel. This was his response – typically both kind and witty.

Contents

List of Articles

Preface

It was at my 70th birthday lunch. Two rocks of my life – not least because they are both called Peter – said that I should write a book. I was, at best, agnostic. My wife, Lynda, was very enthusiastic, mainly because she likes finding things for me to do, so that I don't bug her. I accordingly gave the idea some thought.

I'm not a big name, so I would be very unlikely to find a publisher on a strictly commercial basis (my late and great father Nathan wrote an autobiography – neatly entitled *Thought for Food*[1] – of his remarkable career, not least as Marks & Spencer's [M&S'] chief food technologist, but this only succeeded because M&S financed its publication). Nor did I think that a conventional autobiography would be appropriate. But it did occur to me that I could usefully write about (and maybe a bit around) my involvement with various organisations, not least because, with a multifaceted career, I had learned from each organisation and – I hope – used that learning and experience to the benefit of the others.

So, this book starts by setting the scene with a brief autobiographical note of my life up to graduation, and then reflects my experiences of the various "worlds" in which I have engaged: law, politics, business, charity and religion. One of the key issues is that they are all too often very separate worlds, which are so rooted in their own cultural silos that they are incapable of understanding

---

1   Published by Food Trade Press Limited, March 1989, ISBN 0 900379 35 9, and see also the charming textbox at pp 127/9 of *The Grocers* by Seth and Randall, published by Kogan Page in 1999 ISBN 0 7494 2191 6.

each other. I then write a brief note on anti-Semitism, which exists, should not be swept under the carpet and which has – without doubt – had an adverse effect on my career path. At the end, I attempt to derive some conclusions from my observations. I have appended some articles by or about me to some chapters, and at the end.

One additional point: I did think fairly hard about both the principle of "naming names" and the detailed application of that principle. I concluded that this book would have little validity if I had anonymised all the references (except that I have, in Chapter 4, omitted the names of almost all TSA staff), but I hope that I have been fair, reasonable and constructive in my observations. I have at any rate tried! And, of course, many comments relate to distant events, so may not now apply.

Lastly, one of the other speakers at my birthday lunch was my former assistant and subsequently Conservative MP, Jonathan Djanogly. He kindly wrote a hagiography of me for *The Guardian*. It appears at the end of this preface, and I'm happy for it to stand as my monument.

Philip Goldenberg
MMXIX

Caring concern is vital to the understanding and support of the handicapped child

DISCOVERING that one's child has a serious medical problem is something that happens to other people — until it happens to you. Then the 1 in 10,000 statistic becomes a 100 per cent reality, writes Woking councillor Philip Goldenberg

Jonathan was born on May 28, 1986: the much wanted first child of Lynda and myself in what was a second marriage for both of us.

During August and September, he developed a habit of jerky movements at the time of feeding. Health visitor and GP both assumed colic. But the medicine did not cure the problem and there were signs of arrested development. Eventually the worried parents kicked sufficiently hard that they had to be pacified by a referral to the local consultant paediatrician.

The paediatrician looked, prodded and thought. His mind, too, was stomach-directed. Then Jonathan suddenly gave a demonstration of the symptoms. An immediate provisional diagnosis of infantile spasms followed, to be confirmed the following day by an electro-encephalogram test. One day later, Jonathan was in hospital for a week with a cortisone-type treatment which had limited, but beneficial, effects.

The symptoms, however, continued, and were treated with pheno-barbitone — the only anti-convulsant for a small baby. Unfortunately, however, as a central nervous system depressant, this reinforced the developmental problems.

The paediatrician gave us the odds. 20 per cent of babies with infantile spasms simply grew out of them; in 50 per cent of cases they continued into adult epilepsy with no known cause; and in the remaining 30 per cent of cases a cause would be identified.

We wanted greater certainty, and were worried not so much by the epilepsy — Alexander the Great, Julius Caesar and Napoleon had coped — as by the developmental prospects. Could we please be referred to Great Ormond Street? Yes, of course.

While this was pending, the paediatrician, having a routine look at Jonathan, felt something peculiar about the shape of his kidney. An ultrasound scan, which an unprepared and horrified Lynda saw as it was done, showed one kidney nearly non-existent and the other with a number of holes. At this stage, we suspect in retrospect, the paediatrician guessed the truth.

At Great Ormond Street, a kindly top child neurologist looked, prodded and thought. To our surprise, he asked to look at Jonathan all over, and inspected his skin closely. Depigmented patches told him what he wanted to know, but he was not going to tell us until the diagnosis was confirmed. Jonathan would be admitted for a week of tests.

Within two days of admission, and coincidentally when I had just walked in from the office, the neurologist appeared in Jonathan's cubicle. He gave us a confirmed diagnosis of Tuberous Sclerosis, saying that a definitive developmental prognosis was not possible. "Sometimes" he said by way of intended consolation "there are quite pleasing late developments." The significance of this comment only sank in slowly. "Would the phrase 'Pessimism tinged with cautious optimism' be right?," I inquired. He assented and disappeared.

It is difficult to say exactly how we came to realise that our son was, in fact, severely mentally handicapped. I suppose it was a gradual process, and the doctors probably intended it to be so. And we can — at times — rationalise our distress by reflecting that a physical handicap would have concerned Jonathan more, while a mental handicap distresses him less, whatever it does to us. I suspect this is a rationalisation, and he is becoming more aware that something is wrong — which is in itself a good sign of development.

Since then, we and our paediatrician have been trying — and it can only be empirical — to find the optimum combination of drugs to control Jonathan's fits (which hinder this development) without so depressing his activity as to hinder his development. We have so far failed, but err on the side of lower dosages if he can thereby be more active without the fits being too severe. We are about to try a ketogenic diet, which seems to work in some cases for reasons that nobody quite seems to understand.

The most difficult thing to cope with is the uncertainty. We simply don't know — nor does any doctor — where on the scale of mental handicap Jonathan will end up. We have learned — or we have tried to learn — not to be excessively encouraged (or discouraged) on a short-term basis. His special school — into which we got him at the age of two-and-a-half! — has clearly helped. So has a very caring nanny. And we have had to learn the patience to take his development at his pace, and be thrilled by occasional improvements which would be unnoticed in a normal child. One certainly develops a sense of proportion!

We have found it easy — surprisingly so — to be open about the problem with our contemporaries. A support group can be — and the TSA has been — a source of strength. But an older generation still has a sense of irrational shame about mental handicap. And I can feel in myself a psychological resistance to going public, as I am today, almost as if I was "coming out," reinforced by a fear that, as a prominent member of my own community and a small player on the national stage, I may be thought to be courting some kind of public sympathy.

Lynda and I decided to do so for two key reasons:

— to make our own contribution to combating the irrational stigma that attaches to mental handicap

— to help the TSA's appeal for funds for medical research, so that the condition will be capable of in utero detection and others can avoid our problems.

As parents of a TS child, we do not ask for sympathy. Indeed, we find it difficult to cope with sympathy — it makes us feel sorry for ourselves, which is an emotion that saps our energies. We do ask for support — from family, friends and colleagues, and from a wider community.

The Tuberous Sclerosis Association (TSA) aims to act as a mutual support group for parents and sufferers, sharing problems and ideas; provide information on TS to families, doctors and others and sponsor medical research into the treatment and prevention and cure of TS. Established in 1977, funding for research began in 1980 and research commenced in 1982. Recently the TSA launched a national appeal and donations can be sent to The Honorary Appeals Officer, Tuberous Sclerosis Association of Great Britain, 127 Boxley Drive, Wilford Hill, West Bridgford, Nottingham NG2 7GN.

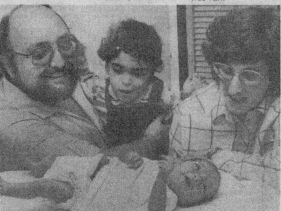

Philip, Jonathan and Lynda Goldenberg pictured with new baby sister Phillippa at their Woking home last year.

1989: Woking News & Mail,

article about Jonathan

GETTING THROUGH THE SYSTEM

Jonathan Goldenberg - now in residential care and schooling

Jonathan, now aged 9½ presented with infantile spasms at three months and was thereafter diagnosed with TS. His fits and anti-convulsant drugs inevitably retarded his development further. His pharmacist Mother, Lynda, eventually stabilised him on vigabatrin and epanutin. He was admitted to special school at 2½ and learned to walk at 6. He clearly has moods and emotions, and can communicate them; subject to that, he is aphasic, and needs total care. He has severe behavioural problems, including self-injury. His mental age is about 2½. His Father, Philip, takes up the story.

Jonathan's medical care was superb; his (day) Special School good; and Social Services back-up non-existent until 1993, when a word by Philip in the right political ear caused Social Services to take a sudden interest in his case. However, his fragmented care package was clearly inadequate, and Jonathan regularly lost developmental momentum during school holidays.

How was this to be achieved?

It was clear - albeit emotionally painful - that the right solution was residential schooling, preferably as part of a village for the severely handicapped.

The Education Authority were unsympathetic. They argued that his educational needs were adequately met by day schooling with normal term lengths.

Social Services, with a new locality purchasing manager, were much more responsive, being prepared to take a holistic view of Jonathan's needs. They offered to fund half the cost, with some help from the Health Authority (at Social Services' request).

All this came together in February 1995, with the (somewhat delayed) annual review of Jonathan's Statement of Special Educational Needs. Supported by Social Services, we put forward the case for residential schooling. This was considered, but subsequently rejected, by the Education Authority.

I therefore formally dissented from the new draft Statement proposed by the Education Authority. In doing so, I took specialist legal advice. The solicitor concerned had been rendered cynical by his experience; one local authority officer had said to him, on an off-the-record basis, that they prioritised special needs as follows: (1) those whose parents had instructed solicitors who had appealed against the authority's statement to the Special Educational Needs Tribunal (2) those whose parents had instructed solicitors who had threatened to do so and (3) anybody else! He also taught me that authorities' (unlawfully) write statements that do not specify the *actual* service needed (eg a specified number of hours of speech therapy each week rather than just a general need for speech therapy).

Following our refusal to accept the draft Statement, the Education Authority produced a definitive Statement which, although somewhat altered, was in effect unchanged. We appealed it to the Tribunal, which has now built up a six-month waiting list (parents are gradually becoming aware of their rights).

At this stage, I went   see a senior Councillor on the Local Authority. He and his political colleagues had long believed that, in the case of children with special needs, Education and Social Services should work together. He was appalled to find a case in which there was to be an appeal against their own Education Department with their Social Services department giving evidence on the other side.

He said so (as a matter of general principle rather than being an advocate in our particular case) in a letter to the Head of Special Educational Needs. A few weeks later, as I was about to incur the expense of an independent educational psychologist to report on Jonathan's needs, the telephone rang at my office. It was the Head of Special Educational Needs, conceding gracefully, and agreeing that the Education Authority would fund its share of Jonathan's residential schooling.

This broke a vicious circle, in that the residential school which had previously indicated that it would take Jonathan would not award a place without a guarantee of funding. It now offered a place, and Jonathan, after a transitional period, moved in finally on 29 October.

To be blunt, we were lucky. As Jonathan's parents, we combined the resources of a solicitor and former Councillor (Philip) and a pharmacist and former member of the Community Health Council (Lynda). Social Services only took a serious interest in us after political pressure. We had a Social Services Manager who was persuaded of our needs, and a doughty advocate. We knew how to, and did, find specialist legal advice. We persuaded the Education Authority that it would look foolish defending its position (a general benefit has been that the Local Authority has now changed its policy, and has integrated Education and Social Services assessments). And finally, we interested the INDEPENDENT in publishing an article on the whole issue of unmet special educational needs (31 August 1995).

I hope that other parents in a similar situation will find this article of use in enabling them to obtain for their child, as we have for ours, the support he needs.

1995: SCAN, article about Jonathan

My legal hero: Philip Goldenberg

A man who saw the legal profession and politics as twin routes to solve problems and create the wheels to get things done

Jonathan Djanogly

Thu 2 Dec 2010 14.03 GMT

Philip Goldenberg at the Weizman Institute International Board Meeting. Photograph: Assaf Shilo/Israel Sun Ltd

What makes a good lawyer? The underlying discipline was drummed into me by my first boss on qualifying as a solicitor, Philip Goldenberg. A man who, like me, saw the legal profession and politics as twin routes to solve people's problems and create the wheels to get things done.

It was 1990 at the international law firm SJ Berwin when I first visited Philip's office as his new junior lawyer. It was like a bull being provided with a farmhand dressed head to toe in bright red. He described himself physically as looking like a "walking Trotskyite conspiracy". Office talk was that he was intellectually intimidating and didn't suffer fools. I would need to learn quickly.

Philip's legal reasoning was as fast and cutting as his wit. I have never met anyone who could quite so formidably and effortlessly take a complicated scenario, think so comprehensively around the issue and then apply such a combination of logic, strategy and practicality to creating a solution.

He taught me that it's not good enough just to have a powerful argument. A lawyer has to present it powerfully too, whether on paper or in person. He had that knack of finding the perfect words to inject the maximum meaning in the minimum space. He then wrapped his argument in impeccable grammar so that the raw nub of any issue was exposed to the full, without interference.

Shoddy grammar was unforgivable. Had he been elected to parliament on one of his half-dozen attempts, I'm sure he would have wasted no time in introducing a bill to criminalise the unprovoked use of split infinitives. Letters to clients drafted other than with the use of the conditional tense where appropriate were invariably described as inelegant.

If anyone else failed to meet his high standards, they had to improve quickly because that was the quality the client was paying for. My first piece of work was returned to me awash with red ink and a big 0 out of 10 at the bottom. My second piece of work was equally rosy with two red circles drawn in the middle. I enquired what this meant. Without breaking concentration from his Latin verse drafting (which constituted his lunchtime relaxation), he simply said "it means it's balls". Maximum meaning in minimum space.

So from a hard taskmaster I learned to deal with hard tasks and eventually rose to be a partner myself. Along the way our separate political careers were proceeding alongside our professional and personal relationship.

Philip has made massive contributions to politics over the years. He has served the Liberal Democrat cause well both nationally and as a long-serving councillor in Woking. Much of politics is about legislation and agreements and he showed me not just the value of a lawyer but the value of a lawyer to politics.

His prolific public policy work over the years has included a key role in the conception and enactment of the profit-sharing provisions in the 1978 Finance Act, and his work on directors' duties as legal adviser to the RSA's Tomorrow's Company inquiry, which found its way into the 2006 Companies Act.

He advised the former Liberal party on its merger with the SDP and co-authored the original Constitution of the Liberal Democrats; and his 1990s work for Paddy Ashdown on the machinery of government needed for a coalition government has been used for the Scottish Executive in 1999 and the present coalition government in which I serve.

This is a pleasing sequel to our passionate debates on whatever happened to be in the papers on any given day, which normally concluded in the much-heard mantra: "Shut up, Jonathan, and get on with your work."

I did get on with my work and bit by bit I learned what was needed to become a lawyer and a politician. Philip was always very strong on always looking for lessons to be learned - as you might expect from an Oxford classicist. I'm sure he still is. I fully expect to receive a copy of this article in my post tomorrow morning with the grammar corrected and very possibly a pair of red circles drawn in the middle.

Jonathan Djanogly is Conservative MP for Huntingdon and parliamentary under-secretary of state at the Ministry of Justice with responsibility for legal aid and HM courts service

2010: The Guardian, *"My Legal Hero"*

1

Me

Family and Home

I was lucky to arrive at all. My parents' wish to have children had been hindered by a stillbirth, followed by a miscarriage. They decided to have one more try. As the late Lord Hailsham observed when asked why he should be a legislator by the accident of birth, "My birth was not an accident!"

My parents[1] had an interesting background, being – directly or indirectly – products of the Pale of Settlement. This is the area stretching from Odessa at its south-eastern extremity through Ukraine[2] to the Baltic States, and is the place in which Catherine the Great of Russia confined the Jews (whom she disliked) in rural poverty, as poignantly recorded in the musical *Fiddler on the Roof*. I set out this background in the following speech at the Weizmann Institute in Israel in 2010, when, in the presence of its President, I dedicated a Career Development Chair to their memory using a large legacy that my mother had (with my full agreement) left to the Weizmann Institute, Israel's premier scientific research institution:

---

1   Obituaries of my father appeared in *The Times* and *The Jewish Chronicle* in February 1995, and the obituary of my mother appeared in *The Independent* in January 1910. The second and third of these are reproduced at the end of this chapter.

2   For the history of Ukraine, see *Borderland* by Anna Reid (2015).

Mr President, I am told that you have a Belgian background. At the end of the Second World War, Winston Churchill visited Brussels. Addressing a large crowd in the central square, he commenced with, "Messieurs, Mesdames, prenez garde – je vais parler français! [Ladies, gentlemen, be warned – I am going to speak French!]"

So, Adon Hanasi, rabotai, gevirotai [Mr President, ladies, gentlemen], don't worry; for your sake and mine, this will be in English!

I am here to discharge my duty under the fifth commandment, lechabed et horai [to honour my parents], whose names this new career-development chair will permanently memorialise. It was a very appropriate bequest by my late mother, of which I wholly approved. It reflects my parents' joint commitment to the State of Israel, and also my late father's commitment to scientific excellence, and to its practical application, which he did so much to promote – both generally in his work as Marks and Spencer's chief food technologist, in which he revolutionised the British food production industry – and particularly in the help and support he gave to the Israeli food industry.

So, let me tell you a bit about them: a classic story of two lives shaped by the fate of European Jewry.

My father, Nathan, was born 99 years ago in a small village called Bohuslav[3], outside Kiev. It is painfully remembered in an SS signal on 15 September 1941, exhibited in [the Jerusalem Holocaust Museum] Yad VaShem, reporting that, "As a result of the execution of 322 Jews and communist functionaries, the town of Bohuslav is now free of Jews." His family escaped after the 1917 revolution. His father went ahead to London; there are photographs of him and others boarding a small boat at an unidentified location.

---

3   My wife, Lynda, and I took our 2018 holiday in Ukraine and fitted in a visit to Bohuslav. See the article reproduced at the end of this chapter.

In 1921, my father's mother, and my father and his next brother, hired a cart and driver, travelled by night, slept by day, and were shot at as they crossed the Polish border. In Warsaw, after they had acquired Nansen passports and were about to travel to London, my father contracted scarlet fever. His mother, who – surprisingly for a Jewess – was a doctor in the Red Army, nursed him across Europe on a 1920s train, without notifying the authorities.

Arriving in England without speaking a word of English, he attended secondary school and then became a research chemist at Lyons, while obtaining his BSc, then MSc in chemistry, through night study at Birkbeck College.

Of Russian and Latvian ancestry, my mother, Edith, was born in Johannesburg in 1913. The family came to England in the 1920s, and lived in the East End. Edith's dentist father, Boris, in whose memory my late mother endowed the Boris Drusinsky office here at the Weizmann Institute, died during my mother's teenage years. There is actually a Drusinsky genealogy on an Israeli website, and I recently discovered from my mother's papers that I had a second cousin of whom I was previously unaware: a lawyer called Tony Leon, who was leader of the Opposition in the South African parliament. So, clearly, law and politics entered my gene pool at an early stage!

A highly intelligent girl, Edith would – in a different era – have starred at university. But family and general culture, and a very dominant mother, denied her this privilege.

Following her father's death, my mother's family moved to Palestine, where Edith was a secretary with the Jaffa Port Authority. But, before they moved, Edith – who was a very beautiful girl and a very sociable animal – had met Nathan through HaBonim. The move did not prevent a continuing friendship, and, eventually, Nathan travelled [steerage!] to Palestine to propose. They returned to be married in London in 1937, although Nathan was actually offered a job here at the

Weizmann Institute by Chaim Weizmann, which makes this bequest particularly appropriate. Nathan was an active Zionist, being – in the 1930s – president of the British Federation of Zionist Youth. Indeed, the Chanukiah given to him on his wedding was inscribed inter alios by his friends Abba Eban and Abe Harman, names recalling an era when Israel had visionary statesmen rather than its present pygmy ministers.

My parents worked for, and rejoiced in, the establishment of Medinat Yisrael, and were committed supporters for the rest of their lives; in particular, my father – as well as his technical work – was ever-active in fund-raising through the Joint Israel Appeal.

So, as their only child, I find it entirely right that their names should be remembered for ever by the establishment of this career-development chair. I was very impressed, Mr President, by the thought, care and humanity with which you engaged in a personal and lengthy email dialogue with me as to the best use for my parents' bequest; a dialogue in which we both concluded that it is people rather than buildings who are at the heart and forefront of scientific progress. And thank you also for extending nomination consultation rights not only to me but to my wife, Lynda – a mathematician and physicist who is with me today – and thereafter to my daughter Philippa, who has just graduated in physics from Durham University. As I am a mere classicist, their judgment will be much better than mine!

It is, therefore, with a mixture of both pride and humility, and sadness and joy, that I now formally endow the Edith & Nathan Goldenberg Career Development Chair, and welcome Dr Assaf Vardi as its first distinguished incumbent.

School

As with many immigrants, my parents' hopes rested in my success. They gave me a secure home background, although it was coupled with a well-meaning but wrong wish to run my life for me – I learned from my experience not to repeat this approach with my own children.

At age seven, they removed me from the local primary school, where I could coast along happily, to the much greater intellectual challenge of the preparatory school for St Paul's: Colet Court.[4] This represented a significant financial burden, and curtailed their lifestyle – particularly, holiday – choices. I did at least make a contribution by winning a scholarship from Colet Court to St Paul's itself.

The Pauline education at that time was based, in vehicular terms, on trams rather than taxis. There were set and invariable combinations of subjects to be taken in the sixth form (curiously called the eighth form there), and a distinct hierarchy – those thought best on the arts side were directed to classics, the next tranche to history with French, and the alleged dullards to geography and economics. The idea of grouping together modern languages, which I would have selected given a free choice, was a bit too revolutionary for a school that had been founded in 1509, by Dean John Colet, to teach Latin and Greek to 153 scholars – the number of fish found in the New Testament's "miraculous draught". It was a rather good joke at the school's Annual Review in 1959, when a spoof TV interviewer interrogated the ghost of Colet as to what changes he foresaw 450 years later, and received the reply, "Some of the staff may have aged slightly!" Indeed, the whole school reeked of antiquity: churchy, sporty, corporal punishment and with a number of staff with paedophiliac tendencies, which in those days were less well controlled than they should have been. (Rather like with clerical institutions, those who misbehaved were moved elsewhere without being required to make any behavioural changes). Only very belatedly in 2017 was there a proper safeguarding inquiry, to which I gave evidence.

I had shown promise in Latin and Greek in my first year, so was directed to the Classics Department.

After a year in which there was at least some residual connection with other subjects, there followed two years in which alternate weeks

---

4   The most amusing moment during my prep-school attendance was when a Latin master said, "Boy, translate '*melius est amari quam timeri*' [it is better to be loved than to be feared] – to give you a clue, it's how we as teachers govern our behaviour to you."
The pupil replied, "It is better to be armed than to be afraid."[!]

of 35 periods included 29 periods of either Latin or Greek. The simple objective was to produce the annual yield of Oxbridge classical scholarships, which the school could advertise to prospective parents. In my case it worked well; by the time the objective was attained, I could translate Shakespeare sonnets into either Latin or Greek verse. In the case of Greek, this was in spite of the fact that the Greek master was a member of the British bridge team (he also captained England at croquet!), and taught us both Greek and bridge simultaneously.

But it left me woefully ignorant of so many of the building blocks of life. I had no real knowledge of non-classical literature, of history after the Golden Age of Rome, or of science or its methodology. I had never been challenged to think conceptually; a narrow-minded academic forcing house had given me no real opportunity to do this.

And, beyond the sheltered world that I had hitherto inhabited, I had no knowledge of civic society or how organisations worked; and my interpersonal skills were positively antediluvian. This was remedied in some small part by my parents' decision to give me life experiences, by sending me abroad twice between leaving school in December 1963 and starting university in October 1964.

So, I had a two-month *stage* (traineeship) in Paris, where my father used the power of M&S to allow me to infiltrate the head office of the French retailer Monoprix. On my first day, I was directed to the sub-department dealing with the buying of lingerie – at least that was the better explanation of the collection of diaphanous garments in its head of department's filing cabinet! I then spent a further four months in Israel, of which the first two were on a non-English speaking kibbutz, where I learned both Hebrew and viticulture.

University

To what extent would four years in Oxford remedy my deficiencies?

I was now in a position to pursue my interest in politics. The Oxford University Liberal Club ("OULC"), and the Oxford Union, were certainly two bedrocks of my time there. I enjoyed the company of like-minded people, while gradually coming to realise the extent to which people had personal agendas that were not always compatible with the best interests of the organisations they purported to serve. I held office in both organisations.

In the latter, I developed an aptitude and liking for public speaking. I discovered that the sense of power experienced by a speaker carrying an audience with him is truly amazing. In my final year, I was invited to propose – in the freshers' debate – a motion advocating the decriminalisation of the personal use of cannabis. I had simply not thought how much the audience, who were attending their first Oxford Union debate, would want it to match its reputation, and therefore would will the speakers to succeed. My opening line, "Mr President, it has been argued that this motion is disreputable, and that – accordingly – a person of unimpeachable integrity has been selected to propose it. I resolutely deny both these allegations," brought the house down, and carried me through the rest of my speech.

I also encountered the intrigue that is an unavoidable aspect of politics; as the late Dick Crossman pointed out in a speech to the Cambridge Union, "politics" is not confined to Westminster and Whitehall, but is part of the lifeblood of most organisations.

Additionally, I developed a talent for what subsequently became known as "media management". To exemplify this, the OULC held an annual election for vice presidents, assisted by the consumption of a modicum of Pimms. Harold Wilson had been treasurer of the club while he was an undergraduate, and was shortly thereafter elected to one of these posts to mark his appointment as Prime Minister. He was de-selected the following year, at which time one of his successors was a witch who had also addressed the club.

It was an obvious gift to me as the club's press officer, and I obtained six column feet of national coverage for the story "Witch beats Wilson in Oxford Election", some American coverage to boot (in *The Washington Post*, as a result of which I received a letter from an American nutcase who listed the witches in his family!) and the following cartoon in a national newspaper:

The Prime Minister today lost an election for continued honorary membership of the Oxford University Liberal Club. His place was taken by Mrs Eleanor Bone, High Priestess of the Worshipful Coven of London Witches.—"

One use of my media management skills was, however, more controversial. An incoming president of the club naïvely considered that it would be a good exercise of the liberal principle of free speech to invite a German neo-fascist as a speaker. He gave no thought to the consequences for German politics of thus giving status to this dreadful person. I used my media contacts to give this national publicity, and the resultant pressure forced the cancellation of this undesirable event. I lost some support over this, but had no regrets.

One of the curious features of the OULC, which is shared with other long-standing university Liberal clubs, is the right to propose members for the National Liberal Club ("NLC"), which a number of us joined in this way. Incredibly, for a Liberal club, the NLC at that time did not admit women as full members. So it came to pass that the OULC proposed, among others, one Hilary Wright. The NLC secretary wrote to me, as OULC secretary, seeking my confirmation that the applicant was a male.

With my tongue firmly in my cheek, I replied that the application "conformed in every respect with the rules of the club" (which it did under the standard rules of interpretation). Hilary received a letter accepting the application, and asking that he sign the Members Book when first visiting the club. The visit duly occurred in March 1967 on the day before Jeremy Thorpe was to be honoured at a luncheon as the incoming leader of the Liberal Party, with Miss Wright being accompanied by me, together with a reporter and photographer from the "William Hickey's Diary" section of the *Daily Express*, which led with the story the following morning. This did not escape Jeremy's notice, and he enjoyed gently teasing the club establishment, some of whose more outraged members suggested that I should be locked in a room with a bottle of whisky and a revolver, and left to do the decent thing!

Academically, I trod water in the first half of my classics course, getting a decent second in my first public examination. At that time (with shades of St Paul's), the classics course was inflexible, and I was very uncertain as to how (if, indeed, at all) I would cope with the conceptual thinking that would be involved in the history and philosophy of which the second half of the course consisted. So, I opted to move over to Hebrew and Arabic, which rapidly turned out to be a mistake, as the Hebrew was incredibly badly taught by English clergymen who had no feel for the language. I retreated back to classics, and the philosophy course eventually succeeded in endowing me with conceptual thought; I emerged with a reasonable second.

I had not given early consideration to my career choice. My father had always thought I was a natural for law, but he had the sense not to suggest it until – in a conversation with him – I mentioned it as a possibility. He then moved with lightning speed, and – through M&S – I was given some summer work experience at the end of my third year with their City of London solicitors, the "magic circle" firm of Linklaters. That led to an application, and acceptance, for articles, at a time when the largest City firms had not yet been leaned on to take on appropriate numbers of articled clerks, so only hired six or so a year. In retrospect, I was very lucky.

NATHAN GOLDENBERG

Born Boguslav, near Kiev, September 4, 1911. Died London, January 26, 1995, aged 83.

Nathan Goldenberg was a key figure in the development of food technology and, in particular, the growth of Marks & Spencer's food business. As head of the company's food technical services from 1948-72, he broke new ground in food procurement, raising stands for the industry both in Britain and Israel.

He inherited his scientific ability from his mother, who had graduated as a doctor from Kiev University — a remarkable achievement for a Jewish girl in Tsarist Russia. His father was an ardent early Zionist, whose love of Israel and the Hebrew language he continued in his own career.

He was the first president of the Federation of Zionist Youth in 1936, campaigning for Jewish immigration into Palestine, and was a member of the Zionist Federation executive for 23 years.

In 1920, the family fled the Ukrainian pogroms in a narrow escape, described in Nathan's autobiography, "Food for Thought." He went to Latymer Upper School in London and obtained a first-class science degree and MSc at London University's Birkbeck College. He studied at night, while working by day as a junior research chemist at the food company, J. Lyons and Co. He continued his work on foods during the Second World War, and became a senior research chemist for Lyons.

Through his ZF involvement, he met Sir Simon Marks, chairman of Marks & Spencer, who engaged him in 1948 as technical executive and chief chemist to the food division, with responsibility for the company's food development.

Nate, as he was known, set up an analytical laboratory against considerable opposition from those who

Nathan Goldenberg: raised standards of British food

thought that food production was a craft, not a science.

He played a key part in establishing hygiene standards for all M & S staff catering units. This work formed the basis for similar standards in the production and handling of food products for sale in the stores.

He demanded that raw materials were traced back to source. Despite the difficulty of persuading growers to change their ways, he was uncompromising and succeeded in overturning time-honoured practices, such as drying fruit on the ground. With his incisive mind, he was always courteous but firm.

In setting the pattern for the methods of today's M & S technologists, he indirectly influenced other large food retailers. He made numerous trips to Israel, where he contributed significantly to the country's developing agriculture and food-processing industries.

A founder member of the food trade committee of the Joint Israel Appeal, he was its deputy chairman for six years, as well as a member of the JIA national executive and cam-

paign executive committees. He was a founding member of the food committee of the British-Israel Chamber of Commerce in 1969. He became joint chairman when Lord Sainsbury retired in 1974.

From 1964-75, he was a member of the food additives and contaminants committee of the Ministry of Agriculture, Fisheries and Food, and of the UK Baking Industry Consultative Committee. He was the author or co-author of some 90 scientific papers on a huge variety of subjects within the food industry.

After retiring from M & S in 1972, he remained as scientific adviser until 1985 and also advised a number of major suppliers to the company. He was appointed OBE in 1976, made an honorary fellow of the Haifa Technion in 1977, and awarded the President of Israel's medal for industry in 1979.

He is survived by his wife, Edith, son and grandchildren.

Rabbi Dr Louis Jacobs writes: Outwardly shy and reserved, Nathan Goldenberg soon revealed his warm, caring nature to his many friends. Critical and unswerving in his pursuit of truth, he was at the same time emotionally and unquestioningly involved in the life of the Jewish people.

He and his life's partner, Edith, were among the founder members of the New London Synagogue, assisting us in its early struggles and far beyond.

1995: The Jewish Chronicle, *Nathan Goldenberg Obituary*

Lives Remembered

Edith Goldenberg

EDITH GOLDENBERG, who died on 12 January 2010 a month before her 97th birthday, was very much an individual. But she was above all a classic Jewish matriarch who cared deeply about her family.

Of Russian ancestry, Edith was born in Johannesburg in 1913. The family came to England in the 1920s and lived in the East End. Edith's dentist father died in her teens. A highly intelligent girl, Edith would, in a different era,

have starred at university. But family and general culture, and a very dominant mother to whom Edith was notably more obedient than was her somewhat colourful sister, denied her this privilege.

Following her father's death the family moved to Palestine, where Edith was a secretary with the Jaffa Port Authority. But before they moved, Edith, who was a very beautiful and a very social animal, had met Nathan through the Jewish youth movement HaBonim. The move did not prevent a continuing friendship, and eventually Nathan travelled (in steerage!) to Palestine to propose.

They returned to Britain and were married in 1937, although Nathan, who was then a research chemist at Lyons (having arrived in England aged if not

speaking a word of English), was offered a job at the Weizmann Institute. I was born in 1946, their only son following a miscarriage and a stillbirth. In 1948, Nathan moved to Marks & Spencer to head up their new Food Technology Department – a job in which he revolutionised the British food production industry.

Following her marriage, Edith worked for the Ophthalmic Benefits Council. After a maternity break, she was a company secretary and director with a medium-sized business. She was a brilliant dancer (Gold Star in both Ballroom and Latin American). But she was also a wonderful support to Nathan in all his work - although Nathan kept in his desk a piece of paper saying "Behind every successful man is a woman telling him that he's

doing the wrong thing"! Edith took enormous pride in my own progress, in law, politics, business and the voluntary sector. If her pride sometimes shaded into attempted over-possessiveness, it was nevertheless well-intentioned. Interaction between us was not always easy. On one memorable occasion, Edith said "You're very obstinate," to which she got the scathing yet loving retort, "And where do you think I got that from?" But Edith, who had a sharp sense of humour, had the grace to laugh.

After Nathan's death in 1995, Edith remained firmly - or obstinately - independent. She survived one piece of medical mismanagement by the NHS, and two falls - the second of which necessitated a hip replacement at the age of 93. Eventually, in spring

2009, to my shocked relief, she accepted the inevitable, and moved into Clore Manor, where she was well cared for. Her move made our relationship infinitely easier, and we really enjoyed her last months until she went into steep decline a month ago.

She died in peace, comfort and dignity in the superb care of Barnet General Hospital.

Philip Goldenberg

2010: The Independent, *Edith Goldenberg Obituary*

As journalists are taught, a picture is worth a thousand words. This one shows Philip and Lynda standing in front of a statue of the Jewish storyteller known as Shalom Aleichem. But where are they? The answer is in a small town in southern Ukraine called Bohuslav, where Philip's father Nathan was born in 1911, and from where he and his family escaped in 1921 in the aftermath of the Russian Revolution. And who are they with? Yevgeny and Elena, who run a (probably the!) tourist business in Bohuslav, and whom Viking River Cruises kindly found to take us *off piste* for a personal tour. So, as you will have gathered, our holiday this year took us to Ukraine, where we cruised down the Dnieper from Kiev to Odessa, learning about its difficult history in general, and the tragedy of its Jews in particular - the current Jewish population, at 56,000, is a mere 2% of the 1941 figure of 2,800,000. Its present is also interesting, as - at least in the west - its younger generation is asserting its cultural independence from years of Russian dominance. But its politics remain mired in corruption.

Kiev itself, a city way older than Moscow and indeed once the capital of Russia, was largely rebuilt after the Second World War, and its modern wide boulevards feel almost Parisian. Its architecture ranges from the glorious historic, through the crumbling historic, and Stalinist brutalism, to some really attractive modern buildings. From there we cruised downstream via Dnipro, the historic Ecaterinoslav where Philip's maternal grandmother was born, and again went *off piste* to the new Jewish Menorah Centre with its impressive, if inevitably poignant, museum.

Our third interesting stop was the wonderfully cosmopolitan city of Odessa; its Jewish population is some 3,000 out of 1,200,000, whereas historically it was 50%, not least because it welcomed immigrants to help its early growth. Because its foundation was much more recent than Kiev (think Catherine the Great and Potemkin), and its WWII damage much less, its architecture is less variegated and more consistently elegant, and its Opera House is truly magnificent! I rank the city alongside St Petersburg, Stockholm and Prague, so well worth a visit.

Final linguistic comment. I had not previously realised that the Cyrillic alphabet was an entirely artificial creation. When the Russian authorities decided that they needed written records, they commissioned a monk called Cyril to design an alphabet. His approach was eclectic; he incorporated letters from both the Greek and Latin alphabets, plus the odd one or two from Hebrew, but not always with the same sounds!

2018: Guildford Synagogue Newsletter, *Bohuslav*

2

Law Firms

Linklaters & Paines

"Now," said my mother, "you're moving into a serious job. Please make sure you behave accordingly. In particular, you've developed a habit of using bad language; please stop it."

Well, she was a bit premature. I was to go nowhere near Linklaters & Paines (Linklaters) for the first six months. Instead, I went to law school to study for what was then known as Part 1 of the Solicitors' Examinations. This was because I was a non-law graduate, which in retrospect was as much a plus as a minus: as a classicist (or indeed any other linguist), I had been forced to learn my own language thoroughly, and – in the end – law is about words. As difficult as it may be to believe now, at that time (1968), not only non-law graduates but also non-graduates were welcome as trainee solicitors.

The course was dire, consisting of rote learning. It required the memory of an elephant, the stamina of an ox and the regurgitation skills of a parrot. I reflected – and indeed wrote a somewhat precocious letter to The Law Society to this effect – that this was great training for running a zoo, but not well targeted at the skillset needed as a solicitor. I received a predictably dusty reply.

Having completed the course, I arrived for my first day at the office. My mother's admonition proved inappropriate, as my first "seat" was with a managing clerk (before the breed somewhat pompously renamed themselves "legal executives") called Donald Benjamin, who had previously been a chief petty officer in the Royal Navy, and who turned the air blue for a radius of 100 yards every time he opened his mouth. As he was the first to admit, he was – as many litigation lawyers were and are – a proceduralist to his fingertips, but with no knowledge of substantive law. I was therefore his legal researcher, and a new audience for his stock of racy stories. It was a good first three months.

I then moved to sit with my principal (to whom I was personally articled) – a tall, bony Scot called Iain Murray, who specialised in company law. This had a much greater intellectual component, and I really enjoyed the learning experience, both in terms of strict law, and how to handle people and situations. The latter element was honed much further in my next seat, with Mark Sheldon, who was the senior tax partner, but also did corporate work and really excelled in client-handling, with his extrovert and engaging personality. I gratefully modelled myself on him.

My last seat was with another legal executive – Harold Russell in probate. He had been a general office boy, and Linklaters had the benevolent paternalist approach of encouraging these boys to higher things. He had been prayerfully waiting for an articled clerk to disentangle a very messy estate, which involved constructing and evidencing a family tree going back to the previous century; I was the answer to his prayer. Three months later, I was back at law school for Part 2 of the Solicitors' Examinations.

I duly completed these in February 1972, having experienced for the second time the rigours of a week at Alexandra Palace, which was the ill-judged London venue for this event. Alexandra Palace is an enormous barn of a place, with a glass ceiling; in the February exams it is freezing, and in August boiling, and on both occasions I could only hope that the pigeon droppings would miss both me and my exam scripts!

Before leaving the Probate Department, there had been no indication as to my future career prospects. In the end, and not having heard anything, I asked for a meeting to ascertain my position. "Oh!" I was told, "Of course we want you back, in the Corporate Department."

My relief was matched by surprise at this approach. I began to understand that Linklaters was an institution of supreme self-confidence, where everything was expected to fall into place. It was the classic Rolls-Royce definition of an after-dinner speaker: smooth, well-oiled and interminable. Communication – with its staff or clients – was not its strong point; it had an illustrious clientele that had been built up over the years, and rested a bit too easily on its laurels (which were, however, real in terms of technical legal excellence). For instance, its pay levels for articled clerks assumed parental support, and my successful application for a local authority top-up was considered a tad undignified. Indeed, on one occasion when I was sporting a very 1960s shirt, which was bright orange with a white collar and cuffs, and a black tie with matching orange spots, a senior partner enquired sarcastically if I was working as a navvy on the M1 in my spare time, and my instant reply – to the effect that, with what they paid me, I needed to – was perhaps not best calculated in terms of career enhancement.

So I came back to the office as a newly qualified solicitor, and began to work under supervision on corporate transactions. One of these involved advising the auditors of a secondary bank called London & County in relation to its accounts, which were manifestly on the dodgy side (it was sometimes referred to it as the "Bank of Toytown").

Jeremy Thorpe, then leader of the Liberal Party, had recently become a non-executive director of this bank. I smelled a large rat, and rang Jeremy's office. A few days later, I found myself in his office at the House of Commons. I explained my concerns. He pointed out that the party was not wealthy, and his £5,000 annual fee (for doing very little) was helpful. I decided to be brutal and told him, "They're not paying you for your services, Jeremy. They're buying your reputation. And you're selling it cheaply and riskily." He got the message and, shortly thereafter, resigned from a number of external appointments, pleading pressure of work. A bit later, the Bank of Toytown went bust. The consequential reputational damage was tangible, but it was a lot less than if he had stayed.

My work had an unusual feature, which was to be of future personal significance. The Heath government had just introduced tax relief for executive share options and, on the basis of "new guy, new topic", I was instructed to draft the office precedent. This meant some fast learning about the law relating to both options and their taxation.

This gave me an expertise in the niche subject of employee share ownership. This became of sudden relevance during the Lib/Lab Pact of 1977–8, when one of the commitments given to the Liberal Party – in return for supporting the Callaghan government – was tax relief for employee share ownership, to which there had been a long-standing Liberal commitment since Lloyd George's Yellow Book of 1929. I was by then well established in the Liberal Party, having contested both general elections of 1974, and having served on its National Executive Committee. I told Treasury Spokesman John Pardoe MP of my knowledge, and was promptly asked to assist him in delivering this commitment.

John was given a draft Green Paper, and I rapidly concluded that both its proposed systems were technically clumsy and counterproductive. I suddenly found myself, with John, explaining this to Chief Secretary to the Treasury Joel Barnett, in his office, with officials giving my words flatteringly serious attention as I recommended a technically superior method. The next draft of the Green Paper contained my recommendation as an additional proposal, and the word was that it would be the basis of the proposed legislation.

John was allowed to launch the Green Paper at a press conference (the first Liberal Party launch of Government policy since the fall of Lloyd George in 1922), with me on the platform to deal with technical questions, on 2 February 1978. I wrote an article for the next day's *Times*, with many more to follow in various publications.

I had a real sense of personal achievement, but much more was to follow. The Inland Revenue – at John's request, through Joel – consulted me on the draft legislation. This would involve office time, so I appeared in the office of Jeremy Skinner (Mark Sheldon's successor as senior tax partner) clutching some papers.

Whitehall was, at that stage, a closed world. It was only to learn to align its culture with that of Brussels gradually, where representations on "law in the making" were positively encouraged.

"Jeremy," I started. "There will be legislation in the Finance Bill for tax reliefs to encourage employee share ownership. As we will be asked by clients to draft their schemes, may I have some office time to work on this?"

"Are you sure? How do you know?" he asked.

"I have the draft clauses here."

"That's not possible!" he exclaimed.

I handed him the papers.

He read them with astonishment, and said, "You'd better sit down, and tell me what's going on."

I did, and he agreed to my request for office time to work on the legislation.

So I helped shape the legislation, which had by then been published as part of the Finance Bill. As we negotiated improvements, the Inland Revenue invited John to table agreed amendments in the Standing Committee, which Joel promptly accepted – this was unprecedented in the legislative process. Indeed, at one stage late in a sitting, the Tories complained that their amendments – on any topic – were being rejected, while the Liberal ones were being accepted. Joel Barnett, in reply, suggested that maybe the Liberals had better legal advice. I tried to make my laughter as inconspicuous as possible, and probably failed.

Once the Finance Act was passed, much of my work consisted of advising clients on their new schemes, for which I had drafted the office precedent. I also, as the originator of the legislation, became an established speaker on the professional conference circuit, as well as writing for professional journals; for example, my 1980 piece "Budgeting for Employee Shares" in *Business Law Review*. In 1991, the *Legal Business Magazine* ran a page on share-scheme lawyers; my piece, with another about me, appear at the end of this chapter.

Linklaters appointed new partners once a year, normally six to seven years after their qualification. The system then was effectively "up or out". I approached the 1979 round with a reasonable degree of confidence. My technical ability was recognised, and I had effectively pioneered a new-and-developing area of law that was of direct relevance to clients.

I was to be disappointed. I reflected gradually on my rejection, and concluded that it had been cultural rather than technical.

Like many long-standing institutions, in my opinion Linklaters operated on the "clone" principle. To be accepted as a partner, it seemed that one had to be a clone of the existing partners: male, upper-class, WASPish (white Anglo-Saxon protestant), quietly spoken and restrained. I just didn't fit. I was European and Jewish, and "quietly spoken" and "restrained" were hardly my hallmark, then or subsequently.

Exactly how these elements were assessed, I don't know, but it was difficult not to feel the whiff of anti-Semitism.

My focus then turned to finding a different firm in which to carry on my career. This took some time. Meanwhile, work carried on, and my speciality acquired a new dimension as the incoming Thatcher government began to privatise massive chunks of the public sector.

This started with British Petroleum (BP). Until then, it had been 100% state owned. It was decided to offer 25% of the company to the public. This hit my desk with some force. A midday telephone call from the senior partner informed me that he was sitting with BP's managing director, whose car would pick me up in 10 minutes. I joined their meeting. BP's managing director explained that there was a meeting at the Treasury that afternoon, at which he would advocate a scheme to incentivise employee participation by offering a free share for each one subscribed. I inwardly groaned, as this concept (known as "buy one, get one free" [BOGOF]) had already been raised in discussions between BP's human resources (HR) people and me in relation to a "normal" scheme for BP, and we had agreed it was wrong in principle, as it advantaged the wealthy. Indeed, I had chatted about it informally to the Technical Department of the Inland Revenue, and guided them to the same answer.

I decided that a tactful silence on this point would be good, and headed off to the Treasury as the very junior member of an impressive team. Facing us were the Second Permanent Secretary, Sir Lawrence Airey, who was later to chair the Inland Revenue, with serried ranks of civil servants in support.

Airey started by saying that the relevant Cabinet Committee minutes "recommended employee participation, perhaps supported by loans..." BP made its counterproposal. Airey turned to the Inland Revenue representative with the question, "Does this work?"

"I'm very sorry, Sir Lawrence," he replied, "but my expertise is in the taxation of loans, not employee share participation." He pointed at me, and asked, "Why not ask BP's solicitor, who wrote the legislation?"

I got the same question, with the addition of a raised eyebrow. Trying – and probably failing – to conceal my egotistic enjoyment of the moment, I answered, "Yes, in principle, but there are some technical issues that will need to be resolved with the Technical Department."

"Right," said Sir Lawrence to the Inland Revenue representative, "please arrange an urgent meeting at which Mr Goldenberg can resolve these issues."

This was duly done, and the senior partner and I headed for Somerset House, where – higher authority having pronounced – the selfsame civil servant I had persuaded to take one view had little hesitation in adopting the opposite one.

BP set the precedent for a raft of employee schemes on subsequent privatisations, which kept me heavily occupied for the following year or so. One amusing occurrence was when we acted for the Government in relation to Cable & Wireless: the relevant minister (Kenneth Baker of the Ministry for Technology, and MP for Dorking) demanded a full brief from his civil servants, who rang me for help. I offered a shortcut: to take me into the meeting with them. Having inspected me to check for sanity, cleanliness and robustness, they did just that. We jointly decided not to mention that I was the prospective Liberal Parliamentary candidate in a neighbouring seat!

One other interesting matter during this period was when The Law Society (an elephantine body that fought for years against the inevitable division between its incompatible roles as both a trade union for solicitors and their regulatory body) referred to Linklaters a solicitor seeking legal advice on a relationship breakdown in his law firm.

I was brought in by the Linklaters' partner into whose lap this hot potato had been dropped, and who wanted to pass it on as speedily as possible. To my astonishment, the client – Keith Howell-Jones – had been at school with me, and we formed a good working relationship.

The issue was sorted in the end by an agreed dissolution of Keith's law firm, but the voyage of mutual discovery that we shared was more important. We were both solicitors, and he could have dealt with the technical issues as well as I could. So what value did I add? The answer was what I came to define as "detached empathy"; in other words, "feeling his pain" but detached from the cocktail of emotions in which he was understandably drowning. Thereafter, that became my definition of professional advice in fraught situations. For Keith's part, he appreciated the fact that I actively kept him informed of progress, and developed his own motto of "An informed client is a happy client."

SJ Berwin (SJB)

I continued my search for a new professional firm. Luck again came to my aid, in that a Linklaters partner called Christopher Haan had been asked to leave, and had decided to join a new firm that was being established by Stanley Berwin, by taking over a small West End firm specialising in commercial property. Stanley had asked Chris to recruit corporate lawyers and, knowing of my position, Chris put me at the head of the list. I was duly interviewed by Stanley, who was – as ever, as I was to learn – surrounded by empty coffee cups and wreathed in cigarette smoke. He looked at my hands, and said, "Hm. Small hands, but long fingers – just like your father." I was impressed by this power of observation, but also by the deliberate ingratiation attempt, which I was also to come to recognise as one of his hallmarks. Indeed, he informed no less than a dozen early clients that each was the first client of his new law firm!

So, as the year turned from 1980 to 1981, I both moved house from Watford to Woking and moved jobs from the Rolls-Royce of Linklaters in the heart of the City to the Mini of SJB just behind London Bridge Station in Southwark. "Adjacent to PricewaterhouseCooper's back passage" was my favoured description of the location. Indeed, when I had been at Linklaters, one of PricewaterhouseCooper's predecessor firms, Coopers & Lybrand, had its head office in a nearby road called Gutter Lane. A pompous incoming senior partner had written to the City of London Corporation asking for a name change to one more appropriate and less insalubrious, perhaps Coopers Lane. Back came the deadpan reply: "Sir – Gutter Lane antedates your esteemed firm by centuries. If you wish to harmonise the names, perhaps you could rename yourselves 'Gutter & Co'!"

But the geographical move paled into insignificance compared with the cultural one.

Linklaters had been WASPish, complacent and conformist. SJB was its diametric opposite.

Firstly, there was Stanley himself. He was a larger-than-life character, which meant that both his good and bad qualities (not that he would have acknowledged the latter) were similarly magnified. On the plus side, he was highly entrepreneurial, insisted on technical excellence and was committed to client service. But he was also greedy, vain and a control freak. He endowed his new firm with all six features. He played a fierce game of "divide and rule". When he extended the equity in the partnership beyond himself, the partnership deed gave him sole powers of management, but made no provision whatsoever for what would happen after his death.

Stanley's career progression had been unusual: he had left his first firm because he was refused a second secretary to cope with his workaholic habits; he next set up a new firm, which became Berwin Leighton; and then left to become a director of N M Rothschild. When his position there became untenable because he backed Jacob (later Lord) Rothschild in the disagreement that led to Jacob leaving N M Rothschild to set up on his own, he had a discussion about returning to Berwin Leighton.

Stanley's version of this was simply that an agreement was not reached. Theirs was that he wanted an unacceptably high proportion of the equity. This greed was matched by his vanity: he had the legal power to withdraw the name "Berwin" from Berwin Leighton, and – indeed – this would have been commercially sensible when setting up a new firm with that as the partnership name, but his vanity could not resist the delight of having two firms of solicitors bearing his name.

Then, on the corporate side, he brought in two assistants, who were driven – in their different ways – as much as himself. One was technically very able, but his Jewish angst and insecurity made him both greedy and a control freak – he was Stanley Mark 2. The other was an intellectual dullard for whom truth was a malleable commodity, and with a relentless talent for self-promotion, even exceeding that of Stanley, albeit with much less justification.

If all this sounds negative, much of it was not immediately apparent, and SJB had the very real merit of providing a challenge to the complacency of established City law firms by its commitment to speedy and excellent client service.

Stanley's core corporate client base was two-fold: Jacob Rothschild, whose corporate deals were the core of my 1980s workload, and John Ritblat of British Land (where Stanley was deputy chair). For some strange reason (perhaps countercultural), the elegant Jacob Rothschild later formed a business partnership with the roughneck Jimmy Goldsmith.

This led to one of the most remarkable telephone conversations of my professional life. A deal involving both of them had proved difficult to get to the wire. I received my one and only call from Goldsmith, who demanded an explanation for the delay. I gave one, but he was not minded to hear it and expressed his view in unseemly language.

The firm grew rapidly in the 1980s, in terms of both people and activity. I became an equity partner in 1984, and my income shot up from £30k to £70k in a year, rising persistently thereafter until the dotcom bubble broke at the end of the decade. My workload was high and of good, mainstream, corporate quality. Stanley was very good at passing on his clients to his partners, while adding new ones himself.

However, the culture of the firm had many unsatisfactory elements. Its competitive ethos was too often internal rather than external, and some partners were never happier than when undermining their colleagues with the motive of self-promotion. Stanley relished all this, as it reinforced his dominating personal power. In addition, staff were paid top whack, but too often treated like dirt, so there was no reserve of loyalty in a downturn.

But there was a more fundamental problem: the firm was outgrowing Stanley's management style, which was best described as a benevolent autocracy without the benevolence. He commissioned a report on the future of the firm; when it came back entitled "A tale of two transitions" (one of them being the necessity of a change in his leadership style), the writer was summoned to his office and despatched into outer darkness, the report was never mentioned again, and he did not visit the office for a fortnight, by which time his bruised ego had at least partially recovered.

This burgeoning problem was solved by his well-timed death in 1988; if it had occurred much earlier, the firm would have been too immature to survive, and if much later, it would have probably exploded in conflict.

This was the classic case of what I later discovered was a "founder culture", where the skills needed to establish a business (or, as I was also to discover subsequently, a charity) are radically different from those required for its sustainable maintenance. Managing the transition into an institutional culture is genuinely difficult. On Stanley's death, SJB was to mutate instead into the dysfunctionality of warring satrapies.

Chris Haan assumed the role of senior partner, but the Haan dynasty was to be short-lived; he had no talent for leadership, and – in any event – such talent would have needed to have been prodigious to manage the overcompetitive ethos.

Haan's successor was a smooth operator, who saw clearly that his position depended on acting as front man for the overcompetitive partners. This was demonstrated when, after a marked downturn in the firm's profits after the dotcom bubble burst, the six biggest fat cats put through a new profit sharing system to favour their greed and egos. From then on, seniority, experience and technical excellence took second place, and the differentials slowly and inexorably widened at the expense of everybody apart from the greedy fat cats and their acolytes. Effectively, the firm had ceased to be a partnership, and had become instead a collection of sole traders using common services.

At the same time, there had been a parallel cultural shift. In common with much of the financial services industry, the firm had replaced a commitment to genuine client service with the aim of making as much money as possible.

In other words, the "means" and "ends" had fundamentally altered; instead of a principal end of providing an excellent client service with profitability flowing in its wake, the principal aim became profitability with the clients as the means of achieving it. I put this brutally in a lead letter in *The Independent* in 2012, which appears at the end of this chapter.

Some partners, whom I respected, left at this juncture. But I stayed. It's fair to ask why, as clearly the whole operation was fundamentally offensive to my personal values. The answer was severely practical – money. Although my profit share was constantly and unjustifiably reduced to satisfy the demands of the greedy fat cats, it was much more than I was likely to earn elsewhere at my age, as I had been, in the jargon of law firms, a "grinder (hard-working), minder and binder (sustaining existing client relationships)" rather than a "finder" (bringing in new clients), so I did not have the client "following" sought by all law firms looking at lateral hires in their late 40s. SJB was also a useful base from which to undertake a whole raft of activities that also interested me: not only politics but also public policy engagement.

That my non-executive directorship of the Confederation of British Industry (CBI) (Chapter 3), my role as legal adviser to the Royal Society for the Encouragement of Arts, Manufactures and Commerce's (RSA's) Tomorrow's Company Inquiry (Chapter 4), and my work on company law reform, were each sneeringly labelled as "yet another Goldenberg non-chargeable" spoke volumes for the firm's short-termism and exclusive focus on moneymaking. This attitude ignored favourable publicity for the firm derived from articles in newspapers, periodicals and professional journals on *inter alia* company law, directors' duties, corporate governance, and both European and constitutional law – a selection of which appears at the end of this chapter. There was also the odd bit of humorous publicity too:

AGM was a piece of cake

■ SHAREHOLDERS' meetings have been a bit hairy recently for company directors, so it's nice to hear of one where everyone seemed happy. The Safe Store AGM this week descended not into angry recriminations and votes against the board but a party for chairman Giles Clarke and his predecessor Philip Lewis after lawyers SJ Berwin informed investors that it was their birthdays (or near as dammit) and produced a huge cake. "There was no booze," says an adviser, morosely, before adding brightly "but there were no children either."

A rare specimen

SJ Berwin corporate finance partner Jonathan Djanogly was brought down to earth with a bump when he returned to his office after walking off with John Major's old seat, the ultra-safe Huntingdon, in the General Election.

There, winking up at him cheekily from his desk, was a copy of the Endangered Species Act.

The Diary can reveal Liberal Democrat corporate colleague Philip Goldenberg as the source of this heartless prank.

Then again, there are so few Tories left, Djanogly stands a good chance of making the shadow cabinet.

I also took on the editorship of CCH Editions Limited's *Guide to Company Law*, where – with the assistance of a younger colleague, and in the aftermath of the fundamental legal reforms of the mid-1980s – I fundamentally rewrote a dusty and weary tome to make it much more user-friendly (this was recognised by its reviews – see one given at the end of this chapter), and updated it periodically until CCH was acquired by a conglomerate that (with equal promptness and unkindness) remaindered it!

One of the few occasions when my range of external activities came in useful was when SJB pitched for the work of local authorities to devise schemes to bypass controls on capital spending. We had a partner with local government experience, so the pitch team consisted of him, a tax partner and me.

On one memorable occasion in the late 1980s, the meeting started with the local authority's officers explaining that what we proposed had to be capable of being understood by their (impliedly) dim-witted councillors.

"What's your political composition?" I asked to move the conversation along.

"We're hung," came the reply. "Roughly equal numbers of Tory and Labour, and this wretched little group in the middle which can't make its mind up what to call itself." (This was just after the Liberal / Social Democratic Party [SDP] merger.)

"Let me introduce myself more formally," I said, "I am the Liberal Democrat chair of highways on Woking Borough Council."

Lesson: always know to whom you speak!

In the end, I made the fatal mistake in 2002 of taking the three-month sabbatical break that had just been instituted for long-serving partners. My temporary absence put too much temptation in the path of the greedy fat cats, and – on my return in autumn 2002 – I was invited to accept a managed retirement, with a year to sort out my direction of future travel. Declining this kind invitation was not an available option! I reflected that – as with the father who had been asked by his son what he had done in the French Revolution and had received the reply, *"Je suis vécu [I survived]"* – I had quite remarkably survived 23 years.

Michael Conn Goldsobel (MCG)

What I had rightly thought would be difficult 10 years previously now proved near-impossible. Who wanted a 58-year-old lawyer with – again, the dreaded word – no significant "following"? SJB paid for a firm of consultants to assist me, but they proved totally useless. However, one of my clients came up trumps.

Howard Goldsobel, whom I had coincidentally known in my childhood because our respective parents lived near and were acquainted with each other, had become company secretary to a property company client of SJB, which was originally floated as Sinclair Goldsmith and had subsequently been subsumed into Conrad Ritblat, another of John Ritblat's enterprises.

Howard had merged his tiny firm of solicitors into another slightly larger one, with the resultant firm thereupon being renamed Michael Conn Goldsobel (MCG). I had done a lot of work for this property company, and Howard was a decent person, although unlikely ever to set the world on fire. We negotiated a consultancy, and I turned up there in March 2004.

Work started a bit slowly, but gradually built up over a few years into a reasonable volume. I was pleased to have escaped from a bearpit of intrigue into what was essentially a home for five or six lawyers, who all seemed pleasant to a greater or lesser degree. I well understood that I would have none of the support services of a large firm, and survived the shock of learning to do my own word processing.

However, the firm's information and communications technology (ICT) system was of the MRE[5] variety, and the partnership was no more willing to get a grip on it than on any of the firm's other deficiencies: an accountant whose work was a shambles; a total absence of competent practice management; no objectives, key performance indicators (KPIs) or strategy; and no leadership whatsoever (one partner rightly described the senior partner as having his head so far up his rear end that he couldn't see where he was going).

Howard was the ICT partner, and was unwilling even to contemplate changing suppliers; the other partners surmised that the supplier was his love-child or vice versa, but could not decide which, and there was no management structure to enforce a change.

Howard regularly fed me the excuse that I couldn't expect more from a small firm; there was an element of truth in this, but overall it was unconvincing.

---

5   Combat rations for US military personnel are called "meals ready to eat" (MREs). They were of dubious quality, and – in a time of famine in the Horn of Africa – some politically incorrect wit renamed them "meals rejected by Eritreans".

I put all this to one side as being "not my problem" as a mere consultant, and got on with my work (although I did hang on my office wall a Mickey Mouse clock, which had adorned the bedroom of one of my children at a young age, explaining to all and sundry that it was part of the office's ICT "system"). There was a reasonable flow of corporate work, and I brought in a few new clients, including diversifying into a couple of really difficult estates, one being that of the playwright Anthony Shaffer, who had died in 2001, but whose estate was only brought into some semblance of order by me and others in 2015.

This business relationship worked well from 2004 until the back end of 2014. In particular, I enjoyed working with the family law partner, David Rose, on a couple of fraught demergers of family companies, where our respective skillsets combined to provide a good client service in a difficult emotional context.

But that timing is retrospective. I had not perceived any change, because – in the nature of relationships – when you think everything is OK, you ignore the inevitable bumps and scrapes; whereas, when you know that a relationship is in difficulty, those niggles become magnified and you disregard its positive features. The workstream from the firm dried up, with files to which I could have added value being withheld from me. There was a general atmosphere of disengagement. My office was (reasonably) relocated, but then unjustifiably used as a dump for various clutter (it had come to resemble the office of a legendarily untidy property partner, but his was by choice). A junior employee let slip that he knew I was leaving, at which stage warning bells belatedly began to sound.

I worked out what had happened. For some unfathomable reason, the partners had decided to bring my consultancy to an end, but – even more unfathomably – hadn't actually had the courtesy to tell me so. That only happened in late 2015, when the untidy property partner hauled me into the boardroom and told me, in expletive-laden language that was as unpleasant as it was unprofessional, that I was no longer welcome in the office. To put it mildly, it would have been rather more helpful if I had been told that courteously and without profanity a year earlier, so that I could have found another perch for my work or at least organised a dignified exit.

Philip Goldenberg
SJ Berwin & Co

'Share scheme law is difficult to define. For a lawyer, it is a mixture of corporate finance (company law, Yellow Book, institutional shareholder qualities, securities law and regulation), trust law (on ownership schemes or ESOPs), tax and employment law. But it is more than this. It is about employee participation and, above all, for all-employee schemes, good communication with a workforce is a *sine qua non* of a successful scheme.

'I came at this field politically as well as professionally. The first tax reliefs for all-employee share schemes were contained in the 1978 Finance Act, which flowed from the Lib/Lab Pact. I worked with John Pardoe on the conception and enactment of the proposals. And all-employee share schemes have a strong political content – documents for employees have to be written in language which is clear and concise, while remaining legally watertight – the former by no means the universal hallmark of the legal profession, but writing election literature is a good discipline.

'Against this background, clients need broad advice. No company should go into all-employee share schemes lightly, wantonly or ill-advisedly. To do so is emphatically not a panacea for lousy industrial relations. And it must sit well with the company's employee remuneration package, and general attitude to employee relations.

'On this basis, one has to exclude from consideration outfits in the share scheme field that market packages, rather than give advice. Self-styled "specialist consultants" too often fall in this category.

'It is also difficult to judge other lawyers, because share scheme law tends to be client/lawyer rather than lawyer/lawyer – there is rarely negotiation, let alone conflict. So one rarely meets, and never has to refer!

'If I had to, I would go for my partner Adrian Shipwright, who is a tax guru with a particular bent for complex corporate structures. Michael Jacobs at Nicholson Graham & Jones has an affable solidity. And, if communication skills are as important as I suggest, then the self-publicising abilities of David Cohen of Paisners should stand him in good stead.'

Michael Jacobs
Nicholson Graham & Jones

'Arrangements for employees to obtain shares on beneficial terms have been around for a very long time, but share scheme lawyers as such were rare until the late 1970s. Two of the leading lights from that time who are still much involved in the field are Philip Goldenberg of SJ Berwin & Co, a larger-than-life character who helped create the all-employee profit sharing scheme, and Francis Sandison of Freshfields who wrote the first useful book about share schemes.

1991: Legal Business Magazine, *Share Scheme Lawyers*

Government faces a corporate powers struggle

By Philip Goldenberg

THE Government's attempt to reform the law of corporate ultra vires, which prevents companies acting outside their powers, is likely to be frustrated by its drafting of key provisions in the Companies Bill which is being considered at report stage in the Commons this week.

The problem arises because of the interaction of two provisions of the bill relating to the objects of a company as set out in its memorandum of association.

A company's memorandum of association is a long, boring and, normally, unread document. A company is a creature of statute and only exists for the objects set out in its memorandum. For this reason, and because of a body of case law, lawyers have drafted ever longer and more complex objects clauses to ensure a company's capacity to undertake any particular transaction cannot be impugned.

Although every paragraph in an objects clause is expressed to be a self-standing object of the company, there is a conceptual division between "objects" and "powers". Accordingly, objects clauses will set out in two or three paragraphs the principal (genuine) objects of the company; contain a further paragraph giving it an object of doing anything that is ancillary or conducive to those principal objects; and then go on to set out a range of powers to cover every conceivable transaction into which it might wish to enter.

The existing law is set out in Section 35 of the Companies Act 1985 which says: "In favour of a person dealing with a company in good faith, any transaction decided on by the directors is deemed to be one which it is within the capacity of the company to enter into, and the power of the directors to bind the company is deemed to be free of any limitation under the memorandum or articles."

It has long been recognised that there are a number of difficulties with the operation of this section.

The fundamental difficulty is that the "good faith" test has been interpreted by the courts as meaning that mere knowledge by a third party of any limitations deriving from the constitution on the authority of the directors to bind a company will remove the protection intended to be conferred.

The Government is undoubtedly right to alter this and it was the recommendation of Dr Dan Prentice of Oxford University who was commissioned by the Department of Trade and Industry to advise on the implications of abolishing the ultra vires rule.

The Government proposes to substitute for the existing Section 35 a new provision. The key paragraph of this provision is: "The validity of an act done by a company shall not be called into question on the ground of lack of capacity by reason of the fact that it is beyond the objects of the company stated in the memorandum of association."

The word "objects" is the crucial one to note. It is crucial because the Companies Bill goes on to provide for a substituted Section 4 in the Companies Act 1985.

The principal provision of this Act is: "A statement that the object of the company is to carry on business as a general commercial company means that the object of the company is to carry on any trade or business whatsoever, and in such a case the company has power to do all such things as are incidental or conducive to the carrying on of any trade or business by it."

The intended effect of the latter provision is that lawyers can put away their word processors and companies can have one-sentence objects clauses. This effect is achieved as regards "objects" in the genuine sense of the term but it does *not* achieve its intention so far as "powers" are concerned.

Solution is to give the power to do anything subject to express limitations

This is because, in the second part of the substituted Section 4(2), the "powers" conferred on a company which state that its object is to carry on business as a general commercial company, are limited to such things as are "incidental or conducive to the carrying on of any trade or business by it."

It must be uncertain what exact powers are thereby conferred. For example:

● A general commercial company will clearly be able to sell assets out of its trading stock as part of its day-to-day business. Suppose, however, that it wishes to sell a large property interest, which may no longer be relevant to its business activities, or to sell the whole or a main part of its undertaking and assets – perhaps to effect a merger or because it is part of a group of companies and a strategic decision has been taken to discontinue that business.

Is the power to do so "incidental or conducive to the carrying on of any trade or business"? Hardly, and a solicitor acting for the purchaser would be unwise to rely on the proposition.

● As a corollary of its power of sale, a general commercial company can clearly buy assets, for example as part of the manufacturing chain or property in which to conduct its business. However, suppose it wants to diversify, by acquiring either a different business or a company carrying on a different business. Is that "incidental or conducive to the carrying on of any trade or business by it"?

The answer is uncertain, as it is not clear whether the phrase refers to an existing business. A vendor who was taking a cash consideration might take a chance but a vendor receiving shares would almost certainly not rely on a marginal construction of the statute.

● A general commercial company would clearly have power, say, to guarantee the obligations of one of its suppliers to that supplier's bank if it felt that thereby it was securing a source of supply which was commercially necessary.

By contrast, take the normal situation of a group of companies where the group's principal bankers require that each company in the group gives an unlimited multilateral guarantee – particularly where the group's treasury function is totally integrated. In other words, the group guarantees the bank borrowings of every other company in the group. Is that "incidental or conducive to carrying on its trade or business"? Probably not.

● A group's banker which takes security for the group's bank borrowings will normally require not only a charge from the parent company over all its assets but from all subsidiaries. Is the giving of that charge "incidental or conducive" to the business of each subsidiary? Almost certainly not – and in any event no bank is going to take the risk.

● The Government encourages charitable giving and companies now have a simplified procedure to make tax-efficient charitable donations. Is a charitable donation "incidental or conducive" to carrying on a business? Probably not, unless the company relates in some way to the company or its activities.

The solution, if, the Government is to achieve its objective of eliminating unnecessary legal verbiage from companies memoranda of association, is to alter the substituted section 4(2) to provide that a general commercial company has the power to do any act whatever, subject to any express limitations on its powers contained in its memorandum of association.

It is to be hoped that the Government will accept this concept when an appropriate amendment is moved at the report stage this week.

Philip Goldenberg is a corporate finance partner in City solicitors S.J. Berwin.

Dangers lurk for directors

Members of a company board are not automatically exempt from blame and personal responsibility for their actions. **Philip Goldenberg** explains the pitfalls

Liable: Kevin Maxwell after bankruptcy order was made against him

Kevin Maxwell's £406 million bankruptcy may have sent a shiver down the spines of some of Britain's board directors. To what extent can company directors find themselves personally liable for the debts of of the companies they manage?

The sums in the Maxwell case are exceptional but all company directors can be victims of the same legal pitfalls.

The first lesson for any student of company law is that a company is a distinct legal person and accordingly that those who own or manage it are not personally liable for its debts. This privilege of trading with limited liability was, from the 1870s onwards, a significant engine of economic growth, matched by a concomitant obligation of public disclosure.

The veil of incorporation, however, may be lifted and those involved in running a company's affairs, in particular its directors, may be exposed to personal liability, in a number of ways.

● **Guarantees:** Banks and other large creditors are not devoid of sense. Accordingly, where a small company is managed by its owners, personal guarantees may often be sought. This is also true in the case of a small subsidiary of a large group of companies, where the parent company may similarly be asked for guarantees.

● **Without authority:** A director who enters into a commitment on a company's behalf without proper authority may well incur personal liability. Even signing a company cheque not carrying the company's correct name will render the director personally liable. Although generally a third party dealing with a company can assume that a transaction authorised in what seems to be a correct manner will bind the company, there is an exception where the third party is connected with the director concerned.

In addition, even if a company is bound *vis-à-vis* a third party by the unauthorised act of a director, that director may be personally liable to the company.

● **Breach of duty:** A director will also be personally liable if he is in breach of his duties as a director — because there is a conflict of interests, for example. In essence, a director must not make a "secret profit", and must disclose any such conflict of interests to his fellow directors.

● **Directors' dealings:** The shareholders' consent is required for the purchase or sale of an asset between a company and one of its directors if the value of the transaction is at least £100,000, or, if less, 10 per cent of the company's net assets, with a minimum of £2,000. More onerous requirements apply to a director of a company whose shares are listed or quoted on the London Stock Exchange. There are also strict limitations on the extent to which companies can make loans or quasi-loans, as defined by statute, to a director. This is quite apart from the criminal and regulatory prohibitions on dealing on a stock exchange where a director has the benefit of inside information.

● **Corporate Transactions:** If a company raises capital on a stock exchange, or seeks equity investment from a financing company, directors may bear additional personal responsibilities in two ways.

First, directors as a whole will have increased responsibilities. In the case of a prospectus or listing particulars, statute law imposes criminal or civil liabilities if information is inaccurate. This is extended by the Financial Services Act covering a range of other documents that are deemed to consti-

tute "investment advertisements". Second, in the case of any such transaction, directors, particularly those directly involved in managing the company, will be asked to give warranties or indemnities or both relating to the company's affairs to those providing or raising the capital.

Because of these potential liabilities, companies invariably have a detailed verification process for a prospectus or listing particulars, under which all factual statements are confirmed as true and all expressions of opinion are confirmed to be honestly and reasonably held. No doubt those involved in the Robert Maxwell affair are even now looking carefully at the flotation document for Mirror Group Newspapers. Information on the appointment of independent trustees of the pension fund would be of special interest.

Directors whose company is in difficulty must take professional advice

● **Keep it green:** There are also statutory obligations on a company where, to achieve greater compliance, the law says penalties for non-compliance may be personally exacted from individual directors.

This is particularly true on environmental matters, and it is a foolish board of directors that does not, in circumstances where the company's

activities make it appropriate, commission an environmental audit and thereafter adopt appropriate policies and designate a director to be responsible for them. This applies equally to safety matters.

● **Insolvency:** The key area where the personal liability of directors has come to the fore is that of insolvency. If a company carries on trading when it has no reasonable prospect of paying its debts as and when they fall due, then directors who authorise this conduct or negligently fail to prevent it may end up being made personally liable without limit for all or part of the company's debts.

Any board of directors whose company is in a difficult financial position must protect themselves by promptly taking appropriate professional advice as to how best to proceed. Rather like unfair dismissal, what will be tested is not so much what was done or not done, but rather the procedures that were followed.

Becoming a company director is a little like getting married. One would not go to the extreme of the traditional Advice to Those Getting Married: "Don't"; but one would at least say that becoming a company director should not be done lightly, wantonly or ill-advisedly.

● *The author is a partner with the City solicitors S.J. Berwin & Co.*

1992: The Times, *Dangers for Directors*

PLC
May 1997

book reviews

Title: CCH Guide to Company Law

Author: Philip Goldenberg
Publisher: CCH Editions Limited
Price: £35
Format: Paperback

I am sure that we can all think of a number of well established books on company law. There are the ones which require half an hour of preliminary reading of the index before finding everything that anyone ever wanted to know on the subject of, say, protection of minority shareholders' interests. Then there are the ones which set out in detail how to fill in form 288. Both serve their purpose well. But sometimes all that is needed is a balance between these two extremes. Philip Goldenberg has succeeded in bringing together the simple and the complex under one roof.

The book provides all the basic practical knowledge required to incorporate and administer companies, as well as explaining the constitutional documents of the memorandum and articles of association. The management of companies, in particular, directors' duties is helpfully illustrated by specific case examples. There is much legislative and case law theory on this issue but for those who actually need to be aware of theirs or their client's job description, practical examples are often the most comprehensible guide.

The book goes on to consider share capital, its maintenance and dividends. The potentially tricky issue of financial assistance is again illustrated with a case example. Obviously, a book with such a wide remit is unable to cover such areas in great detail and a more focused analysis may be required once the reader has got to grips with the main issues which are covered here. There follows analyses of accounts and audits, reorganisations, and winding up.

Throughout the book there is a good balance between detailed theory and practical advice. I would recommend this book as a company lawyer's companion to be used when the exhaustive library books cannot be faced or their level of detail is not required. *AM*

1997: PLC, book review

Life in the City piranha tank

Messrs Welch and Yell (letters, 16 March) are absolutely right about the culture of Goldman Sachs. But the problem sadly goes much wider than merchant banks.

When I entered the world of City solicitors, it was a liberal and learned profession, with a pleasant hallmark of collegiality. By the time I emerged, it was a trade carried on in a piranha tank.

Profits were no longer shared between partners; they were fought over between warring satrapies, on an "eat what you kill" basis, with all the consequences as to unpleasant adaptive behaviour your correspondents recite.

Staff were paid top rates to be treated poorly, so there was no loyalty when boom turned to bust.

And the nature of the business turned from earning money by providing a client service to making money with the service as secondary.

It would be good to think that a generation with better values would change this, but this is difficult when the greedy fat cats at the top set the self-enriching rules.

PHILIP GOLDENBERG
Woking, Surrey

2012: Lead letter to The Independent

3

Business

The Confederation of British Industry (CBI)
Shortly before his death in 1988, and in a superb piece of marketing, Stanley Berwin had – on behalf of SJB – tendered for the legal slot in a CBI initiative to prepare British business for the upcoming Single European Market. Ten British businesses were to run a roadshow and contribute a book, on key topics; this was to be at their expense, but with the benefit of public exposure under the aegis of Britain's premier business organisation. In a major coup, the tender succeeded, to the fury of larger law firms that felt upstaged by this neophyte success – one of which even spat out sour grapes in public.

I played my part on the company law side, and this started my involvement in the CBI – a somewhat dated name for a somewhat dated organisation. I went onto the London Regional Council as the SJB representative, and thence to the National Council.

That put me onto the CBI lunch and dinner circuit, which sometimes provided interesting speakers and occasionally the odd lighter moment, as below (I leaked! – but the CBI was not unhappy, not least as the infamous Cecil Parkinson had arrived already under the influence, and somewhat misconducted himself).

I would normally have served on a Policy Committee, but – reasonably enough – this was considered inappropriate for a known

CBI chief touches a raw nerve

Sharp words at the London regional dinner of the Confederation of British Industry on Monday night.

As dinner engagements go, this one had looked a relatively safe port in a storm for Cecil Parkinson, the guest of honour. But the Secretary of State for Transport had not bargained on a late joke from Sir Trevor Holdsworth, the CBI's president.

In thanking his other guest, Professor Witold Trzeciakowski, a member of the Polish council of ministers and Solidarity's chief economist, Sir Trevor alluded to the Cabinet rift.

"It is interesting to note, Professor, that you are both Economics Minister and your Prime Minister's personal economic adviser", he said. "It sounds like a good system. We should try it over here sometime."

Whether the professor appreciated the wit remains unclear. But Parky looked mortally wounded.

political activist, and so I was invited to join the Finance and General Purposes Committee (FGPC): another dated but, as it transpired, entirely appropriate name for the body allegedly responsible for the management of the CBI.

The director general (DG), and his deputy, attended this committee, and so the other members were effectively the CBI's non-executive directors (NEDs). I once described myself in this way when declaring an interest while speaking at a conference, and the CBI person there sneaked on me to Digby Jones (the then DG), who – in turn – wrote me a rushed and ill-considered letter of reprimand, for which I insisted on – and obtained – an apology. At the next

FGPC meeting to consider and approve the annual accounts, Gerry Acher (the senior partner of KPMG, who attended as audit partner) referred to the FGPC members as NEDs, and looked baffled as I tried – and failed – to suppress a degree of merriment. Digby was less amused.

This gave me an unexpected insight into another institution, in this case one of a paradoxical nature, where the image of competence that it presented to the outside world was not matched by its internal workings. For example, having been asked to witness its corporate seal on a couple of occasions, I made so bold as to enquire how the use of its seal was managed. "We keep it in a locked cupboard," was the reply. My insistence that there should be a register of the documents to which it was affixed was greeted with disbelief, followed by reluctant acceptance.

More importantly, I began to investigate the CBI's finances. My conclusion was that it would go bust within five years, because it had taken a head lease on Centre Point at the height of a property boom, and then granted subleases of shorter duration, which were about to come to an end at the diametrically opposite end of the economic cycle.

I was infuriated to learn informally that, during a previous boom, it had refused a multimillion-pound offer to surrender its lease – on the advice of one of its members, who was a chartered surveyor! In the present circumstances, its lease had a negative value of a similar multimillion-pound amount.

I shared my thoughts on paper with my three FGPC colleagues who had the competence to understand it: a senior accountant and a couple of finance directors. But we came up against a blank wall – effectively, nobody wanted to know.

I began to ask myself why this was. I concluded that successive DGs (rightly) saw their key role as lobbying Government on behalf of British industry, which was obviously important as well as satisfying, with pretty automatic access to any relevant minister. They had been appointed based on their talents in this regard:

those I worked with (John Banham, Howard Davies, Adair Turner and Digby Jones) were well qualified for this responsibility. But, wrongly, the first two had given inadequate time to minding the shop or even ensuring that somebody else minded it. Howard had, however, become aware of my concerns and – as almost his last act before his translation to the deputy governorship of the Bank of England – replaced all the ineffective members of the FGPC with more robust successors, effectively and deliberately lighting the blue touchpaper as he departed.

Howard was just about the most acerbically witty person I ever encountered. After I narrowly failed to be elected to the European Parliament in 1994, he said airily to a CBI dinner, at which I was a prominent attender, that the European Parliament's loss would be the CBI's loss too. When he moved to the Bank of England (his predecessor had resigned in ignominy after being outed for "carpeting" a female financial reporter on his office floor, giving rise to witty cartoons about "The bank that said, 'Yes, yes, ooh yes'"), my letter of congratulations to him said that the CBI's loss would be the Bank of England's too. Notwithstanding this, when I failed to win the Woking constituency in the 1997 general election, and the incoming Labour government gave the Bank of England independence over monetary policy (a good LibDem proposal) while removing its regulatory functions – causing the Bank of England to work over the weekend to deal with the consequences – I subsequently received a handwritten letter on the deputy governor's personal notepaper, written on the Sunday, expressing his regrets in the most generous of terms.

I occasionally matched Howard's wit. At a dinner for Graham Watson MEP (Member of the European Parliament), Howard devoted a section of his response to comments about Italians. In my vote of thanks, I commented that his remarks would have been particularly appreciated by Graham's Italian wife Rita, who was sitting next to him!

Shortly after Adair took up the reins as DG, I sent him my FGPC paper. Almost immediately, his office rang me to ask if I could I please come to meet him for 45 minutes. I obviously accepted, noting that 45 minutes was an impressively long time slot in his crowded diary.

Adair started by finding out about me. I answered, then added, "Incidentally, I know more about you than you think. You attended the founding congress of the SDP, gave a rather good speech on economic policy and were thrilled to receive a handwritten note from Roy Jenkins inviting you to join the Economic Policy Working Group."

Adair went slightly pale, as obviously the higher echelons of the CBI were blissfully unaware of this, and the DG had to be non-political (although "Conservative" was deemed to be "non-political"!). "How do you know that?" came his strangulated voice.

"It is my business to know useful facts," I replied.

He rapidly decided that I was an ally, and said, "Well, I've looked at your paper, and you're absolutely right. What do I do? I could just about get through my five-year term, but I think that would be chickening out."

I strongly concurred.

And so began an immense period of change management at the CBI, including a major cash call on key members to sort out the property fiasco. It all had to be kept confidential, because Adair was strongly pro-European, including advocating the UK joining the nascent Euro, and several far-right members would have ruthlessly exploited the CBI's weakness in pursuit of their ideological objectives, even at the cost of its destruction. The necessary changes involved not only finance but also organisational and cultural issues: the telephone system was antediluvian, with no inward direct dialling; there were many internal restrictive practices; and it was difficult to avoid the suspicion of a staff Masonic ring, with all that meant in terms of a closed culture. That Adair managed to change all this – and to do so under the radar – was enormously to his credit, and effectively saved the CBI. Our working relationship was excellent, and I was even occasionally used as an impromptu CBI media spokesman on European issues, as well as using *CBI News* as a publicity vehicle for SJB. I later reviewed his book *Just Capital* for *LibDem News*, and then, much later (both publicly, and privately with ministers), advocated his appointment as governor of the Bank of England. See the articles at the end of this chapter.

I also became an occasional supplier of jokes to Adair. In 1996, when Tony Blair was clearly the next Prime Minister-in-waiting, the CBI's London region hosted an overflowing dinner with him as the speaker. I faxed Adair with the following gag for his speech of thanks: "Well, Tony, this has been a remarkable occasion. So many people have wanted to listen to you that we've had to move the venue seven times, and this room in the Café Royale is the largest function room in London. So, this evening is a sell-out, although not perhaps in the way that a number of your Parliamentary colleagues would use that expression!" Adair delivered this verbatim, to the amusement of both the audience and the speaker.

I even had my own moment. At the CBI conference in 1992, just after Black Wednesday, I made a speech in the economics debate in which I observed that, had the Conservative general election manifesto of that year been a Companies Act prospectus, the entire Cabinet would now be in gaol! I had not realised how many bored industrial correspondents were covering the conference, for whom this soundbite was gold dust; the resultant national coverage (including "quotes of the day" in two national broadsheets – reproduced at the end of this chapter) reached the House of Commons, where it was cited by a Labour MP as showing the business community's view of the Tory government. The LibDem benches collapsed in giggles.

Adair was succeeded by Digby Jones, who was of an entirely different ilk. He had been the senior partner in a Birmingham law firm, where – very like Stanley Berwin, and with the same hallmark of self-ingratiation – his job had been to attract and keep clients. So Adair's leadership was replaced by Digby's followership; his principal mindset was to keep the members happy, rather than to challenge them. My involvement with the CBI faded out gradually.

Mission Capital

It was lunchtime in a slightly-better-than-average West End restaurant in early 2008. I had been invited to lunch by Robert Burrow, whom I had known as a fellow corporate law partner at SJB. He was a highly intelligent and entrepreneurial lawyer, but with the character flaw – typical of an upper-class Englishman (or, in Robert's case, Irishman) – of being all over you like a rash if he wanted your help, but unavailable if you were not on his priority list for the day (shades of David Cameron!).

"I have a problem," said Robert. (As we had lost touch with each other for the preceding few years, I had assumed that already!) "I'm one of three NEDs of a small property company called Mission Capital PLC. The other directors are Neil Sinclair as chair [the "Sinclair" in Sinclair Goldsmith I mentioned in the MCG section of Chapter 2, who had departed in pretty short order after John Ritblat had become chair], and his daughter Emma as managing director. They've been mismanaging the company, and we may have to fire them. What do you think?"

We discussed various angles, and caught up generally and pleasantly. In particular, Robert explained that the company had been a start-up for the Alternative Investment Market (AIM) (the section of the London Stock Exchange for smaller companies, with lighter-touch regulation), and that most of the shares had been subscribed by either his friends or Neil's.

I thought no more about it, until I received an urgent phone call in March.

"Philip," said Robert, in a pressing manner. "We've just fired them, and all hell has broken out. We have the AGM [annual general meeting] coming up on 30 April. Would you like to chair it?"

"As what?" I enquired.

"You can be the alternate for Michael Guthrie [one of the NEDs]."

"No, Robert," I said swiftly. "This is a quoted company, and that looks too tacky for words."

"OK," he said, "you can be appointed a NED or even chair."

I demurred on the second suggestion, but on the first enquired, "Does the company have D&O[6] cover?"

"No."

"Well, get it if you want me aboard – I want insurance cover in what is clearly a litigious situation."

"Dealt," he said.

I had written enough about the law relating to NEDs (see Chapter 4 in relation to the Tomorrow's Company inquiry) that I thought I should experience the reality. So, I prepared for the AGM, which clearly would be heated.

The normal City AGM lasts about five minutes, and is attended mainly – if not exclusively – by those invited to the subsequent lunch. There is, of course, a different pattern for large companies, which either have a strong individual-shareholder base (the questions about ladies' underwear at M&S's AGMs were legendary) or attract protest groups. But, otherwise, I had never known an AGM (and I had attended many as the company's solicitor) go beyond 45 minutes.

Not this time! My appointment as a NED had been announced overnight, and I walked into a room that was packed, both literally and metaphorically: the Sinclair camp had taken advantage of the recent legislation permitting the appointment of multiple proxies by one shareholder, Their obvious intention was to win votes on a show of hands, even if they lost on the subsequent proxy count. I had anticipated this, and I used my power as chair to move straight to a proxy vote on all resolutions.

"On a point of order, Chairman," Sinclair opened (it was to be the first of many), "You have become chair in a contentious situation. You have a duty to be fair to everybody. How can you be when you are a former partner of Mr Burrow?"

"Well, Mr Sinclair," I replied, "you used to be a client of the firm where Robert and I were partners, and – indeed – I personally acted

---

6   This is directors and officers liability insurance: no sane person should ever become a company director, or a trustee, without considering whether this is advisable; in this case it was essential!

for your company. So all of us have a past which we cannot rewrite. I will just do my best!"

Milking the "new kid on the block" theme for all it was worth (and perhaps a bit more), I survived the next couple of hours of historical revisionism, when the Sinclair camp indulged in what was to be their permanent trope: that the company had been brilliantly successful under the Sinclair dynasty, which had been cruelly, abruptly and wrongly terminated by the NEDs for no justifiable reason.

After the meeting, where all the votes were won 55/45, I took stock. The company had a couple of property assets, one of which was clearly a write-off, with the other teetering on the brink. There was a trading subsidiary called KML, which was profitable, but it managed car parks, and its leases were running down. And the litigation that the company had started to force the Sinclairs to leave the company's premises had effectively become an action by them to claim compensation for their dismissal. It was draining in terms of both time and expenses. Plus, as the company had almost no cash reserves, it was in a very weak tactical position.

Robert (with Chris Phillips, an experienced property practitioner whom Robert brought onto the board) dealt with the property issues. I took over managing the litigation and the responsibility for telling the shareholders the objective facts. I haven't detailed my circulars to shareholders in this book, as they are all on public record, and – as shareholder communications – they are all protected by qualified privilege, which they would not be if repeated here!

It was clear to me that we faced an ongoing guerrilla war. It was therefore essential to sell KML, both because it was a declining asset and because the proceeds of the sale would give us the strength to see off the Sinclair litigation. This took a year or so, during which the Sinclairs added to their list of grievances the fact that KML was a declining asset about which we were taking no action. The litigation was mired in stalemate.

In early summer 2009, we signed a tolerably good deal for the sale of KML, and announced it in a circular convening an extraordinary general meeting (EGM) to approve it. Suddenly, the Sinclairs – having worked out that their stranglehold had been weakened in consequence – settled the litigation at a difficult day-long mediation. And, at the EGM, they predictably – albeit shamelessly – attacked the board for disposing of the company's only income-generating asset!

We now had a cash shell worth some £750k. We obviously sought the only viable exit to give value to shareholders, namely a reverse takeover by an unquoted company seeking an AIM quotation. This took a bit under two years, which was longer than I would have wished, not least because it brought with it yet more two-hour revisionist AGMs.

The problem in a situation such as this is that the cost of this type of transaction is very considerable; lawyers and accountants do not come cheap, as I now discovered from the other side of the fence! Effectively, a cash shell worth some £750k has just one shot in its locker, so had better get it right.

The counterparty we alighted upon was called Quindell, and I am not going to add to the acres of print about its subsequent history. But a reverse takeover, which offered an initial value of over 2p a share as opposed to the notional 0.75p value of the cash shell, was a proper course of action in terms of the directors' duty to advance the interests of shareholders; as Maurice Chevalier once observed about old age, it was better than the alternative!

I neither received, nor would have accepted, an invitation to join the Quindell board. I did not understand its business model, and its boss Rob Terry did not inspire my confidence.

So, I exited with modest self-satisfaction, and the benefit of having undergone an interesting experience. I had contributed a cool head and a balanced judgment, together with two attributes that I had imported from my political experience: an ability to communicate (in letters to shareholders and at AGMs) clearly and concisely in relation to complex issues, and the ability (learned from Jacob Rothschild, and carried into in local government – see Chapter 7) to chair a meeting with repressive courtesy.

It was always said of me that my circulars to shareholders sounded too much like election leaflets, and vice versa. Maybe the truth was (and is) that all communications need to be clear and concise, but that there is a spectrum regarding how they should be pitched.

CBI NEWS
FEBRUARY 1998

Not so confidential

City solicitor Philip Goldenberg warns that impending constitutional change may have some unexpected consequences for business

We are in an era of constitutional change; and the business community has not yet begun to appreciate its impact on their activities.

Take two key changes. First, the incorporation into domestic UK law of the European Convention on Human Rights (ECHR). Two ECHR Articles are crucial.

Article 6 gives a right to fair process, including a right to a public hearing in the determination of civil rights and obligations. Bang go regulatory hearings in private, potentially throwing the whole of the present City regulatory framework into chaos. And a company aggrieved by a decision will have a right to judicial review of that decision if it can reasonably allege breach of due process.

Article 8 gives a right to privacy. Unless Parliament itself legislates a privacy law, the effect of incorporating the ECHR will be to create a new tort (or civil wrong) of privacy. This should be an interesting period for the media.

The second key change is the proposed Freedom of Information (FoI) Act. FoI is as much a sword as a shield: 40% of all US requests for information under FoI are by companies seeking information either about government decisions that affect them or about other (competitor) companies.

Looking to US practice, companies should clearly identify confidential information as being such; and anticipate, in the light of the exemptions from disclosure contained in any FoI legislation, the reasons why a government department could be justified in not disclosing such information.

Any FoI legislation is likely to contain a third-party procedure, whereby a person supplying information will be allowed to object to its disclosure. But the fact that information is commercially sensitive or subject to copyright will not, in itself, be likely to constitute a mandatory exemption from the disclosure obligation. Companies seeking to prevent disclosure will need to be able to put forward compelling arguments to support their views. Watch this space!

Philip Goldenberg is a partner in City solicitors S J Berwin & Co and is a member of the CBI's National Council.

1998: CBI News, *"Impact of ECHR on Business"*

Book review

Philip Goldenberg

on

JUST CAPITAL

by **Adair Turner**

THE late Sir Maurice Bowra, an Oxford Don renowned amongst other (more unpublishable!) things for his wit, was once asked for a collective noun for Heads of Oxford Colleges. Without a moment's hesitation, he replied "A lack of principals"!

Whatever the correct collective noun may be for Directors-General of the CBI, two of them are visiting our Bournemouth Conference. The present DG, Digby Jones, is addressing Conference from the platform on the Tuesday. His predecessor, Adair Turner, will be visiting on Monday for Corporate Day, speaking on his book JUST CAPITAL, and participating in an EMU debate.

JUST CAPITAL (despite its title, a robustly non-Marxian book!) challenges Liberal Democrats as to whether or not they are economic, as well as social and political, liberals. That so distinguished liberal as Ralf Dahrendorf should have written the Foreword speaks for itself.

Turner's book is a wide-ranging and intellectually coherent review of a nexus of interlocking issues in the field of politics and economics. It deconstructs the over-simplification of "globalisation"; asserts the importance of national economic and social policies in establishing the balance between the public and private sectors; looks at a number of economies, arguing against over-standardisation of economic and social objectives; argues for reform, rather than rejection, of the European – as against the US – economic model; and asserts that Britain's economic priorities should now be more about investment in capital and skills than yet more deregulation.

Turner then addresses environmental objectives, and how market instruments can be used to promote them; supports global capitalism but not always liquid financial markets; and criticises the unrestrained neo-liberalism wished upon Russia by certain western economists. He declares free trade to be in the interest not least of developing countries, and argues for the integration of environmental issues into global trade policy. He also asserts the importance of human rights, and says that it is no part of liberal economics to sell arms to dictatorships.

What is impressive in all this is the analytical quality of Turner's writing. Too many writers on this sort of topic fit the facts to their theories; Turner is scrupulous in distinguishing the facts, the probabilities and the policy choices.

In the tailpiece to his book, he neatly demolishes any intellectual pretensions of the so-called Third Way, and asserts that the correct method of reconciling the twin objectives of economic dynamism and an inclusive society is long-established, and called – simply – liberalism.

At Bournemouth, he will challenge Liberal Democrats to share his views.

Philip Goldenberg is, and was during Adair Turner's period as Director-General of the CBI, a member of its Management Committee.

(JUST CAPITAL is published by Macmillan @ £20)

2001: Liberal Democrat News (LDN), *review of Adair Turner's book* Just Capital

Strengths to lead the Bank

I am surprised that Steve Richards (29 October) has been briefed by unnamed sources that Lord Turner lacks the combination of policymaking and organisational skills necessary to be an effective Governor of the Bank of England.

My direct experience is the opposite. I was a member of the CBI's management committee when Adair Turner became that organisation's director-general. His day and public job was to be an effective spokesman for British business; in this role he was both effective and courageous. His private role was to take a failing organisation, and change its

management structure and attitudes, its ICT, its property arrangements and its finances; in this role he was radical and innovative, and made the CBI fit for the future. Without his leadership it might well not have survived.

So his alleged weaknesses are in reality formidable strengths.

PHILIP GOLDENBERG
Woking, Surrey

WHAT THEY SAID

"If it had been a companies act prospectus, it would have landed the entire cabinet in jail."
Philip Goldenberg, of SJ Berwin, on the government's general election manifesto

CBI press cuttings

48

4

Charities

The Royal Society for the Encouragement of Arts,[7]
Manufactures and Commerce (RSA) and Tomorrow's Company
Established by Royal Charter in 1754, with luminaries such as
Benjamin Franklin among its founders, the RSA is the oldest think-
tank in the UK. I had not been aware of its existence until late 1992,
when a phone call out of the blue invited me to apply to become a
fellow of the RSA.

"Is this a fund-raising approach?" I enquired with a touch of
cynicism.

"No," I was firmly told, "We seek out prospective fellows[8] on
a targeted basis, and you interest us because you are a corporate
lawyer and you have also just become a member of the CBI's
National Council, which is an unusual combination."

Feeling impressed and slightly flattered, my cynicism abated. I
accepted, and was sent a package of information. In this was a reference
to a newly established inquiry into the purpose of companies. This
appealed to both my professional interest in company law and my
political interest in public policy. I booked in to meet the RSA's then

---

7   Meaning "skills", as does the Latin word "*artes*" from which it derived.
8   Fellows are entitled to put the letters "FRSA" after their names. A subsequent
    modernising chief executive of the RSA, Matthew Taylor (of whom more later),
    suggested that "member" was less archaic than "fellow", but abandoned his proposed
    change when it was pointed out to him that "MRSA" was a somewhat unfortunate
    acronym.

programme director, Mark Goyder. Although I did not tell Mark at the time, I had listened to his father George Goyder – who, in the 1950s, had written a striking book called *The Responsible Company* – speak to Oxford University Liberal Club on the topic.

Mark and I got on well together, and he explained that the Tomorrow's Company inquiry would involve major corporates, which would part fund it and – more importantly – provide input at chief-executive level, together with professional firms that would not put up cash, but would provide partner-level input. The legal role was currently on offer to one of the top City law firms, but they had yet to reach a decision. Mark rang me a week or so later to say that the decision had been negative, and would SJB/I be interested. Knowing that SJB's reaction was likely to be negative (it was – see Chapter 2), I promptly accepted without consultation.

It was one of the best decisions of my life. The inquiry was brilliantly chaired by Sir Anthony Cleaver of IBM, with whom I developed an intellectual empathy, which was explained when I discovered that we shared the mindset of Oxford classicists. Key issues were discussed at weekend gatherings. At one of these, over dinner with tables of six or so, I mentioned *en passant* that it was wrong – in terms of company law – to assert (as City merchant banks constantly asserted, to the benefit of their fee income) – that company directors owed their duty to shareholders, and moreover on a short-term basis. The better proposition was that they owed their duty to their company, and that duty was to act in the interest of shareholders on a sustainable (so not short-term) basis.

Tony Cleaver's jaw dropped. He called the room to silence, so that I could repeat what I'd just said. There was general astonishment. Accidentally, we had hit upon a key element of the inquiry's eventual findings.

Not that the process was plain sailing: just before the report was finalised in 1995, one participant took separate legal advice from an intellectually challenged partner at Linklaters, who wrote an unimpressive letter that totally failed to grasp the argument. Tony rang me at home to resolve the issue. I was firm; that was my view, and it was supported by Professor Gower, who was the country's then foremost expert on company law. If my view was not accepted, I would resign from the inquiry. Tony was magnificent; "That's what I hoped you would say," he said.

Following publication of the report, I rejoined the professional lecture circuit as the newly minted expert on directors' duties; I had a short article published in *The Times*, and, in 1998, gave my first (and only) academic lecture to the recently formed Institute for Advanced Legal Studies (IALS), which I had joined at its inception as an associate fellow. The lecture[9] was subsequently published, although not without incident; a concomitant editorial appeared, penned without the courtesy of consulting with me to ensure that the writer at least understood my argument before criticising it – this necessitated one of the fiercest "letters to the editor" I have ever written. The institute kindly promoted me to a full fellowship, so the letters "FSALS" [Fellow of the Society for Advanced Legal Studies] could now be added to my "FRSA".

The RSA saw itself as a promoter of ideas that should then be taken forward by others. So, Mark departed to establish The Centre for Tomorrow's Company (which, for simplicity, is today known simply as Tomorrow's Company), and I wrote its constitutional documents. We have had a warm personal and professional relationship ever since, as I have worked with Tomorrow's Company on a whole raft of corporate-governance issues (in particular, as noted towards the end of Chapter 6).

The Tomorrow's Company inquiry was not, in my view, a "big bang" approach; rather it would send out significant ripples across the pond, which would gradually return results. It certainly stirred up discussion, which might have stalled had the incoming Labour government in 1997 not announced a full-scale Review of Company Law, with one of its key objectives being to resolve what came to be

---

9   Published in *The Company Lawyer* and reprinted in the appendix. To my astonishment, a Google search of my name shows it still being used in university courses around the globe.

known as the shareholder/ stakeholder debate – the subject of my 1988 IALS lecture.

It seemed to me to be important to carry through the work of the Tomorrow's Company inquiry on directors' duties. This would be helped by the presence of Sir Stuart Hampson, an inquiry team member and chair of John Lewis, on the Review's steering group. But that would deal with high-level issues; we needed to be in the engine room too.

So, I lobbied hard – and successfully – to be there. Working Group 1 was to deal with shareholder and stakeholder issues. It took up a lot of my professional time (with the boringly predictable negative reaction by SJB), but was absolutely worth it.

The key decision, drafted by me at the request of Jonathan Rickford as the review's director, was the doctrine (as I entitled it) of "enlightened shareholder value". In other words, directors could lawfully, while discharging their duty to the company of advancing the interest of shareholders in terms of sustainable value, have regard to other material factors. Indeed, not to do so might well be a breach of that duty.

This doctrine was, in due course, given statutory force by the Companies Act 2006 s.172(1), which I set out as follows, as I conceived it, in proud parental mode:

A director of a company must act in the way he considers, in good faith, would be most likely to promote the success of the company for the benefit of its members as a whole, and in doing so have regard (among other matters) to:

(a) the likely consequences of any decision in the long term,
(b) the interests of the company's employees,
(c) the need to foster the company's business relationships with suppliers, customers and others,
(d) the impact of the company's operations on the community and the environment,

(e) the desirability of the company maintaining a reputation
    for high standards of business conduct, and
(f) the need to act fairly as between members of the company.

I regarded (and still regard) this – I hope, reasonably – as a significant achievement along the road to good corporate governance.

My favourable experience with the Tomorrow's Company inquiry had drawn me into the more general work of the RSA. In 2004 (its 250th anniversary), for the first time it introduced an open election process for trustees. I stood, and was pleasantly surprised to be one of four successful candidates. I discovered my success by means of a phone call from Penny Egan as its then DG. "But you must keep it an absolute secret until the formal announcement at the AGM," she enjoined. "I've been directed to tell you this by the chair."

I thought this a bit silly, and my view was confirmed when I received a letter from the mailing house dealing with the Anniversary Day at the Albert Hall informing me that, following my election, the somewhat down-market seat I had paid for had been upgraded to something more fitting for my elevated status!

I met the chair just before the AGM, when I was summoned to join the trustees in the Green Room. I decided on the spot that Sir Paul Judge was clearly a dominant figure, used – not least as the former head honcho at Conservative Central Office – to having his every whim instantly obeyed. His persona reminded me of a former Attorney General called Sir Reginald Manningham-Buller, universally known around the Inns of Court (behind his back) as "Sir Reginald Bullying-Manner".

It was a strangely dysfunctional board. Judge, as chair, behaved as if he was the chief executive, while Penny was more of a chairman-type; in particular, she ran the senior-staff team (all of whom attended the board) in a very collegiate style. As Matthew Taylor discovered when he succeeded her, in practice this meant the place was full of silos rather than working together, with no targets, let alone KPIs.

There was always a pre-meeting of the chair and the senior-staff team, at which a line was agreed (as the chair perceived it) or imposed (as the staff saw it) from which there could be no deviation at the meeting.

In addition, Judge had an eye for vanity projects (his vanity rather than the RSA's). He wasted £20,000 on a coat of arms (although dealing with the Lancaster Herald was fun – I sourced a classical quotation which he had half-remembered). More seriously, he commissioned architects to produce a plan for the RSA's house in John Adam Street, which would have cost at least twice as much as the value it would have added.

This caused the first breach in the wall of conformity, as the finance director – Philip Bunt – nervously looking down, read a prepared statement as to (the lack of) value for money. Judge tried to resolve the issue by delegating it to the FGP, a smaller body that he also chaired. Sitting opposite him, I simply said, "No, Chairman." (I reflected that this might be a new experience for him.)

One amusing issue of contention arose subsequently when it was suggested that Vicky Pryce (a senior economist) become a trustee. The senior staff, who now briefed me regularly when they thought I should be aware of something, told me that Judge was vetoing this, as he had discovered that Vicky was Chris Huhne's wife, and was therefore politically affiliated by association with a (non-Conservative) politician. It so happened that Judge's second wife was Barbara Thomas, a well-known senior figure in the world of nuclear energy, dubbed "The Atomic Kitten" by *Private Eye*. In my (now deliberately selected) position opposite him, I confronted him on the issue. "May I please mention, Chairman," I began, when any other business was called at the end of the board meeting, "that I've picked up a rumour that Vicky Pryce is being vetoed as a potential trustee because of the identity of her husband. I hope this isn't true, as I'm sure The Atomic Kitten would rightly regard this view as unacceptable." It was the first time in my life, as he glared at me in defeat, that I had experienced a look that would cheerfully have killed me on the spot.

We could not remove Judge without serious cause, and – in any event – the majority of the trustees were of a compliant nature. But I formed an early alliance with Gerry Acher (see Chapter 3), and we agreed that we just had to sit out Judge's chairmanship in damage limitation mode, and that Gerry should become the next chair in due course. In addition, following the resignation of one of the treasurers, and in default of any other contender, I put myself forward for the vacancy, thereby increasing my authority within the board.

It was clear to senior trustees that there needed to be a new broom as DG. A selection panel was duly established, which would then present a shortlist of three to the board for consideration.

This process was not followed, however. An email from Judge informed the board that the panel had identified a superb candidate, who would be leaving a sensitive post to join us, and had therefore requested that his name was not released beyond the panel. Accordingly, the panel sought authority to make the appointment without reference to the board.

I was outraged. The trustees could keep a secret. What sort of appointee would seek this denial of information? What did this augur for his/her relationship with the board? So I demurred, as did one other trustee. I was called in to see Judge and an uncomfortable-looking Gerry. A request was made that would I please not be awkward and agree. I explained the issue of principle and politely declined.

The appointment went ahead, and was in due course revealed to be Matthew Taylor, fresh from 10 Downing Street where he had been Tony Blair's head of policy. It was an excellent appointment. When I met Matthew, I asked him whether he had indeed insisted on confidentiality. He was clear that he had not. I told him what had happened. He was visibly uncomfortable. So, I was forced to conclude that Judge was not just overbearing but he was also economical with the truth, not least – by inference – with Gerry as his co-selector.

Judge completed his term of office, and Gerry succeeded him. The start of his term was inevitably difficult, not least because Matthew was heavily engaged in restructuring the organisation, breaking down the silos, and building the concept of defined objectives and co-operative working. He needed Gerry's full engagement in this, and the resultant concentration on this priority made some of the more self-important trustees feel unloved by the chair. I gave Gerry my full and active support during this difficult period, from which we all emerged into a very positive period of activity and progress. And, as treasurer, I made it a priority to explain the RSA's finances in clear terms to its AGM, distinguishing between core activities and non-recurring items. I also led the rewriting of its creaking constitution.

When Judge himself came up for reappointment as a trustee, the matter was considered by the Nominations Committee. Gerry argued for reappointment, but explained to me afterwards that he had promised to do so. I was very firm: Judge would misuse his position to promote his personal agenda, and the RSA needed to move forwards. The meeting agreed with me. The usual platitudinous statements were made, but the reality appeared with curious accuracy in the "City Diary" column of *The Times*.

Gerry was now moving to the end of his term, and a successor was needed. The process (transparent on this occasion) produced Luke Johnson, who first became deputy chair. I was uncomfortable with him; as with many right-wing Conservatives, he understood money (and was really good at reviewing the RSA's catering operations) but not people, and caused very significant frictions, both within the board and with the fellows as a whole. It was clear to me that I would not enjoy remaining on the board, and would be unlikely to achieve anything useful. I had a new and potentially time-consuming appointment pending (see opposite), so exited gracefully.

The Tuberous Sclerosis Association (TSA)

As mentioned in the dedication at the front of this book, our eldest son Jonathan was diagnosed early on with tuberous sclerosis complex (TSC), which is a genetic condition with a spectrum of severity: the earlier it manifested itself, the more severe it was. The TSA was the charity dedicated to the benefit of sufferers and carers, and we had been profoundly grateful for its help and support.

I had received various tentative approaches to become a trustee, which I resisted while my life was too crowded; however, when – in the late 1990s – I concluded that I would not contest another Parliamentary election, I made myself available and was duly elected.

It was a highly unusual board, which reflected the way in which the TSA had developed. It was originally founded by parents of TSC children who had been told by the medical profession that there was no treatment or cure, and neither was likely to be found; they transferred their collective grief into establishing an organisation to fund research, and to provide both practical and emotional support. It's right to say that, without their hard work and dedication, the organisation would never have come into being.

Having received a very large legacy serendipitously, they established a charitable company, with three key personnel becoming paid executives and others becoming trustees. In practice, the organisation was managed by the three heads of department (the Research Department by Ann Hunt, the Support Services Department by Janet Medcalfe, and the Appeals and Publicity Department by Anne Carter), who were a closely knit team, and the board had an ill-defined consultative role on a quasi-constituency basis: trustees felt themselves to be representative either geographically (Scotland, Wales and Northern Ireland) or by sector (Research, Support Services or Appeals and Publicity).

But there was no sense of strategy or priorities, let alone KPIs, and the board's collective nose was firmly excluded from management. All this was shown by the fact that, as a board of 20(!), it met three times a year for a full day's ill-directed *witterfest* [*wide-ranging conversations with no discernible outcomes*], with no committee structure.

I got through some changes – principally three service committees, and a fourth one to deal with finance and attempt to co-ordinate the others – but that did not resolve the problems. These became more evident as Ann Hunt retired, Janet Medcalfe sadly died young and Anne Carter passed her sell-by date, but was protected from criticism by her husband Tom from his position as president. But what was to be done? My predecessor as chair, Christine Naylor, instituted a strategic review, which would begin to work as she stepped down in early 2010. A successor chair was needed to see it through to conclusion and subsequent implementation.

The timing was emotionally difficult. Jonathan had died in June 2009, and I had an understandable emotional wish to turn the page, close the book and move on. I had a long discussion with my wife, Lynda. She was very clear, and said, "Look. You're telling me that this organisation, which has helped us and others so well, is in danger of falling apart. And that, for some strange reason I find difficult to understand [supportive wives are wonderful!], you might be able to sort out its problems. You just don't have a choice."

The truth was that there were two trustees who might have done the job, but the other – as I explained to disbelieving friends collapsing with hysterical laughter (notably Gerry Acher in the august surroundings of The Mansion House) – made me look tactful and diplomatic by comparison. I had to agree with Lynda.

I became chair in early 2010. I used the board meeting that appointed me to seek an express mandate for change; in particular, to change the nature of board meetings from unproductive all-day *witterfesten* to half-days with a purposive agenda, relegating all the informational clutter to a monthly email. And I warned that the strategic review would not necessarily be a comfortable process.

As that review began to take shape, I took stock. As company secretary (which I had remained), I had assumed responsibility for legal issues, compliance and HR (shared with the previous chair). I now became aware that being chair entailed also being managing director and finance director: the former role entailed managing (or rather trying to manage) the heads of department (see the following), and the latter required managing the finance controller and the audit function – tasks that for some reason the treasurer did not think were his.

A helpful crisis arrived when the finance controller handed in her notice; I viewed this as an opportunity, and found an experienced accountant as a temporary replacement, who reported to me with justified horror on her incompetence.

The longer-term solution arrived as part of my board recruitment campaign; I had decided that it was easier to find good new trustees who would indirectly drive out the sub-standard ones rather than engage in a frontal assault. One of my early picks – from a list that Tom Carter had helpfully provided of those who had indicated an interest – was Rob Vaughan, a Swansea accountant whom I brought in as deputy treasurer, with a view to succeeding the then inadequate appointee. Another appointee was Martin Short, an Anglican priest whom I rapidly saw as my successor in due course.

Rob's appointment was, however, indicative of our cultural problem. "But we don't know him!" was the cry from parts of the board. I groaned inwardly, and emphasised that he had a TSC daughter as well as (and I thought rather more significantly) being a qualified accountant, who was also prepared to have a partner in a different office manage our finances on a permanent basis. It was a clear and manifest win-win situation; that I had to deploy my full persuasive authority as chair, and lose some goodwill in the process, was troubling. Indeed, Christine Naylor (who had kindly agreed to produce draft minutes) argued fiercely that he had not actually been appointed as deputy treasurer. I squashed this attempted sabotage firmly.

The heads did not take to the concept of joint working. On the Research side, the head was a trustee: Chris Kingswood, a busy consultant renal physician specialising in TSC, who delegated organisational functions to one of his senior staff as deputy head. After Janet Medcalfe's death, her successor as head of Support

Services was a lady whom I came to regard as a beacon of sanity, but who was later to fall spectacularly from grace. Anne Carter was still head of Appeals and Publicity, but she was not amenable to any form of management; indeed, when – as her line manager – I sent her an email asking for a rough breakdown of how she spent her time, I received a reply from her husband, President Tom, saying that it was not my place to ask such an impertinent question!

The strategic reviewer then reported. He had fulfilled the standard task of an external management consultant: to tell blindingly obvious truths that would have been brushed aside if I, or any other insider, had voiced them. His review was welcomed by the Support Services Department, and deeply resented and resisted by trench warfare on the part of the Carter household. At the board meeting, Tom and Anne delivered a joint paper complaining about the publicity function ceasing to be Anne's personal fiefdom.

The review was not, in truth, as strong a document as it should have been. It totally failed to address the fundamental cultural issues, which took me a lot longer to unravel; at least I had the defence of being an amateur. But it did make a fundamental recommendation: that the TSA should, for the first time ever, appoint a chief executive officer (CEO). I had been sceptical of this proposal initially, but a few months as chair had caused me to have a rapid change of mind: even if I could bear the burden at that particular time, it was wholly unreasonable to expect anybody else, without my professional skillset and experience (not least including fierce time management), to do so in the future on a voluntary, unpaid basis. And I simply did not have the management skills that I had come to realise were needed.

I aligned myself with the growing board consensus on this point, and we engaged specialists to find suitable applicants. After a thoroughly competent process, we cut down the 120 applicants to a manageable handful (most, in truth, eliminated themselves) and interviewed a shortlist of five. The outstanding candidate was Dr Jayne Spink, who – after some hesitation on her part, and much persuasion on ours – came into post at the start of 2011.

I very carefully phased Jayne's induction, as throwing everything at her in one go would have been wrong for both of us. For example, I withheld any financial issues until she had sorted out the organisation and management. But neither of us had the faintest idea just how extensive this exercise would prove to be.

To put it bluntly, we discovered gradually that the organisation was unmanaged, unmanageable and overwhelmingly dysfunctional.

Immediately upon Jayne's appointment, and a week before the 2010 AGM, Anne Carter had resigned as head of Appeals and Publicity, and ruthlessly and shamelessly stage-managed that AGM as her swansong, trailing clouds of glory with a video of her past triumphs. It was actually a blessing in disguise, as she was not prepared to tolerate being managed, and we would have had a miserable two years of disciplinary processes, which would have damaged us. When we found a replacement, her requested handover was more akin to a chuck-over-the-garden-fence.

The Support Services side seemed reasonably managed, but it was not to be long before they went into whinge mode. They had been enthusiastic supporters of appointing a CEO; in practice, however, they were no more willing to be managed than Anne Carter was. What they effectively wanted was not a CEO, but a chief operating officer (COO), who would provide them with administrative support but not interfere with their activities.

That administrative support related not least to ICT, where services were provided cheaply by a TSA member. But his systems were wholly inadequate, and he inevitably lost out when Jayne put our ICT requirements out to tender. He was very miffed by this, and wrote me a lengthy letter of protest to the effect that the TSA was no longer what it had been (i.e. chummy rather than competent); I reflected that we were clearly making progress!

He was also involved on the communications side, and – with a (very) part-time editor – was responsible for producing our *SCAN* magazine. This had to be – and was – injected with the necessary professionalism.

On the research side – where Jayne's own expertise lay – it was clear that there had been an almost complete rundown. The strategic review had identified this as an area for expansion, and the board had agreed, but it became apparent that the deputy head was incapable of delivering this. Being a dedicated researcher, her thoroughness and perfectionism meant that nothing administrative happened on time, if at all. She was simply inappropriate for her allotted role, and was – with Chris Kingswood's support – gently eased out.

We thought we had solved most of the problems and could now move forwards. We were deluded. The storm was about to break, giving rise to an existential crisis.

That break was in the form of a long whinge (63 pages, including appendices) from the head of Support Services, thinly disguised as a formal complaint against Jayne as CEO. To give one example of its inadequacy, the Support Services Department in general, and its head in particular, had long been – justifiably – vociferous about the inadequacies of the ICT service. Suddenly, for whinge purposes, our alleged unkindness to the failing supplier was used as a *casus belli* to complain about the authoritarian attitude of the CEO. But, however thin the allegations were, it was clear that there had been a relationship breakdown – the head saw her role, not as managing the Support Services Department as directed by the CEO (which was what she was paid to do), but acting as the team's shop steward.

I had to tell a distressed Jayne of the complaint, which I endeavoured to resolve informally. Any prospect of this was damaged by the situation around the deputy head of research, and it became clear to me – in various conversations with the Support Services Department in April 2013 – that a formal process would be necessary. The Support Services Department kindly informed me that they would graciously accept a trustee-led inquiry and nominated the trustees whom they magnanimously considered acceptable.

My parents on their wedding day

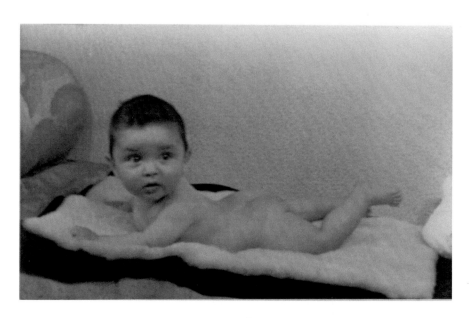

A very early me!

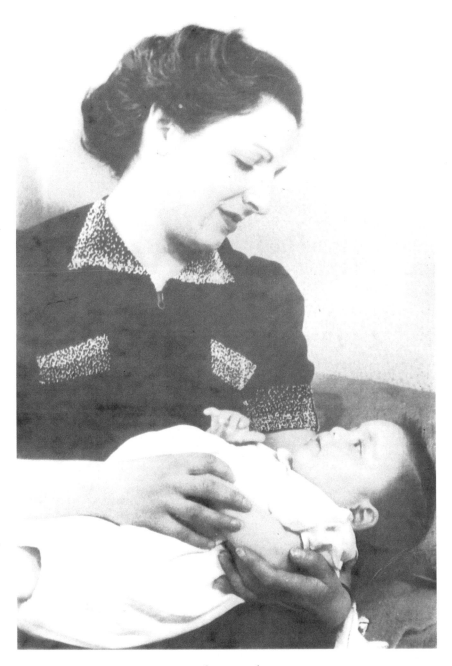

With my mother

My father

*Taking my MA
at Oxford*

*With my parents at
Buckingham Palace
after my father was
awarded the OBE*

A later me

My mother in her later years

With Lynda at my 70th birthday lunch

Over the weekend, I considered my options. One of my problems was that, just as Tom Carter viewed his wife Anne through rose-tinted spectacles, Christine Naylor had the same optical defect in relation to the Support Services Department. Her view was that, if push came to shove, it was Jayne who should go rather than the Support Services Department. I had to neutralise her. So I decided to bring back our previous strategic reviewer, on the twin basis that (a) whatever his inadequacies, it was pretty inconceivable that any management consultant would not come to the only sane conclusion; and (b) as he was Naylor's nominee, she would find it difficult to criticise his (inevitable) recommendations. I sat down and drafted a long email to the board, thinking we were now at last on the right track. I could not have been more wrong.

The grenade was hurled by one of the Support Services Department on the Sunday evening. In a document preparatory to her annual assessment by her head, she took the opportunity to launch a root-and-branch critique of Jayne's performance as CEO. This was of itself inappropriate, but her circulation of what she had written to all her Support Services Department colleagues, with a copy to various trustees and to Jayne herself, could only be seen (given that the Support Services Department moved as one) as a co-ordinated attempt to force the CEO's resignation.

Jayne had, in fact, spent the Sunday afternoon supporting TSA entrants in a London fun run, and was distraught to find this poisonous document in her inbox on her return. I was due to meet her the next day, with my deputy chair – Martin Short – for her annual appraisal, for which she turned up visibly – and unsurprisingly – distressed. We gave her total support. I explained that I had appointed an investigator to report to a special board meeting (in place of the regular, scheduled, June one), and asked her to submit a formal complaint against the grenade-hurler and a formal response to the sesquipedalian whinge by the head of Support Services.

The report – inevitably – dismissed the whinge and upheld Jayne's complaint. At a fully attended board meeting, the right outcome emerged, although not as strongly as I would have wished. I deliberately opted for 100% support for 75% of the right answer, rather than only 75% support for the totality of the right answer. Too many trustees were either too nice to recognise the stark reality of what had happened or were too loyal to the Support Services Department (from whose support they had, of course, benefited over the years).

I circulated the outcome to all concerned, coupled with a formal request to the grenade-hurler to apologise. She resigned instead, to be followed in due course by three further colleagues, including the head.

We had saved the TSA for its beneficiaries – the TSC community. Although much remained to be done, we could now move forwards as an organisation that had replaced amateurism with professionalism, and where it was recognised that the "empathy and enthusiasm" – which Tom Carter had said was all that a trustee needed – was nowhere near adequate as the test of a trustee's effectiveness.

I handed over the chair to Martin Short in March 2014. The TSA was on an even keel, with Jayne as an increasingly effective CEO. And, as I said to Martin, it had always been our agreement that I would shovel the shit, and he would reap the glory. Less scatologically, I had been a warrior, but the TSA now needed a healer. I remained a trustee, overseeing Jayne moving on after five years to lead the Genetic Alliance.

But, just when I mentally said to myself "mission accomplished"…

Martin was due to retire in 2018 after his four years in the chair. There was no obvious internal successor. So we engaged headhunters, reduced their long list to a short list, and interviewed three applicants. We were technically seeking to appoint a trustee, with a view to that person then moving on, subject to board assent, to deputy chair and then chair. Into our agreed list of questions, Martin brilliantly inserted what proved to be a killer: "If we took the view that you could help us as a trustee, but did not think you were a likely chair, would you still be interested in us?"

Two men effectively disqualified themselves by a negative answer; clearly, their primary interest was not in us, but in adding a charity chairmanship to their respective curricula vitae (CVs). So, a seemingly highly impressive lady virtually appointed herself by giving a positive answer, and duly became a trustee and deputy chair.

Sadly, behavioural difficulties emerged. A busy person in career terms, her attention span for the TSA was inadequate, with peremptory emails, sometimes to the point of offensiveness. Her approach was confrontational, and her habit was to lay down the law (literally as well as metaphorically), leaving the details to others. After one particularly egregious exchange in early 2018, my patience finally snapped and I rang round most of the board, following which I told Martin that there was a clear majority against her becoming chair at that time or indeed subsequently, unless there were changes in her behaviour.

All this came at a time which was difficult for two other reasons. Firstly, Jayne's successor as CEO, Louise Fish, had promptly become pregnant upon her appointment, so we were running with an extremely good interim CEO in the form of Maxine Smeaton (who was as concerned as I was by the deputy chair's behaviour, not least in terms of staff cohesion). Maxine was uncovering – and sorting at full stretch – some administrative and organisational issues that had been left untended for too long. And, secondly, our fund-raising operation was failing to produce the requisite results, even after a long developmental period, so we needed to reduce our spending to match our income in reasonably short order (but not, as the deputy chair insisted peremptorily to the board, in one disruptive fell swoop).

Martin kindly agreed to stay on for an extra year, but – in pastoral mode with good intentions, albeit wrongly – decided to tell the deputy chair that this was to ensure financial stability, rather than confronting her more directly about her behaviour. His view was that "time would tell". Mercifully, it did and, after a key board session at which the deputy chair made a good contribution to adopting revised strategic objectives, he came up to me and said,

"You're right. She's a great gadfly in discussion, but does not have the key skillset of a chair to lead inclusively, take people with her[10] and find compromises."

Towards the end of June 2018, there was a key board meeting. It was preceded by a meeting of the Nominations Committee (consisting of the chair and his predecessors), which formally recognised that the deputy chair would not become chair on Martin's retirement. It also had identified a prospective new trustee from among those who had expressed an interest in joining the Research Committee, and I volunteered to meet him with Maxine later that week.

The board itself approved a really good paper from Maxine on the "enablers" we needed for the future, and had an interesting half-hour discussion – impressively led by my daughter Pippa (whom I had introduced to Maxine) – on adapting the TSA to the digital age, which was a process that Pippa had helped lead at Asthma UK.

The prospective new trustee – Sanjay Sethi – was clearly outstanding, and readily agreed, in principle, to join the board. I also suggested that the deputy chair should be gently eased out, but this proved unnecessary! She was mysteriously unavailable for the board meeting, but had sniffed the wind emerging from the Nominations Committee, and resigned out of pique, with a ludicrously overstated email critique of the functioning of the board. In Martin's absence (on holiday), I could not leave that critique unanswered, so I responded in a tone that was sympathetic in general, but strongly refuted her allegations. This brought forth a torrent of personal abuse, which at least had the positive result of

---

10 In the early Thatcher years, just after the Iranian Embassy siege, which was relieved when the Special Air Service (SAS) stormed the building and rescued the hostages, she complained to her Cabinet Secretary that senior civil servants hadn't "got it" in terms of what she wanted to achieve. "Well, Prime Minister," he responded, "They love the formalities, so have them all in to a black-tie dinner at No. 10, and try to take them with you." Some hope! At the coffee stage, she let fly with a 30-minute harangue. At its conclusion, the Permanent Secretary at the Ministry of Defence left the room for a comfort break. "Where's Frank gone?" one colleague asked. "To get the SAS to rescue us!" came the reply from another. The story was so good that I gave it to *The Times* diary, which kindly published it.

demonstrating to the board why her potential chairmanship was a disaster waiting to happen.

With harmony thus restored, and Louise back from maternity leave and buying into the agreed direction of progress, we held an extra board meeting in October for a big discussion on the new strategy and looked at upcoming board changes. I told the board that it needed new blood, and I had more than done my duty. We signed off the new strategy at the November board meeting on the eve of the annual members' "Big Day" in Sheffield, and appointed Sanjay as a trustee and deputy chair. Martin used his presentation at the Big Day to promote the new strategy and to appeal for fresh trustees. As the strategy was rolled out, I retired from the board in mid-2019.

Customers and staff count, too

But directors' duties are to their companies, says **Philip Goldenberg**

Company directors are awaiting a report on what duties they have to shareholders and stakeholders. They have already had their accounting practices scrutinised by The Accounting Standards Board, which cleared up the excesses of 1980s UK company accounts — too often designed to mask rather than reveal the truth.

Then came the Cadbury Report on the financial aspects of corporate governance which has had a significant impact on financial controls and reporting, and enhanced the role of non-executive directors. Today, The Royal Society for the encouragement of Arts, Manufacturers and Commerce launches the findings of its Tomorrow's Company inquiry.

Its theme is that the companies which will sustain competitive success in the future are those which focus less on present shareholders and on — inevitably historic — financial measures of success, and more on their relationships with stakeholders (employees, customers, suppliers and the community), and a broader range of measurements in the way they think about their purpose and performance. This is called the inclusive approach.

Is this yet another burden on directors? On the contrary, it is an end to the sterile debate of "shareholder versus stakeholder". Only by giving appropriate weight to all stakeholders can directors maximise the sustainable growth of their companies for the benefit of shareholders, both present and future.

What consequences does this analysis have for directors' duties? We were struck, during the inquiry, by the number of directors who thought that company law pushed them towards pleasing the current body of shareholders rather than securing the long-term health of the business.

The opposite is the case. Directors' duties are to their company, not to any third-party group. This is true even of their legal statutory duty to have regard to consider the interests of employees. In discharging that duty, they must have regard to the interests of shareholders (or, if the company is insolvent, of creditors). This obligation is not related to the actual shareholders at any particular moment but to the general body of shareholders from time to time. Accordingly, the duty of directors is to maximise the company's value on a sustainable basis.

There is nothing in law to prevent directors from considering the interests of third parties with whom the company has a relationship, if they judge that to do so will aid its success. Indeed, for directors not to give weight to their company's relationships could inhibit the discharge of their duty.

The end of shareholder versus stakeholder

This means that a company that skimps on environmental protection risks losing money and reputation — part of its intangible "licence to operate". One which pays out too-high dividends risks not investing adequately for the future, and one which saves on employee costs can lose staff loyalty.

Company law does not prescribe how directors should balance all the factors when they make decisions. It does not tell them to work in partnership with their suppliers, rather than seeking to maintain short-term, adversarial relationships designed to minimise costs. It does not compel them to build up a good record of environmental practice or tell them to value human resources as the key element for their future.

But it does allow them to do so. And clearing up this misconception removes a significant barrier to change.

● *The author, a partner in City solicitors S.J. Berwin & Co, has been the legal adviser to the RSA's Tomorrow's Company inquiry.*

1995: The Times, *"Directors' Duties"*

82   *Business Law Review*   April 2003

Corporate Governance

Reforming Corporate Governance – A Very British Solution

Philip Goldenberg*

Background

Derek Higgs' Report, entitled *Review of the rôle and effectiveness of non-executive directors* and published in January 2003, was not a self-contained event. Rather is it part of a continuing process of the reform of corporate governance, for which the most immediately convenient starting point is the UK Company Law Review; its final report was published in July 2001, followed a year later by a government White Paper entitled "Modernising Company Law".

The Company Law Review was a fundamental review of the totality of company law, whose architecture had effectively remained unchanged since the Victorian era. But included in it were two points which were particularly relevant to Higgs:

- a proposed statutory statement of directors' duties; and
- an obligation (primarily upon listed companies) to include in their annual Reports & Accounts a more holistic overview of their affairs by way of an Operating and Financial Review (OFR), which would go beyond reporting historic financial outcomes to include a narrative review of a company's business, its performance, plans and prospects, and other information judged necessary for an understanding of the business (relationships with employees, suppliers, and customers; environmental and community issues; corporate governance matters; and risk management) – effectively a SWOT analysis, which good companies already undertake in private.

In advance of a new Companies Act, the Accounting Standards Board in January 2003 updated its Statement "Operating and Financial Review" to bring it closer to the anticipated statutory requirements.

It was the intention of the UK government effectively to legislate the near-totality of the Company Law Review. However, in the light of various dramatic corporate failures, the government revisited the two topics of (a) the responsibility of (particularly non-executive) directors and (b) the UK audit and accounting process. The first has given birth to the *Higgs Report*; the second has now produced a final report by the Coordinating Group on Audit and Accounting Issues, published together with the report of the Review of the Regulatory Régime of the Accountancy Profession.

Into the waters of this review process two more streams have recently flowed. Firstly, Paul Myners reported in 2001 on the reluctance of institutional investors to tackle corporate under-performance in their investee companies; this was followed by a 2002 Statement of Best Practice by institutional investor bodies on the Responsibilities of Institutional Investors. Secondly, there has been a significant and growing debate around the twin topics of Corporate Social Responsibility and Socially Responsible Investing (see for example the 2002 report by the Federal Trust).

The Combined Code on Corporate Governance

The Combined Code itself has a history. There was originally (in 1992) the *Cadbury Report on Corporate Governance*, which was a first step towards an appraisal of the responsibilities of company boards. This begat (in 1994) the *Turnbull Report on risk management*, and then (in 1995) the *Greenbury Report on the remuneration of executive directors*; the 1998 *Hampel Report* then reviewed and consolidated these three into the present Combined Code, which is binding upon listed companies only in the sense that non-compliance with any of its provisions has to be declared and explained.

Higgs has effectively built on the Combined Code, advocating significant re-writing on key topics, while maintaining its methodology.

Law and Regulation

The word "law" is actually, upon proper analysis, a hierarchy of obligations. At the top is statute law (either primary by statute or secondary by delegated legislation), which commands the obedience of all, normally with criminal sanctions for non-compliance. There is then regulation, such as the Listing Rules as they apply to companies whose shares are listed on the London Stock Exchange. Beyond that are softer forms, such as international conventions; and below them Codes of Practice.

Law can also have two different functions. It can be prescriptive, for example compelling certain conduct. Alternatively, it can be facultative – creating a situation which encourages certain outcomes in a non-prescriptive way. The proposed OFR is an extremely good example of the latter; by compelling companies to put additional information into the public domain, it will in effect kick-start a whole process of encouraging best practice in doing so.

The British approach is often to use softer forms of law, not least to facilitate a cultural change which is by its nature a process rather than an event. This is to be contrasted with the highly prescriptive (and too often extra-territorial) approach typical of the USA, as witness the Sarbanes-Oxley legislation following the Enron débâcle. *Higgs* is squarely within this very British tradition.

*Partner, SJ Berwin. This article reproduces City Solicitors SJ Berwin's Client Memorandum on Higgs which Philip Goldenberg wrote.

Corporate Governance

Higgs: The Theme

Higgs starts from the basis (widely accepted within corporate Britain) that there should be a unitary board. His aim is to strengthen this by defining rôles not only for non-executive directors (his terms of reference) but also for chairmen, senior independent directors and the functioning of the board as a whole. He rightly acknowledges that an architecture in itself does not deliver good outcomes; his review therefore also focuses on the conditions and behaviours necessary to deliver those outcomes.

The Rôle of the Board

Higgs defines the rôle of the Board in draft wording for his proposed revised Combined Code as follows:

"The board is collectively responsible for promoting success of the company by directing and supervising the company's affairs.

The board's rôle is to provide entrepreneurial leadership within a framework of prudent and effective controls which enable risk to be assessed and managed.

The board should set the company's strategic aims, ensure that the necessary financial and human resources are in place for the company to meet its objectives and review management performance.

The board should set the company's values and standards and ensure that its obligations to its shareholders and others are understood and met."

Effectively, this proposal elegantly sets out the rôle of all directors in being both "strategists and policemen" (a phrase normally applied only to non-executive directors, but equally applicable to all). But this is probably the first time that as authoritative a document as Higgs has suggested an explicit statement which includes a company's values.

' also recommends that boards should publish in the annual reports a statement as to how they operate, and in particular the division between matters addressed by the whole board and those delegated to management.

One of the peculiarities of the ongoing British debate on corporate governance has been the contrast between the near-paranoid insistence on the unitary board model on the one hand, and the actual practices of a number of boards on the other. Too often non-executive directors have not of their own motion acquired sufficient knowledge of their company's business (or been encouraged to do so); and the vaunted unitary board has in consequence operated as an awkward conjunction of two different planets of executive and non-executive directors. Higgs' proposals should remedy this.

The Rôle of the Chairman

Higgs first addresses the rôle of the chairman, whom he describes as "pivotal" in creating the conditions for overall board and individual non-executive director effectiveness. Building on the existing Combined Code distinction between the chairman (responsible for the governance of a company) and the chief executive (responsible for its management), Higgs recommends that the chairman be given specific responsibility for:

- leadership of the board;
- ensuring a good information flow to directors, and effective communication with shareholders;
- arranging the regular evaluation of the individual and collective performance of the board; and
- maintaining a relationship of trust with and between the executive and non-executive directors.

In this context, Higgs proposes that the Combined Code now contain a straightforward statement that the rôles of chairman and chief executive should be separated (as is already the case with around 90% of listed companies), and that the division of responsibilities between them should be set out in writing and agreed by the board. He also recommends that the chief executive should not become chairman of the same company, and that the chairman on appointment should meet the test of independence (see below). Annex D to the Higgs Report sets out some of the attributes and behaviours of an effective chairman.

Higgs also makes specific recommendations as to the process for appointing a chairman.

The Rôle of the Non-Executive Director

As mentioned above, much existing literature describes the rôle of the non-executive director as being both a strategist and a policeman. Higgs' research found that the oft-cited conflict between these two rôles did not in practice exist, so long as there was a proper balance between them.

Higgs then sets out a proposed Code provision detailing the rôle of the non-executive director as follows:

- *strategy:* constructively challenging and contributing to the development of strategy;
- *performance:* scrutinising the performance of management in meeting agreed goals and objectives and monitoring the reporting of performance;
- *risk management:* satisfying themselves as to the accuracy of financial information and that financial controls and systems of risk management are robust and defensible; and
- *people:* determining appropriate levels of remuneration for executive directors (see below) and leading on the appointment (and where necessary removal) of senior management, and on succession planning.

Higgs rightly goes on to argue that the key to non-executive director effectiveness lies as much in behaviours and relationships as in structures and processes. As well as skills, experience and integrity, non-executive directors need to be sound in judgement and have enquiring minds; they should also have appropriate interpersonal skills – without which their other abilities will be ineffective. In addition, they must acquire the expertise and knowledge (of both the company itself and the markets in which it operates) necessary to do an effective job.

Higgs recommends that new non-executive directors should have a comprehensive, formal and tailored induction; that subsequently, on an ongoing basis, there should be a programme of professional development for directors to develop and refresh their knowledge and skills; and that this should be linked with an evaluation process of regular appraisal. These pro-

84   *Business Law Review* April 2003

Corporate Governance

grammes should be overseen by the chairman and facilitated by the company secretary.

Higgs then reviews issues relating to the liability of non-executive directors. Noting the proposal of the *Company Law Review* for a statutory statement of directors' responsibilities, he annexes to his draft revised Code additional guidance on the liability of non-executive directors. He then recommends that various institutional bodies draw up guidance on directors' and officers' liability insurance, so as to bring together the present somewhat disparate approach to this important topic.

Finally, Higgs discusses the topic of resignation by non-executive directors. He rightly regards it as a last resort, noting that it may in certain circumstances be contrary to a director's fiduciary duties. Non-executive directors who have serious concerns should raise them in the first instance with their board colleagues, if appropriate requiring them to be minuted. If a non-executive director feels that resignation is the only course of action, then (rather as with an auditor) he should give a written statement of his reasons to the chairman, who should then circulate it to the board.

Independence

Higgs recommends that at least half the members of any board (excluding the chairman) should be not only non-executive but independent. He does not rule out non-executive directors who do not meet the test of independence (for example, those with a recent or existing connection with the company), but asserts that they should not be counted for this purpose. He then recommends a definition of independence for the Code which will bring together the present proliferation of different definitions, as follows:

- a non-executive director is independent where the board so determines and there are no relationships or circumstances which could affect (or appear to affect) that director's judgement;
- such relationships or circumstances include where the director concerned:
  - has been an employee (or had any other material connection) with the company within the previous five years;
  - has, or has had within the previous three years, a direct or indirect material business relationship with the company;
  - receives remuneration from the company (including any incentives or pension) apart from a director's fee;
  - has close family or business ties with any of the company's advisers, directors or senior employees;
  - represents a significant shareholder; or
  - has served on the board for more than ten years.

Each board should identify in its annual report the non-executive directors it determines to be independent, and should state its reasons if such independence is asserted notwithstanding relationships or circumstances such as those set out above.

The Effective Board

Higgs' research identified the potential for a virtuous dynamic in which executive directors' perceptions of the value of non-executive directors' experience and contribution encourages greater executive openness which, in turn, allows for greater non-executive engagement. The opposite vicious dynamic is, of course, equally possible! and all this comes back to the need for an environment of trust and mutual respect. To this, both executive and non-executive directors need to make a positive and continuing contribution.

Higgs recommends at least one meeting a year of non-executive directors without the presence of the chairman or executive directors in order to increase the effectiveness of the former, and says that there may be a case for additional meetings of the non-executives with the chairman.

Higgs' three research projects as to existing board composition and practice are available on the Review's web site.

Higgs also emphasises the importance of the r̃ the company secretary in ensuring the effective ṽ ing of the board. He suggests a formal provision in the Code that the company secretary should be accountable to the board through the chairman on all governance matters; in this context, both the appointment and removal of the company secretary should be a matter for the board as a whole.

Recruitment and Appointment of non-executive Directors

Higgs sets out the current population of non-executive directors. The incidence of multiple directorships is less than may have been thought; 80% of non-executive directors hold only one such position in a UK listed company, with a further 10% holding two such positions. However, 13% of chairmen hold more than one chairmanship; a significant minority of listed companies combine the posts of chairman and chief executive; and as many as 24 of the FTSE 100 chairmen were formerly the chief executive of the same company. A mere 4% of executive director posts ar̃ of non-executive director posts are held by women, and only 1% by ethnic minority groups.

Higgs identifies the cause of this in what he calls the "high level of informality" surrounding the process of appointing non-executive directors, with almost half the non-executive directors surveyed for the review recruited through personal contacts or friendships. He accordingly makes significant recommendations for a proper process of appointment:

- all listed companies should have a nomination committee, a majority of whose members should be independent non-executives and which should be chaired by such a person (that is, not by the chairman);
- the chairman and members of the nomination committee should be identified in the annual report, together with their terms of reference and the processes they have used;
- before making an appointment the nomination committee should determine the rôle and capabilities required for the appointee;
- there should be a formal letter of appointment (a *pro forma* is provided in Annex H to the proposed Code);
- potential non-executive directors should disclose to

Business Law Review April 2003 85

Corporate Governance

the chairman the nature and extent of their other commitments; and

- when a new non-executive director comes up for his first election by shareholders, the board should explain why they believe that the individual should be appointed having regard to the rôle of non-executive directors in general and also of the particular appointment.

Higgs makes significant practical proposals for broadening the pool of candidates for non-executive directorships; the London Business School has undertaken to play a key rôle in this process.

Higgs believes that a board should regularly re-evaluate the mixture of skills and experience it needs, and emphasises the rôle of the nomination committee in succession planning. He considers that a non-executive director should normally be expected to serve two -year terms and that, in the exceptional case of a term, any non-executive director should thereafter be subject to annual re-election.

The nomination committee should also have oversight of the time and responsibility of each appointment of a non-executive director (including particular appointments as chairman, senior independent director and/or member of specified board committees), and should review this annually as part of performance evaluation. Given the seriousness of the commitment, Higgs believes that any executive director should not take on more than one non-executive directorship nor become chairman of a FTSE 100 company, nor should any individual chair the board of more than one such company.

As to remuneration, Higgs cites a recent survey that a non-executive director of a FTSE 100 company should be paid between £40k and £60k (the current average is £44k) per annum, and that the comparable figures for smaller listed companies should range between £25k and £40k (current average somewhat on ow side at £23k). There is merit in giving non-executive directors the opportunity to take part of their remuneration in the form of shares rather than cash, but they should not be granted options.

Audit and Remuneration Committees

Independent non-executive directors should play a leading rôle in audit and remuneration, as well as nomination, committees. Higgs considers it undesirable for any one individual to be a member of all such three committees concurrently.

Higgs incorporates the recommendations of the Financial Reporting Council Group appointed following the interim report of the Coordinating Group on Audit and Accounting Issues to develop Code guidance for Audit Committees. These should:

- have at least three members (all of whom should be independent non-executive directors, and one of whom should have had recent significant and relevant financial experience);
- monitor the integrity of the company's financial statements, reviewing significant financial reporting judgements;
- review internal financial control and risk management systems, as well as the internal audit function; make recommendations in relation to the appoint-

ment of the external auditor, and approve their remuneration and terms of engagement;

- monitor and review the external auditor's independence, objectivity and effectiveness, taking into account relevant UK professional and regulatory requirements;
- develop and implement policy on the engagement of the external auditor to supply non-audit services, taking into account relevant ethical guidance; and
- have their rôle and actions separately reported to shareholders.

The remuneration committee should work closely with the nomination committee to ensure that incentives are appropriately structured for directors and for senior executives, and that severance terms are carefully considered. *In the latter case, the broad aim should be to avoid rewarding poor performance while dealing fairly with cases where that is not the reason for departure.*

The remuneration committee should also have at least three members, and all such members should be independent non-executives. It should have published terms of reference, including delegated responsibility for setting remuneration for all executive directors and the chairman. The committee should also set the level and structure of remuneration for senior executives, and be responsible for appointing remuneration consultants. Any support for the remuneration committee by executive directors or senior management should be clearly separated from their executive rôles. The annual report of the remuneration committee should disclose the frequency of, and attendance at, its meetings.

Relationships with Shareholders

Higgs believes that non-executive directors should be more involved in discussions with major shareholders. This should not only be by attendance at the AGM; the senior independent director (who should be formally identified, and should be an ultimate point of contact for shareholders if the normal channels of communication with the chairman and/or chief executive break down) should attend sufficient of the regular meetings of management with a range of major shareholders in order to develop a balanced understanding of the themes, issues and concerns of shareholders. S/he should then communicate these to the other non-executive directors and the board as a whole. Other non-executive directors may also find it constructive to attend such meetings, and should do so if requested by major shareholders; and they should meet major investors as part of their induction process.

Companies should state in their annual reports what steps they have taken to ensure that non-executive directors in particular have a balanced understanding of the views of major shareholders.

Conclusion

Higgs was originally commissioned to review "The Rôle and Effectiveness of Non-executive Directors". It is wholly to his credit that he interpreted his mandate broadly; he has made a valuable holistic contribution

86   *Business Law Review   April 2003*

Corporate Governance

to corporate governance. In effect, he was asked the wrong question, but has given the right answer.

At the heart of what Higgs recommends is a significant cultural change; and, by definition, cultural change is a continuing process rather than a single event. Perhaps the most fundamental such change will prove to be the end of the "crony culture" of non-executive appointments. The most difficult to implement, however, at least in the short term, may well be altering the composition of existing boards to satisfy the requirement for half their membership (excluding the chairman) to consist of *independent* non-executive directors, and at the same time establish a reservoir of potential appointees with appropriate skill bases.

Appendix

Useful Web Links

The full text of the Higgs Report, together with details of the research it commissioned, and copies of consultation responses, can be accessed at:
http://www.dti.gov.uk/cld/non_exec_review
The full Interim Report of the CGAA can be accessed at:

http://www.frc.org.uk/publications
The *Cadbury, Greenbury* and *Hampel* Reports and the Combined Code can be accessed at:
http://www.ecgi.org/codes/country_pages/codes_uk.htm
Information on the *Company Law Review* and the *Company Law White Paper* can be accessed at:
http://www.dti.gov.uk/cld
The *Myners Report on Institutional Investment in the UK* can be accessed at:
http://www.hm-treasury.gov.uk/Documents/Financial_-Services/Securities_and_Investments/fin_sec_mynfinal.cfm
The recent *Statement of Best Practice on the Responsibilities of Institutional Investors* can be accessed at:
http://www.abi.org.uk (under the heading Investment Affairs).
The Federal Trust's Report on *Corporate Social Responsibility and Socially Responsible Investing* can be accessed at:
http://www.fedtrust.co.uk/csr
Copies of guidance on nomination and remuneration committees, and checklists for due diligence and induction (and a specimen letter of appointment) for incoming non-executive directors, produced by the Institute of Chartered Secretaries and Administrators, can be accessed at the ICSA web site:
http://www.icsa.org.uk

2003: Business Law Review, *Corporate Governance*

5

Liberal and Liberal Democrat (LibDem) Politics: Local

Introduction

A political party is structurally no different from any other voluntary organisation, such as a charity or a bridge club. But it is fundamentally different in both culture and purpose.

Culturally, it is inherently tribal. Because it is in competition with other political parties, it does – or should – have the camaraderie needed by successful armies. Furthermore, its purpose is to win power and use it in furtherance of what it stands for or represents. In Britain, the Conservative Party exists to protect wealth and privilege, while doing just enough to stave off a revolution (its Brexit wing is a remarkable abandonment of its historic pragmatism); the Labour Party used to represent the workers, until it was left behind by the changing nature of the workplace – it has yet to resolve the contradiction that the socially progressive views of its leadership are at odds with the social conservatism of large sections of what was its voting base; and the LibDems exist to promote liberal values – open-mindedness, tolerance and generosity of spirit (the last being the meaning of the Latin word *"liberalis"*).

So, in theory, a local LibDem party should have two features: a co-operative internal culture, and members who are committed to liberal values in behaviour as well as ideology.

But the reality can often be different. As the journalist Francis Kinsman pointed out in a brilliant pamphlet entitled "Once upon a Group" (produced under the aegis of the Roman Catholic Church), those who come into voluntary organisations often do so with primary or secondary motivations, which have nothing to do with that organisation. They can instead be using them for displacement activity to address emotional gaps in their lives: the need to feel wanted and self-important is a frequent motivating factor. That may, in turn, give an emotional edge to their involvement that is detrimental to the organisation, because they are more motivated by their personal success within the organisation than by its success against its competitors. In the case of the LibDems, that causes two conflicts: firstly, such people are – by definition – unlikely to be guided by liberal values or behavioural standards; and, secondly, their behaviours can inflict significant cultural damage on the organisation as a whole (the "rotten apple in a barrel" problem).

This problem is aggravated by another feature of voluntary organisations: there is no P45! In other words, getting rid of somebody for bad behaviour is extremely difficult; the LibDem rules on this were written by an enthusiastic, young barrister who was keen on human rights and who stupidly applied the criminal standard of proof to them, which gave rise to the difficulties in the Rennard[11] case.

In addition, there is a desperate shortage of committed activists, so that there is excessive tolerance of misconduct on their part.

---

11   Chris Rennard was in his heyday a brilliant – if highly cynical – by-election campaigner, responsible for many of the Party's triumphs. But he had a difficult personality, which hindered his work as the Party's Chief Executive. He continued in this office long past his sell-by date, and resigned after being caught up in the Parliamentary expenses scandal. There were subsequent complaints about his misuse of his authority to engage in serial sexual harassment (for which he was never charged), and his combative LibDem QC ruthlessly exploited the overly onerous requirement as to proof in fighting to retain his Party membership.

Beginnings

I had always been interested in politics and current affairs; my awareness began with the Suez crisis when I was aged 10. My natural empathy was liberal centre-left, and my early heroes were Jo Grimond and Roy Jenkins. That I would end up meeting – let alone working with – both was not then within my contemplation! I left it until the end of my time at school to become practically involved, starting with the St Marylebone (where I lived) by-election when a safe seat was found for Quintin Hogg after he disclaimed his peerage in a failed attempt to become Tory leader. I was then heavily involved at university (see Chapter 1). Thereafter, I became mildly involved in St Marylebone, becoming its Young Liberal chair.

I then translated this activity to Westminster (including standing as a local government candidate) after I moved out from my parents' home. I generated significant local (and, indeed, national) publicity with a formal request to disallow the expenditure by Westminster City Council on a new top-range Rolls-Royce Silver Phantom for its Lord Mayor on the basis that it was unlawful by reason of being excessive, which culminated in a well-reported formal hearing; *The Guardian* neatly headed its piece *Council's Phantom Dignity*!

My first serious involvement was in Sutton and Cheam, after I moved there once I had qualified as a solicitor in 1972. I rang the advertised telephone number and explained that I had just moved in. On hearing that I had been a press officer and local government candidate, I was immediately asked to join the local-party executive, and was appointed a ward organiser. The local party was manifestly in a weak condition! Neither it, nor I, knew that it was about to be hit by a bombshell that would change it out of all recognition.

The national context had been that voters were getting tired of the old, stale Tory/Labour duopoly. Cyril Smith's win in the Rochdale by-election had given the Liberals momentum, and they were developing new techniques for local campaigning, with "Focus" leaflets, led by the redoubtable Trevor Jones ("Jones the Vote") of Liverpool. The party was itching for its next by-election opportunity.

That opportunity arrived in Sutton, with the murder in the Caribbean of its sitting Tory MP. An emergency executive meeting was convened. There was a proposal that Trevor Jones should be the campaign manager. Most of the executive (a number of whom knitted during meetings) clucked their collective disapproval; they had never heard of him, and had no idea what a campaign manager was or did. Eventually, I was asked my opinion. I played it deadpan, saying, "Well, it's very risky." The *tricoteuses*[12] knitted approvingly. "We might win!" I added. The executive appointed him with reluctance.

As history records, we did win, with a very good local candidate in the form of Graham Tope. One of my contributions was to lead the first distribution of the new "Good Morning" leaflets at 05:30 hours on a cold December morning!

At the meeting after we won, a local high-street solicitor gave a solemn warning to the executive: "We must be very careful now we've won. We don't want the wrong sort of person joining this association."

But the campaign did cause me to reflect. We had won on a "community politics" campaign. I analysed it in an article in *New Outlook*, a shortened version of which appears at the end of this chapter.

I helped subsequently with the next year's successful GLC election campaign, in which (as I was by then on the electoral register) I enjoyed the unusual experience of voting for the winning candidate.

While still in Sutton, and by now professionally established, I had begun to look for a Parliamentary seat. I continued this process after moving to Watford in 1973, and eventually ended up being selected by Eton and Slough Liberals.

Slough Liberals were rather less class-conscious than their Sutton counterparts, and a good guerrilla operation in unpromising territory, which had built significant local-government bridgeheads.

---

12 The *tricoteuses* were the ladies who, in the French Revolution, knitted at the foot of the guillotine while it was in operation.

I was happy to join in and – in the February 1974 general election, which was the first impressive performance for modern Liberals – received a 20% vote share, which was pretty good for a seat that had been historically a Tory/Labour marginal seat.

I then fought in the October general election, following the national trend with a slightly reduced vote. My posed photo with Jeremy Thorpe as Liberal leader was elegantly transmuted by one of the local papers with some apt bubbles:

The reporter concerned was apologetic, but I was delighted!

Out of loyalty, I stayed on to fight the unpromising general election of 1979, while also building myself into the national structures of the party (see Chapter 6).

I had, by then, learned quite a bit about real life. As an activist unkindly but accurately said after the February campaign, "Philip, to his surprise, discovered that ordinary people could think quite intelligently." I had escaped from my university and professional ivory tower! But subsequent events rendered unfortunate the front cover of my October election address, bearing as it did a picture of me with Jeremy Thorpe under the strapline "Two Men You Can Trust"!

It was then time to move on to a seat with better prospects.

I thought through my strategy. I had a good, developing professional career, which provided a solid financial base. I would have loved to be an MP, but there did not seem to be much point in joining a gallant band of six, and – more practically – I was unlikely to be selected for a seat with really good prospects, which in any event tended to be well away from London to which I needed to commute. So, I set out to get selected for a seat that we might well win if there were over 50 MPs and was a convenient commute. I identified two: St Albans (near where I lived in Watford) and Woking. I came a narrow second in the contest for the first, and won the second in early 1981, moving there in the autumn of that year.

Woking (1)

Politics was at an exciting juncture. The SDP breakaway from the Labour Party was in full swing. One of my first constituency events as prospective Parliamentary candidate (PPC) was a full-scale leader's rally at Woking in advance of the 1981 county council election. I sat mute on the platform, my offer to do a warm-up act for David Steel having been rejected by the incompetent powers that be, and groaned as the chair said simply, "Your Leader, David Steel!" gesturing weakly to the right while David entered to the left.

Woking Liberals were in what might politely be described as a developmental phase. As I learned, the local-government base it had built up in the 1960s had been allowed to wither on the vine.

It had had a good general election result in February 1974, mainly by hiding the uninspiring candidate from the electorate. There had then – unbelievably – been litigation over who should fight in the October election eight months later. The local party had subsequently gone to sleep until the 1979 general election, at which it had fielded an even more unimpressive candidate, who had lost the party's second place.

Recently, there had been a slight awakening. A borough by-election in a single-member ward had been won by a very personal campaign, which went under the Tory radar, and was masterminded by a seemingly impressive organiser called Bob Somper. Indeed, Bob was my main source of useful information about the local electoral map.

I gradually learned, however, of his flawed psychology: he was intensely narcissistic, and was making himself useful to me in the expectation that he would have my personal attention for 25 hours a day, and would use his working relationship with me to build his own status. Much worse was to come later; Somper was eventually forced to resign from the party after being charged with having grossly indecent images of young boys stored on his computer. They were so bad that, as a first-time offender aged over 70, he was nevertheless given an immediate custodial sentence. He reoffended subsequently, narrowly escaping a second spell inside.

I focussed my attention on the 1981 county council elections, playing a part in helping to win our first county seat for some time and consolidating the local membership base thereafter. I then gave time to strategic thought, as well as ensuring a high local public profile for myself and the Liberals; two examples appear here (and see other material at the end of this chapter):

It's a good job that our photographer always carries a camera. Visiting a friend in St. Peter's Hospital the other evening, he spotted Philip and Linda Goldenberg on a tour of inspection of the maternity unit. The happy couple who were married in October confirmed that they are expecting a new young Liberal next summer.

The borough council elections were by thirds; in each non-county year (so in three out of four years), a third of the borough seats came up for re-election. The wards each had one, two or three councillors, so that a breakthrough, followed by base-building, could have a cumulative effect, and we could run a targeting strategy accordingly, using our limited (but hopefully growing) resources to best effect. We would bring freshness to the local political scene, where very few seats changed hands and there was little serious campaigning, as Labour could not win more than eight seats and the Tories perceived themselves as safe in the remaining 27. So, turnout had been generally low, and disillusioned electors were ready for something new.

We followed this course, helped by adventitious by-elections in useful places. In both the 1982 and 1983 local elections, we broke new ground and consolidated old. In 1983, we had a good general election result, in which we regained our second place and – more importantly – used it to increase our resources by drawing in new members. In 1984, I was elected to the borough council (see Chapter 7) by heavily defeating its Tory leader. In 1985, we gained three of the six county seats in the Borough of Woking, adding a fourth in a 1986 by-election; at the same time, we made electoral inroads into the areas outside the Borough of Woking.

Our 1985 campaign was helped by a really daft Tory suggestion, at the end of a February Council meeting, which was that the council should shell out for number plates "WOK 1" and "WOK 2" for a mayoral car it did not yet possess. This was a gift horse for the media, and I ensured that they did not look it in the mouth. My colleague Ron Hore helped with a brilliant cartoon, which appeared in the local rag as part of a magnificent front page – see the material at the end of this chapter.

By 1986, the Tories had lost control of Woking Borough Council, reduced to holding 15 seats out of 35, with us up to 12, and Labour on eight. It was now possible to travel the length and breadth of the constituency without leaving Liberal/SDP territory.

This fed into a successful 1987 general election campaign, with an increased absolute and relative share of the vote. But this hard-built springboard for success was then thrown away, both locally and nationally: in the latter case by the dreadful mess of the Liberal/SDP merger process (see Chapter 6), and in the former both by the morale-sapping impact of the latter and by a Somper-led stirring in the ranks to get a new PPC, with whom he could have an enhanced status. We lost three years of potentially constructive activity, although I fought a fierce – and successful – campaign in 1988 to retain my own council seat against a local Tory, who had been smuggled in to chair the local Residents Association and then misuse it to undermine me (the Tories did this again elsewhere in 2003–4 – see Chapter 7).

In 1990, I lost a vicious internal battle to continue as PPC; I won a majority of those who attended the hustings meetings, but lost out among other members as the result of an unpleasant Somperled whispering campaign.

The 1992 general election campaign saw us suffer a severe drop in our performance with Dorothy Buckrell (our 1981 county council success, who had been an excellent county councillor) as the candidate. Our voters were demoralised in the local elections a few weeks later, and I lost my borough council seat by 19 votes. I was invited to become president of the local party, and did my best – from that position – to encourage a fragile rebuilding of our strength.

But I clearly needed a new challenge, and the political context had again become exciting, as the Tory government was heavily damaged by the currency crash of "Black Wednesday" in autumn 1992, and thereafter by its internal civil war on Europe.

With my family background, I had always felt as much European as British. The pending 1994 European Parliamentary[13] election might, I reasoned, neatly align my personal feelings with serious political possibilities, and I could keep a connection with SJB (see Chapter 2), which had a Brussels office to whom an MEP would be useful.

I looked at the field. With large single-member constituencies (this was to be the last European Parliamentary election fought under the dreadful "first-past-the-post" system), if I were to have a serious chance, I had to be selected for an area of Liberal strength.

From Woking, that had to be in the South West, where there were four seats: Cornwall and Devon (both too far, and best fought

---

13   Here are my two favourite European Parliament jokes.
     Corridor dialogue with the German MEP Otto von Habsburg:
     "Otto, do you know the football result?"
     "Ach, who is playing?"
     "Austria/Hungary."
     "Ach, against whom?"
     And the perils of simultaneous translation: a florid French MEP from Normandy said to a committee (with a view to local publicity), *"Nous avons besoin de la sagesse des Normains."* Over the British headphones came, "What we need is Norman Wisdom."

by local candidates), Somerset (already taken by my friend Graham Watson) and Dorset (which had the additional advantage of our having a second home there, in Studland, which we had purchased in 1989).

I duly applied for the Dorset seat, and – in early 1993 – was both thrilled and surprised to win the selection battle against three local candidates. My key argument was that, even though we had come fourth in the 1989 election with a mere 10% vote share, subsequent local-election patterns showed that a win was possible. My opening hustings line proved a winner: "I am not here because I wish to be your European Parliamentary candidate. I am here because if, as I hope and wish, you select me in that role, I intend to be your Member of the European Parliament."

My first task upon election was to drive over to the Yeovil Liberal Club for a photocall with Graham Watson and Paddy Ashdown. Paddy had not looked at the list of Dorset applicants and, when a familiar tousled head emerged from his office, he looked at me askance and uttered the immortal words of greeting, "What the f*** are you doing here?" with an octave range that, as I told the Dorset LibDem dinner a month later, would have been rightly envied by the late Dame Edith Evans delivering Lady Bracknell's immortal words "A handbag!" I gave the dinner the BBC version of his exclamation.

My last task in Woking was to preside at the LibDem AGM. As I thought I would never again be involved with them, I shared with them my concern at the amount of faction-fighting and personal-agenda chasing that had been so damaging. After I had finished, Somper rose to present me with a book of political quotations, which had kindly been signed by a number of local members.

My incipient feelings of goodwill were rapidly snuffed out when he then read out some carefully selected vituperative quotations, targeting them at me. I could see that the majority of faces were disapproving. When Somper had finished (to be more accurate, when he had stopped), I rose and thanked him for proving my point so well. It was time to head west!

Dorset

The seat for which I had been selected was called "Dorset East and Hampshire West". It consisted of all the Dorset constituencies apart from West Dorset, plus the two New Forest seats in Hampshire, so it stretched from Weymouth to the outskirts of Southampton. There were upcoming county council elections throughout the area, so – for practical reasons – I put the European campaign on hold while I built myself into the local teams by supporting their target seats. I then had a European workshop in May (to which Graham Watson kindly came), at which I restated my strategy on the basis of the even better results that year.

I look back with retrospective disbelief at my diary for that period. For 14 months, I combined a serious job at SJB with a political commitment that took up most weekends and some weekday evenings, at local events as well as including desk-bound paperwork, as I tried to establish a local media presence.

I drove thousands of miles. I appointed (and personally paid) a campaign organiser in the form of Gerald Vernon-Jackson. Between us, we (much more he than me) wrote a local "newspaper" shamelessly promoting me, although getting it delivered involved overcoming opposition from local members who read *The Guardian* and failed to comprehend that most electors didn't!

Indeed, the newspaper was so good that Tory headquarters circulated it internally as an example of dreadful (for which read "highly effective") LibDem propaganda! It was a very effective part of the "airwar" – a term used by political professionals to describe national campaigns fought over the airwaves and through the media, whereas "groundwar" described local campaigning. In a seat with over 500,000 electors, the former was inevitably more significant.

Challenges kept hitting us. In the summer of 1993, there was a Parliamentary by-election in Christchurch[14] – the most Tory seat in Dorset, and the sixth safest in the UK! Along with the rest of the party, I threw myself into this; our candidate had a massive win.

In the autumn, there was a reduction in the number of the UK's European constituencies, as a rebalancing act following the accession of more countries to the EU. The resultant boundary changes were disruptive, as we lost not only the Hampshire seats but also Christchurch (now a strong positive). Instead, we gained West Dorset and the Honiton constituency in East Devon, where the local LibDems were lovely, but the demography unhelpful, with a significant element of deep-blue *Costa Geriatrica*. My self-interested campaign that the redrawn seat should be the county of Dorset fell on deaf ears.

It was very difficult to meld these disparate seats together. There were good activist cores in some, but there was a paradox: weaker seats were more willing to be led, but stronger ones had a tendency to think that they knew better.

I entered 1994 with a constituency-wide photoshoot (see the write-up at the end of this chapter), and a 50/50 view of our prospects of success. That went up to 75% as I drove down to Poole for an evening meeting in March, only to learn from the radio that the Tory MP for Eastleigh had killed himself in bizarre circumstances, which, to put it politely, belonged firmly after the 21:00 hours broadcasting watershed (after which it was assumed that those of tender years would not be watching).

I went full time from the middle of April, living in Studland. The local elections went as well as possible, and I began to sniff victory.

That hope was soon snuffed out in a wholly unexpected way. The Labour leader, John Smith, died suddenly of a heart attack.

---

14   There was a joke candidate standing on behalf of the so-called "Alfred Chicken Party", who gained media attention by wandering around in a chicken suit. I could not resist the temptation of saying at that year's LibDem conference that, in Christchurch, the difference between the Tories and the Alfred Chicken Party lay in the fact that the latter were running around with their heads still on!

As with Hugh Gaitskell 30 years previously, there was a poignant feeling of unfulfilled promise, which played massively in terms of popular sympathy.

The electoral consequences became apparent as the European election counts took place: Labour won seats from the Tories that were not on their target list, and the tactical vote that should have flowed from Labour to the LibDems was halted in its tracks. We lost Dorset by 2,264 votes (1.2%), which was much less than the total "wasted" votes for Labour and the Green Party.

This was a dreadful disappointment to both the local LibDems and myself. The wash-up campaign meeting the following week demonstrated the old truth that victory has many parents, but defeat is an orphan.

We should have rationally celebrated a genuine advance and an astonishing near-victory; instead, real and imaginary recriminations filled the air. And, in consequence, it became apparent that I would not get selected for a Dorset Parliamentary seat, where I could have usefully capitalised on all the efforts to put me in the public eye.

Woking (2)

I was physically back in Woking, but exhausted and miserable. I had no wish to re-engage with the local LibDems, and so did not apply to be their PPC. Plus I had to rebuild my professional career, to which I also perforce returned.

Woking then selected a PPC in the form of Chris Edwards, a borough councillor. However, it was discovered that one of his opponents, County Councillor Mary Laker, had not been on the approved list of Parliamentary candidates, and party HQ voided the selection. If Edwards had been wise, he would have acted as a quasi-PPC and made his reselection inevitable, but he had always been hot-tempered, so he took umbrage and sought selection elsewhere.

By 1995, the lack of a PPC was becoming a disadvantage, with a general election due by 1997, and the Tories in massive electoral trouble. I was still uninvolved, until – to my surprise – Jamie and

Rosie Sharpley (of whom more to follow) turned up unannounced at my front door. They came in and sought to persuade me to put my hat in the ring.

I was reluctant and sceptical. I had a lot of bruises from my previous local experience, but I have always had a weakness for responding when people I like and respect ask me to do something.

Rosie explained the position starkly, "You are a tried and tested candidate. This is a political opportunity. Chris Edwards isn't suitable temperamentally. We can't, as his fellow-councillors who have to work with him, publicly back anybody else, but a lot of us would be very grateful…"

I talked around the idea with a few key people. Mary Laker was now approved, and would be a competitor, but she didn't expect to win, would certainly give me her second preference and would urge her supporters to do likewise. A number of borough councillors supported me or at least thought I should be in the field. Some local-party officers were also supportive.

I reflected. I still had the political bug. It would only be 18 months. And I was best placed to obtain the optimum result. *Reader, I consented!*

It was a dreadful selection battle. Somper promoted the fourth applicant – a strange character called Chris Jeffries. His second choice was Edwards, who was also supported by Rosemary Johnson as part of her "client politics" (see Chapter 9). Both hustings meetings saw Somper at his most unpleasant.

In the count after the second hustings, Jeffries was eliminated early, with his second preferences going mainly to Edwards; Mary Laker likewise, with her second preferences going overwhelmingly to me. In the result, I won by a handful of votes. The returning officer announced the result. I arose to make a unifying speech. Somper stood up too. Red-faced, he shouted, "I will not work with this man!" I made some mild comments to the effect that LibDems should be tolerant and respect democratic outcomes, but it was not the best start.

It was just before Christmas 1995, and the next constituency event was the Christmas party, at which the result was drawn of the very successful Woking Christmas Draw, which attracted national participation. It was run (with a lot of hard work) by Somper and friends of his. A couple of days before, Chris Jeffries rang me.

"Philip, this is a bit embarrassing," he started. "There really is a lot of feeling that you shouldn't attend the Christmas party."

"Chris," I responded, "are you making this call on your own initiative?"

There was a silence. I drew my own conclusions, and attended.

The next month, Somper – in revenge mode – decoupled the draw from the Woking party (which, as a matter of technical law, owned it), thereby depriving the local party of a significant income stream.

I used the Christmas break to plot the rocky road ahead. I had a massive stroke of luck. A former chair of the western region, Marian Elsden, whom I had got to know through my Dorset exertions, had coincidentally moved to Woking. She kindly agreed to come aboard, effectively working as my campaign manager, but formally as press officer to both the local party and the borough council group. She was prodigiously talented, not least with a Yeovil background, and there was an additional advantage from the fact that nobody knew that we were friends, so she was also a pair of eyes and ears for anything I needed to know about what some of my colleagues were saying behind my back.

I set off to unify the fractured local party as best I could, with the objective of building a broad-based and effective campaign. I had a lot of damage to repair, both at a personal level – following the selection battle – and politically, where our whole campaigning effort had gone downhill since I had last been involved, and our borough council group was much weaker than it should have been – in terms of both numbers and individuals.

The 1996 local-election results showed signs of improvement, and campaigning generally went up a grade, with much better material, including a local "newspaper" produced by Marian. But we still faced obstacles. At Rosemary Johnson's instigation, the central branch wasted an entire evening compiling a list of my sins (real or imaginary), and then demanded a meeting at which its chair, Rosemary McCrum, presented them. Marian and I listened with more patience than was warranted. I responded, "I have a phone, a fax, an email and a letterbox. If anybody has a serious issue, please contact me immediately, rather than letting it fester." I then dealt with the issues raised, showing how many derived from misunderstandings (though I thought to myself they were more probably misrepresentations). As Marian said in her subsequent campaign report, she had never known a local party where there was so extensive a refusal to accept the outcome of a selection process.

In spite of this political equivalent of a grumbling appendix, we ran as well as we could up to and through the 1997 general election. It was helpfully preceded by three prominent defections by present or former local Tory and/or Labour councillors organised by our one-person Political Warfare Department – me! This, and other events, attracted good local (and indeed some national) publicity; see the articles at the end of this chapter, and also this little gem:

AT a conference organised by Shandwick lobbyist **Lord McNally**, the Liberal Democrat panellist was scheduled to be **Alan Leaman**, ppc for **Mid-Dorset** and **North Poole**, the party's strategist. But Alan was delayed, and the panel session started with **Woking** ppc **Philip Goldenberg** – a well-known lawyer – kindly volunteering to stand in.

Introducing the panel, *New Statesman* editor **Ian Hargreaves** quipped: "Mr Leaman has taken the drastic step of sending his solicitor to represent him."

Indeed, the campaign merited an Ashdown visit.

In an excellent result, we reduced a 20,000 Tory majority by 75%. It was the best LibDem result in the South East, and the sixteenth best in England. If we had carried on in the same mode, we could – as Guildford did – have won the seat in 2001.

Some chance! The grumbling appendix had damaged our election campaign. It now exploded into acute appendicitis, with the disaffected minority hitting energy levels, which would have been useful assets for positive purposes during the campaign, but of which the party had been sadly deprived.

The self-appointed leader of this masturbatory tendency was Tony Kremer, with the active support of Somper (who made clear to all and sundry that, in the general election, he had voted for the independent Conservative candidate) and Rosemary Johnson (who had been absent during the campaign, acting as Chris Edwards' agent in a hopeless seat).

The matter had to be settled by contested internal elections, in which – sadly – the Somper/Johnson/Kremer vitriol had sufficient effect to ensure the wrong outcome, with the result that the lunatics took over the asylum and serious local political activity came to an abrupt halt. For the second and – as I wrongly then thought – final time, I exited from Woking LibDem politics, ensuring that I exited publicly on my own terms (see the article at the end of this chapter).

Regional, National and Federal

Between LibDem party HQ and the local parties, there exist regional parties. Their function is to co-ordinate the activities of local parties, to help those local parties improve their performance, and to intervene where called in and/or to deal with a crisis.

Marian Elsden and I had formed a pretty dim view of the South East regional party. So, we turned up at its 1997 AGM and were elected onto its executive. This was part of a wider plot, in which the tame chair proposed by the ruling clique was defeated by the rebels, who also captured the vice chairmanship. The defeated nominee's ego was so bruised by this defeat that he joined the Labour Party, never to be heard of again!

The executive was dire. It was effectively run out of the kitchen of Tom and Jennifer Pearce with the support of their cronies. They were both very active on the candidate approval and selection side, and they simultaneously ran a training business for aspirant Parliamentarians, so there was a clear pattern of institutional conflict.

They also worked in close collaboration with the then candidates officer at HQ to achieve outcomes. There was significant institutional conflict here too. Candidate approval and selection should be a separate HR function, but, under Rennard (see footnote 11), it had been subordinated to the Campaigns Department, where his fiefdom ran unchallenged. Unbelievably, these included delaying Vince Cable's approval, so as to get an HQ favourite into Twickenham before Vince was eligible to stand; the manoeuvre deservedly failed, and I was pleased to help Vince with his internal appeal!

Plus, there was wholesale incompetence. I became treasurer in 1999, replacing Tom Pearce. My first job was to persuade the auditor (the unfortunately named "A Dick") not to resign.

I rang him. He explained that he was perfectly happy to be the auditor, but that meant reviewing recognisable accounts, not creating them from scratch out of the chaotic heap of paper that Pearce kindly sent him. I promised to comply with this perfectly reasonable request, and he stayed in post.

Having sorted the finances, I was the natural successor as chair, which I duly became in 2001 after defeating two weirdos. "Philip, how very sensible of you to have had a hustings debate!" said a grinning Norman Baker MP as we passed in the corridor.

In my three years as chair, I had two principal activities. The first was a rewrite of the constitution, primarily to establish a committee to deal with local-party problems; this took them out of the full executive, where they were disproportionately disruptive, and where the disgruntled former ruling clique could be awkward for the sake of it. The next was dealing with these problems, some of which had been allowed to fester too long.

These problems had a common feature. In each case, a lax approval system had let loose on the unsuspecting public an aspirant councillor who was incompetent, illiberal and/or psychologically flawed (sometimes all three), and whom the trusting public had then unwisely elected (I recognised the problem from my Woking experience).

The consequential difficulties were accordingly in the public domain. This, in turn, meant that the necessary solution involved short-term pain for long-term gain, and the situations needed firmness of purpose accordingly.

I also performed what I have always considered to be one of the key duties of a chair: succession planning. I stepped down as chair after my three years, having locked in our progress for the future, and from the executive in 2006 for the reasons described as follows.

On becoming chair, I additionally became a member of the English party's executive, serving as its deputy chair in 2005–6. In this period, I prised the candidate-approval function out of its corrupt administration at party HQ by repatriating it from the federal party. This was a key reform in terms of transparency of process.

I also led the introduction of a one-year qualifying period before new members could vote in local-party selection processes: there was just too much evidence of entryism (joining for reasons other than the purely supportive) for comfort, and some of the figures I gave to the party assembly drew gasps of astonishment. This entryism was in order to support "friends"; examples included a threefold increase in membership in the run-up to a PPC selection, with a pretty fast subsequent reduction to the previous level post selection. Some of this was money driven: in metropolitan council areas, being a councillor carried an annual allowance of up to £15k. Sometimes it featured an ethnic minority community, whose proneness to electoral fraud and corruption has been shown in the four big election-court cases in recent years – see the legal case cited later in this Chapter.

I retired from both the English and regional executives in 2006, on being appointed chair of the federal appeals panel – effectively the party's chief internal adjudicating body (of which I had been elected a member by party conference in 2000, on the only contested vote: yes, you've guessed – Somper and six cronies forced the vote). I spent four years updating its antediluvian procedures, and chairing four or five appeals.

Two such appeals were important.

The first concerned Simon Hughes MP, who – as party president – had unilaterally appointed various people as "deputy chairs" of the party with specific responsibilities. This was clearly unconstitutional, but I recognised the political necessity of minimising the potential damage of undermining Simon. The neat way out was to say that only the federal executive had the power to make such appointments, but that – by not challenging Simon's appointments – it had effectively endorsed them. The appointments were not renewed a year later!

The second related to what became known as the "triple lock". The LibDem Conference had passed a business motion prescribing internal consents needed before LibDem MPs could co-operate in government with another political party.

However, it was clear that this cut across the independence of Parliamentarians which had been written into the constitution I had drafted at the time of the merger.

This all became a live issue in the run-up to, and after, the 2010 general election. It was addressed by convening a special conference to endorse the coalition agreement.

I subsequently arranged for there to be an appeal to the federal appeals panel to determine the validity of the triple lock, and our ruling is contained in a letter I subsequently wrote to the journal of the LibDem History Group in response to an article there – the letter appears at the end of this chapter. Thereafter, the triple lock was incorporated into the party constitution, with some help from me on the drafting side.

Woking (3)

"Not again," I hear you cry! Quite.

I was coming to the end of my term as regional chair, but was not looking to fill a gap for the sake of it. I was certainly not looking to re-involve myself with the dreadful personal politics of Woking LibDems.

But...

In late 2002, I took a phone call from Jamie Sharpley. "Philip," he said, "we have an unforeseen vacancy coming up in next year's local elections. It's Brookwood, where the Tory councillor is standing down early as he has been selected for a Parliamentary seat. Can you think of anyone who could fill the vacancy?"

It was pretty clear whom he had in mind. We had actually won the ward in 1996, with a candidate I had come across during the run-up to the 1997 general election, when I had formed the view that she was bonkers, if not certifiable. That the local party was not considering her again was mildly reassuring.

Furthermore, I had rather liked Brookwood when I'd canvassed there. It had the additional advantage of being a single-member ward, with an electorate of around 1,900, so a one-person campaign was viable.

"What about me?" I said, playing along disingenuously.

"I hadn't thought about that," said Jamie unconvincingly. "Would you be interested?"

"Yes," I replied, "but I'll only do it if Jenny [Fowler, the key LibDem activist in Brookwood, and utterly untainted by the dreadful Woking LibDem behaviour pattern] positively wants me to."

She did, and – as you will have guessed by now – I accepted. I was clearly not going to fight another Parliamentary election, and I could see advantages in being the sole councillor for a ward, to which I could give the public voice needed by an area at the extreme end of the Borough which would otherwise be easily overlooked.

In our original conversation, Jamie had asked me to not tell anybody, as he needed to manage what may have been a difficult situation.

He wasn't kidding! The campaigns side of the local party was now run by Rosemary Johnson (who was also leader of the borough council's LibDem group), and the meeting at which Jamie recommended that I should be the candidate exploded into a 90-minute row.

The local-party agent – Rosemary McCrum – announced that she would not be my agent. And Rosemary Johnson herself did everything she could to sabotage my approval and selection, even emailing all LibDem councillors for the wider West Woking area with destructive comments (some of them, who were not my greatest admirers, were so horrified that this exercise was probably counterproductive).

When she failed, she refused – at short notice – to re-stand in her own ward of Old Woking (thereby handing it to Labour), and briefed the local press that she was standing down because she could not bear to have me as a colleague. I reflected that, if she had stayed, I'd have had to serve under her as group leader. However, I would have accepted that situation until I could change it.

After a hard campaign, with a significantly high rate of personal electoral contact, I was elected as LibDem councillor for Brookwood in May 2003, and served for five years (see Chapter 7).

That led me back into Woking LibDems' organisational structures, as a council group representative on the local party's executive. So, I had a bird's-eye view of a succession of triumphs and (avoidable) disasters.

We gained the odd seat in the borough elections in 2004, and I held Brookwood with an increased majority. The next year saw combined Parliamentary and county council elections; our candidate, Ann Lee, was hard-working, but incredibly process-driven, with every decision seemingly requiring three bilateral conversations, then a meeting, then a couple more bilateral conversations. Fleet of foot we were not! But the political context was still favourable, with the Tories still in the Blair-triangulated doldrums and the Labour Party in post-Iraq turmoil. I came close to winning a county seat in 2005.

One spin-off from Labour's post-Iraq turmoil was that Woking LibDems acquired a brilliant new activist in the form of Denzil Coulson, who was originally a political activist in his native South Africa, and more recently a Labour constituency chair in Walthamstow, from whence he had moved to Woking. Naturally, Ann Lee (as PPC) and Rosemary Johnson (as campaigns officer), beat a hasty path to his doorstep.

I didn't catch up with him until after I held Brookwood in 2004, and we sat down with a glass of wine in his lounge. I felt myself being interrogated more fiercely than I expected; Denzil, having obtained satisfactory answers, then explained why.

"I've decided that I believe you," he said.

I looked quizzical.

"When Rosemary Johnson came round to see me the first time," he explained, "she spent 20 minutes briefing me about the local party, and the next 40 in character destruction at your expense. So, I wanted to form my own judgment. I now have. Why does she behave like this? What sort of organisation have I joined?"

"One that I hope and believe you will improve," I replied.

Well, he certainly tried, and suffered accordingly.

In 2006, we had a significant electoral success and narrowly took control of the borough council. It was a difficult year (see Chapter 7). And an alarmed Tory HQ sent down one of its senior propagandists, who skilfully manipulated the facts (and invented quite a few) to ensure our defeat the following May.

I found a good-quality Brookwood local to fight the seat in 2008, while I tried to take a Tory seat elsewhere. Both of us sadly failed.

The year 2008 also contained a seeming success, but one built on straw that was to lead to disaster.

We decided to target the Sheerwater Ward, which was originally a GLC overspill estate with permanent Labour representation, but where the Tories had made inroads by means of an alliance with elements of the local Asian community, who often saw politics more as an exercise in loyalty than a contest between political values and ideas.

We had the choice of a highly competent activist or a much less competent (in my opinion) member, Mohammed Bashir. At the selection meeting, the latter revealed no commitment to liberal values, but he was, in my view, selected for two reasons: honourable multiracialism, and client politics by Rosemary Johnson, who saw him as an ideal person in terms of being beholden to her for helping him to win (which she did not least because I was on the other side).

Bashir won the Sheerwater Ward, and his immediate priority was to get his mate Mohammed Amin selected for the county division of Maybury & Sheerwater the following year.

Sadly, he succeeded in his objective: I was the losing applicant on precisely the same basis as the previous year, and I resigned from the local-party executive in protest at the whole sordid process. Amin proved to be a dreadful councillor – idle and incompetent in equal measure, damaging our reputation in the process.

To complete this saga, Bashir won re-election in 2012 by a sufficiently small majority that the Labour Party saw the prospect of success with a formal election petition on the grounds of electoral fraud and corruption. When the case eventually came to trial in 2013 (Ali v Bashir [2013] EWHC 2, 572 [QB], a scintillating and devastating judgment), Bashir was rightly disqualified on the basis of multiple election offences.

We had shot ourselves in both feet, and destroyed our hard-won reputation for honesty and integrity. Why had we done it? This was partly due to client politics (see Chapter 9), but also shameless opportunism. Rosie Sharpley had been selected as the PPC for the 2010 general election, and her husband Jamie thought that ingratiating ourselves with large chunks of the Asian community would be a good quick fix.

It was a disastrous misjudgment, with possible short-term gain always liable to cause long-term pain. When I pointed all this out to the local party executive, which I had rejoined, I was severely censured for uttering inconvenient truths!

Meanwhile, in 2011, I stood for the last time as a local-government candidate. There was a double vacancy in the Goldsworth East Ward, as Rosie Sharpley threw in the towel prematurely after her exhausting efforts at the 2010 general election. Denzil Coulson's wife Amanda was an applicant, and Rosie begged me to join her. So, our names went forward, but we were challenged in an extraordinary way.

In 2007, Rosemary Johnson had arranged for yet another of her "clients", Colin Scott, to be selected for the Old Woking seat she had kindly gifted to Labour in 2003 (as previously described). He was duly elected and, in my opinion, proved utterly useless, both in the council chamber and in his ward.

Norman Johns, who lived in Old Woking, had been a good councillor in the ward where I lived from 2006–10, but had been less than helpful when I tried to gain a second seat there in 2008, seeming to regard the ward as his exclusive territory. It also sometimes seemed that publicity for Norman was an end in itself, without regard to any thought of collegiality. Rightly, he pushed hard and successfully for Scott to be de-selected. He then became chief cheerleader for Scott to be selected for Goldsworth East.

His motivation, it rapidly became apparent, was not pro-Scott; it was anti-me, in allegiance with Rosemary Johnson, who was anti-me and anti-Coulsons in equal measure. In the course of the selection contest (which Amanda and I won in spite of their efforts), Johns made slanderous allegations against me to the selectors, and then lied through his teeth when challenged.

Amanda won, but I didn't, in a campaign that was significantly undermined by Rosie Sharpley in a blaze of self-indulgence, sowing dissent both internally and in the public domain.

You would have thought that, by then, I would have had enough. Not quite! We had found a seemingly excellent new young borough group leader in Will Forster, and I came back as president in the hope that I could work with him to change the local party's dreadful culture.

Some chance! When push came to shove over borough council candidate selections for May 2016, for which I had initiated private discussions with other political parties to see if we could use the opportunity of whole-council elections following boundary changes to get the Tories out of control, Will double-crossed me to side with the local-party chair, Anne-Marie Barker. She, in turn, used her position to get her paws on a good-prospect seat, in the process bumping a loyal colleague – who had a better claim than her – into a less good seat, and me into oblivion. As president, I was theoretically responsible for good governance, so – having tried and failed to stop these sordid manoeuvrings – I resigned. After 35 years, my self-respect had eventually – and belatedly – asserted itself over my patient, albeit misplaced, loyalty.

Sutton – Hopes and Fears

Before the Sutton result fades into oblivion, to be recalled only when hindsight and the next General Election have established whether it is to be regarded as a milestone on the path to a Liberal revival or yet another false dawn, some comment would seem desirable, in the hope that the category in which it does eventually appear may be positively influenced by plans and actions based on a better understanding of what occurred, rather than by the benignity or otherwise of a disinterested providence.

The straight psephological analysis is easy. The vast preponderance of Labour voters (including an above-average middle-class element) backed a potential anti-Conservative winner; and a large number of disgruntled Tories, angry at being treated as safe-seat cannon-fodder over the years, kicked over the by-election traces. That this result occurred, and the unanticipated size of the majority, was due to the psychological brilliance of the campaign, orchestrated by Machiavelli thinly disguised as Trevor Jones.

The immediate reaction of hardened political correspondents (once they had recovered their poise) was to write off the result as irrelevant to Westminster politics other than as a timely spur to the Government.

'Parish Pump Politics' was their verdict.

More Significance

I want to suggest that there is more significance in the result, both for Liberals and generally, than most commentators have so far allowed; and by that I do not just mean an argument as to whether the potential Liberal revival has been underplayed.

Liberals must first realise that this election was not won by a campaign based upon political issues in the conventional sense. Although, in his Election Address, Graham Tope set out his views on some political issues, this was little more than a gesture towards traditionalism. Shocking as it may seem to the Political Editor of The Times, what pass for burning issues at Westminster seem an irrelevant slanging match to most electors.

What came across in Sutton was that Liberals had a different attitude. They cared about people's everyday problems. A new zebra-crossing? Pavements in need of resurfacing? Blocked drains? Fire hazards from a demolition site? Leave it to your local Liberals, Madam, they will get something done about it – and then never let anybody forget who got that something done.

In one way, this approach (though obviously based, at least partially, on cynical self-interest) had a wholly beneficial effect, in that it re-created in Sutton a feeling of community that is fast vanishing from all but the smallest units in society (and the evanescence of this feeling is at the root of most of our current social problems); the democratic process also came alive in a way that is healthy for politics as a whole.

Grievance Politics

The use of the democratic process, indeed, for attitude – as opposed to issue – politics is not wrong simply because it does not fit in with some tidy preconceptions of the nature of politics; it is, in fact, one way in which the Democratic Party built up its strength in the States, particularly amongst ethnic and other sub-groups (and Mayor Daley is one of its products). I also suspect that, although in a system of issue politics a candidate theoretically obtains a mandate based on his Election Manifesto, the practice at constituency level is rather different from the theory.

Attitude – or grievance – politics, however, has its own limitations. At least part of politics consists of a decision-making process, and, although grievance politics may be electorally successful, the end result of that success will be the attainment of a position of power where the main problem is reconciling conflicting grievances.

This is really the most worrying aspect. There is, at a constituency level, a reaction against Westminster politics which engenders a volatility in voting behaviour that would have seemed inconceivable ten years ago. But it is not beyond the bounds of possibility that this volatility could be exploited by others, using the same grievance politics campaign basis; in conjunction with, say, an anti-immigrant platform it might be even more potent. If Powell ever left the Conservative Party (or, as he would see it, if the Conservative Party left him), what havoc could Powellite candidates with the master's backing not wreak using a grievance politics campaign in, say, the West Midlands?

1973: New Outlook, *Sutton – Hopes and Fears*

1985: Woking News & Mail,
"Wok 1 & Wok 2"

● Meeting the Dorset shire horses.

Days of shooting the candidate

Being a Euro-ppc means being photographed more than you ever have been before. Euro-ppc Philip Goldenberg describes a full weekend of shooting.

"SOME photo-shoot weekend," I said to myself on the Thursday evening as I surveyed the thick-falling and fast-settling snow. But the weather forecast at 2130 was better than I feared, and so all was set.

Following a campaign team meeting in Poole, I spent Friday night at our Studland home – which *was* in the centre of the Euro-constituency until somebody kindly changed the boundaries!

An early ferry on the Saturday morning took me across Poole Harbour to meet Diana Maddock at the east Dorset end of Christchurch, where we both did general background pictures and then came together for thematic pictures to support the Dorset Chief Constable's call for 97 more police officers.

Then a rushed trip to Bournemouth, posing at the council's new neighbourhood office in Kinson with leader Doug Eyre and ward councillor Jill Abbot, and at the seaside with Doug and Peter Gregory, chair of the Bournemouth Hoteliers Association – to give visual coverage to my campaign to change a proposed Euro-directive which would adversely affect the hotel industry.

It was now too late for me to do the Poole Hospital shot with a friendly consultant, so campaign director Gerald Vernon-Jackson and photographer Dan Chung headed there, while I took the ferry back to the South Dorset AGM.

There I spoke to an enthusiastic group, including incoming president Ian Scott, making a fast and welcome recovery from a heart bypass.

After a welcome lunch, to a nearby farm with my local county councillor Philip Duffy. Wonderful photos with superb shire horses!

Quizzed about my agricultural knowledge by the farmer: "How long is a cow's gestation period?" Confessed ignorance – always better than bluffing.

"Same as a human" I was told. "My wife will like to know that!" I said, just about regaining control of the conversation.

Then on to Weymouth and Portland, where there are key local

● Weather in Bridport.

elections this May and we are gradually killing off Labour.

I have helped them with Euro-funding under the KONVER programme following the Tory government's announced closure of Portland Naval Base in 1996. With local borough councillors, including council leader Brian Ellis, we battle against fading light to get in all the shots, and then look at the rushes – Gerald wonders which of the more unfortunate ones he can sell to *Liberator* for campaign funds!

Go back to Studland for overnight stay.

LEAVE early on Sunday for Colyford in East Devon, where county councillor Margaret Rogers shows us a rural sub-post-office threatened with closure, and then introduces us to a really lovely lady worried abut her water rates – particularly high in Devon as a result of the Tory government's failure to clean up its beaches before privatisation.

We visit a residential and day-care centre, with the manager explaining how they have all-purpose units – health, social services and all supplies – for handicapped children. Why don't other authorities?

Another lovely lady at the centre, and then one later who is recovering from a burglary. A stop at a police

station, where Gerald charms a senior police officer to join in a photo, as we are supporting Devon's chief constable's campaign for 87 more police officers.

And finally a new estate, with inadequate community services and a road that leads nowhere!

THEN Honiton, where we arrive early – something must have gone wrong with Gerald's programming. Photos at site of planning row, and at local railway station – service under threat – with local activists.

Rapidly on to Axminster as the light fades fast, to meet district councillor Douglas Hull, and a local farmer who kindly allows us to be photographed with some wonderful cows. Will the red ones come out with Dan's flash?

A hurried shot at a closed community centre, and off to Lyme Regis as our final destination.

Bridport's deputy mayor Roger Draper, and Dorset county councillor Gil Streets, meet us in a torrential downpour – probably the only weather conditions in which I just *might* get mistaken for Meryl Streep!

Gerald lets go of my hat, which skids across wet sand with Gerald in lukewarm pursuit. A swift shot with the lifeboat, then with a canoe, and it's just light enough to recognise each other as we part company, and I give a – justifiably – tired Dan a lift to Basingstoke station.

What struck me, as I reassembled kaleidoscopic memories afterwards, was how similar Liberal Democrat activists are.

Not – thank heaven! – as individuals, but in the hard work they do, and the cheerful, and often blessedly irreverent, humour with which they do it.

In a weekend, I've covered five of the seven local parties in my Euro-patch, and it's been a delight to feel the strength of the team – diverse as individuals but united in purpose – that's working to send me to Strasbourg.

Probably on a one-way ticket!
● *Philip Goldenberg is Euro-ppc for Dorset and East Devon.*

'A torrential downpour is probably the only weather conditions in which I just might get mistaken for Meryl Streep . . .'

1994: Liberal Democrat News (LDN), *"Shooting the Candidate"*

Sensation as top Tory joins Woking Lib Dems

IN AN amazing climax to the Surrey Liberal Democrat rally, top Woking Tory councillor Sinclair Webster announced to a delighted audience that he was quitting the Tory Party and joining the Liberal Democrats.

Cllr Webster has represented the Mount Hermon East ward on Woking Borough Council for seven years, and is the Conservative housing spokesman there. The other Mount Hermon East seat is already held by Liberal Democrat David Thacker.

Cllr Webster made clear that it was national, rather than local issues which had motivated him. In a strong attack on the Conservative government, he said: "Federalism in Europe is being presented as centralism: that is a lie perpetrated by the most centralising administration since the 1945 Labour government.

"Local councils are being systematically stripped of their ability to do anything other than act as agents for central government policy. I did not stand for election as the government's agent.

"Every councillor owes an individual duty of care to all the people he or she represents,

particularly those who are most vulnerable.

"We cannot discharge that duty when all we can do is to cut expenditure to make short-term savings that benefit only the rich, by disposing of efficient services run for the benefit of our community."

Attacking the recent proposal of the Conservative group on Woking Borough Council to defer projects that all political groups supported, Cllr Webster said: "We are being asked to be enabling authorities. In truth we are disabled authorities.

"I no longer feel that I belong to a party which has so outrageously deceived the public, and that has betrayed me in pursuit of power for an oligarchy of second-rate men. I now regard the Liberal Democrats as my natural home."

Woking's Liberal Democrat ppc Philip Goldenberg, who chaired the rally, immediately congratulated Cllr Webster on a speech of "courage and integrity", and welcomed him to the platform — where he was warmly greeted by other speakers, including Emma Nicholson MP, Graham Watson MEP and Woking Borough Council's Liberal Democrat leader

Doreen Elliott.

● Six new members joined in all, including former Labour councillor Mrs Perveen Baluch-Jenkins.

"I was a Labour councillor because I felt that their policies most applied to my philosophy, and to the problems of local residents in the Central and Maybury ward I represented," she said.

"What I did not bargain for was the unreconstructed socialism of the Inner Woking branch of Woking Labour Party, and their inward-looking petty politics and attitude to newcomers — no sign of New Labour here.

"I now recognise the Liberal Democrats, with their policies on education, health and Europe, as my natural home."

The rally was a scintillating occasion, with an emotional account by Emma Nicholson of why she had no longer felt able to continue as a Conservative. Her invitation to Conservatives in the audience to follow her obviously had a dramatic effect.

The evening literally ended with a bang, as the H G Wells Suite confetti machine showered the departing attenders with an appropriately yellow shade of confetti.

1997: LDN,

"Defections"

Top Byfleet Tory joins Lib Dems

IN a shock move, Bob Coakes has quit Byfleet Conservatives and joined the Liberal Democrats.

This is a notable coup for the party in Surrey as Mr Coakes was the leading light of Byfleet Conservatives and had been a borough council candidate for over 10 years.

He formally resigned from Woking Conservatives last Friday, saying in a letter to them that his aspirations were no longer fulfilled by their party. "It is not I who have left the Conservative Party," he said, "but it has left me. I have always believed in the idea of one nation, something the Conservatives seem to have forgotten. I also realise that you cannot reduce taxation and maintain the quality of public services."

Mr Coakes said that it was "very difficult" to leave a party of which he had been a member for 36 years, but his aspirations could only now be fulfilled by joining the Liberal Democrats.

Leading local Liberal Democrat Philip Goldenberg said that he was delighted by Mr Coakes' decision to join the Liberal Democrats.

"I know from talking to Byfleet residents how much Bob contributes to his community," said Mr Goldenberg, who is the Liberal Democrat ppc for Woking.

"He is one of many 'one nation' Conservatives who are joining us precisely for the tradition of public services for which they originally joined the Conservatives, and which they can no longer find there."

Philip Goldenberg bows out of Woking politics

WHEN Woking Liberal Democrats select their candidate this autumn for the next General Election, there will be a significant gap in the list of contenders.

For the first time in 20 years, their most successful candidate, Philip Goldenberg, will not be offering himself for re-selection.

In a statement, Philip Goldenberg said: "Life moves on. I have fought three out of the last four General Elections in Woking, and a new perspective is needed. This can best be provided by a candidate from outside Woking who will also have the benefit of the strong base that has been created during my period of involvement — and I hope that he or she will make full use of it."

"In addition, my political commitments at regional and national level — let alone the increasing demands of professional life — make it impossible to give the task the time it needs. I also like seeing my family from time to time," Philip Goldenberg added.

Philip Goldenberg contested the 1983, 1987 and

1997 General Elections in Woking. In 1997, he reduced the previous Tory majority of some 20,000 to around 5,000. This was the 16th best Conservative to Liberal Democrat swing in Great Britain and the best in the South East Region.

Philip also represented Horsell West on Woking Borough Council from 1984 to 1992, chairing the highways committee from 1988 to 1990. When he first arrived in Woking, there was only one Liberal borough councillor. He is a solicitor specialising in company law, dealing with significant transactions of commercial importance.

1999: Woking Review, *"Exit"*

The Triple Lock

Mark Pack's article on the triple lock (*Journal of Liberal History* 72, autumn 2011) referred to me a couple of times, so a few comments seem appropriate.

In the run-up to the 2010 general election, I advised both Danny Alexander and Ros Scott of my *provisional* view that the triple lock was not constitutionally binding. I say *'provisional'* because, as I explained when I gave the same view to the Federal Executive (as Mark notes), I was then Chair of the Federal Appeals Panel, and I was not prepared to give a definitive view in case I subsequently had to consider the question formally.

That actually arose on an application by a party member, and I invited Gordon Lishman to make a submission as to the validity of the triple lock. This was carefully considered by a panel consisting of myself and the respective Chairs of the English and Welsh State Party Appeals Panels.

We delivered our ruling in August 2010 to the Federal President, Chief Executive and Operations Director, leaving it to them to determine how it should be published (sorry to disabuse *Liberator* of yet another conspiracy theory!). In the interests of open government, I am happy to supply a copy to anyone interested (requests to journal@liberalhistory.org.uk).

Please note that we were careful not to say that the triple lock was a nullity, as clearly it represented the general view of conference. And we emphasised the importance of consultation. But we did conclude that it was not constitutionally valid in two key respects – binding the Commons party, and binding the conference – without having been proposed and passed as a constitutional amendment by a two-thirds majority.

Philip Goldenberg

2011: LibDem History Journal, The Triple Lock

6

Liberal and Liberal Democrat (LibDem) Politics: National

Beginnings

I mentioned in Chapter 5 that, while remaining as PPC in Slough in the period from 1974–9, I had built myself into the national structures of the Liberal Party. This took a number of forms:

- A five-year involvement (in the executive and various offices) with the Home Counties regional party. This was a pretty hopeless organisation, whose main problem was a paid organiser – a former Heathrow shop steward with an outsize ego – who believed that the officers should not interfere with what he did. The problem was only solved when local parties began to refuse to pay for his "services", so he was no longer affordable.

- A ten-year stint with the National Executive Committee. A latter-day Voltaire[15] would have observed that it was incapable of

---

15 Voltaire famously observed that the Holy Roman Empire was "*ni saint, ni Romain, ni empire*".

taking a national view, was a hopeless committee, and couldn't execute anybody or anything!

- A period of service on the Candidates Committee, with some strange colleagues (I append to this chapter an article from a magazine called *Liberator*, which I can now confess to having written!) and some even stranger people who thought that they were either literally or metaphorically God's gift as candidates.

- Membership of various party-policy working groups, including industrial relations, which led to my becoming a Parliamentary draftsman for Foster Rochester as the party's House of Lords (the Lords) spokesman on the topic.

- An active part in John Pardoe's leadership bid in 1976.

- The joint editorship of a magazine called *New Outlook*.

- A spell as chair of the National Liberal Club's Political and Economic Circle, which involved inviting speakers[16] and chairing dinners.

- Membership of the aforementioned club's Management Committee during the turbulent 1970s, when it lost the will to manage itself, mistakenly got involved with two crooks and was then rescued by Sir Lawrence Robson.

- A four-year involvement (on its board, and for time as deputy chair) with the Electoral Reform Society (ERS); this was a strange combination of academic theorists, with a gradual intake of serious campaigners, which offered ballot services to various organisations, and used the profits to advocate electoral reform.

The ERS was engaged by British Leyland when it went over the heads of its red-tinged shop stewards by holding an all-employee ballot. Sir Michael Edwardes, its combative CEO, explained that the ballot papers would be distributed to employees at work, and would be passed to the ERS to count after completion.

---

16 One of these was Devon and Cornwall's progressive and intelligent chief constable, John Alderson. I recruited him to the party, and approved him as a Parliamentary candidate. He said to me privately that he was always grateful that the infamous dog in the Jeremy Thorpe saga was shot 120 yards outside his police area!

"Sir Michael," said the ERS's head of ballots, "I recommend posting the ballot papers to employees at home."

"It's too expensive," Edwardes said dismissively.

"What result do you want, Sir Michael?" came the question.

Edwardes looked as if he doubted the sanity of his interrogator.

"Let me explain," came the reply. "If you give them out at work, the employees will come under enormous pressure from the unions. If you post them first-class to their home addresses at 09:00 hours on a Friday, their wives will have 48 hours before their shop stewards can get near them!"

Edwardes' jaw dropped; he accepted the advice, and the rest is history.

I also put myself in the public domain on a range of policy issues:

- Leading a campaign that the 1980 Olympics should not be held in Moscow on human rights grounds, including speaking for the party from the rostrum of the Dutch Parliament in The Hague at an international conference on the topic.
- Forcing a Companies Bill amendment through the Lords to treat shareholders acting with a common purpose as "concert parties".
- Advocating tax reliefs to encourage co-partnership in industry.
- Writing the Party's evidence in favour of a statutory securities commission.
- Through Richard Wainwright MP, becoming a member of the Wider Share Ownership Council, and writing its annual budget submissions – one of which advocated a British equivalent to the French *Loi Monory*, giving limited tax relief to individual stock market investors (I then advised Richard on its drafting).
- Publishing an article in *New Law Journal*, arguing that the European Assembly could only become the Parliament of the Treaties if it were elected by a common electoral system.

Additionally, I was an occasional participant in internal party warfare on Israel/Palestine, arguing against the simplistic extremists in the opposing camps.

All of this was good, solid stuff. The first real excitement came with the 1978 Finance Act (see Chapter 2). The next was to be one of many serious roles relating to the party's relationship with the nascent SDP.

Seat Negotiations

It was a routine meeting of the National Executive Committee in early 1981. David Steel had had a leader's slot before lunch, in which we had all mused whether there really would be a split in the Labour Party. When we reassembled after lunch, we were surprised to see David take his place again.

"I'm back," he explained, "because, having listened to radio interviews over lunch, it's clear to me that all this is for real." He was right. Within hours, a Social Democratic Council had been established as a potential precursor to a new party.

Following the 1981 formation of the SDP, there was an inevitable issue to be resolved: which party would contest which Parliamentary seat at the 1983 general election? The Liberals had many claims based on years of local work; the novelty of the SDP had the wind of public support at its back. A messy national deal was struck and imposed. The 1984 European elections were much easier: there were fewer than 100 seats to divide and larger areas, where the local factor mattered less. The issues were reasonably sorted.

But it was clear that sorting out candidates for the 1987 general election would be more difficult. Campaigning together on the ground had led to a welcome fluidity of co-operation; at national level, there were significant differences. In effect, those who thought merger inevitable in the longer term wanted to see as much joint working as possible, whereas those determined to resist it took the opposite view; as a result, the modalities of seat allocation became a proxy war for these two camps.

So there was a formal national negotiating format, but with – at the Liberals' insistence, and rightly so – a higher local input. The National Executive Committee elected three of its members to join the Liberal negotiating team. Somewhat to my surprise, I topped the ballot (perhaps helped by my developing reputation for cutting through nonsense: I could be sent off to annoy the SDP instead of my long-suffering colleagues!).

Sitting through the negotiating process, and indeed at its centre as the agreed draftsman, was fascinating. I was an experienced negotiator as a corporate finance lawyer for whom dealmaking was a daily exercise. Politicians simply do not possess this skillset, because our whole political process is – as a result of our dreadful winner-takes-all electoral system – adversarial by habit, and therefore tribal by attitude.

And that adversarialism was reinforced by our legal system, not least because of the number of barrister MPs – who are by nature fighting cocks (the smaller number who are solicitors tend to be more constructive) – and flowed into the whole of our industrial relations.

The best form of negotiation is where each side is competent, knows what it must have, has worked out what the other side must have and trades on that basis. The worst form is negotiation by attrition – the style of too many City lawyers, particularly at SJB (see Chapter 2).

And playing politics does not help. One morning, Bill Rodgers (whom I liked in general terms and found constructive) came in looking thunderous and, quoting something that the Liberal General Secretary had been reported as saying, demanded that we denounce it before he would allow the meeting to proceed.

My political colleagues were thrown by this, as Bill had intended, and looked at each other in uncertainty as to how to respond. I decided to fill the void. "Bill," I said quietly. "I understand what you are saying and how you feel. But you are asking us to denounce a respected colleague without the courtesy of first talking to him and hearing what he has to say. For a start, he may have been misquoted. You wouldn't do that, and neither will we. We will, of course, take the matter further after the meeting. May we now proceed?"

Bill acknowledged, by a reluctant smile, that his gambit had failed, and the meeting duly proceeded.

The process was lengthy and time-consuming, but the mutual trust gradually increased. Indeed, by the end, the two sets of negotiators often worked together to overcome obstinacy at a local level.

Merger

After the 1987 general election, the merger of the Liberals and the SDP (of which I had been a public advocate since 1982) became inevitable, although there was kicking and screaming on both sides. The SDP had a traumatic special conference followed by an all-member ballot, which gave its support, after which David Owen and various of his acolytes threw their collective toys out of the pram. The new leader was Bob Maclennan, whom I had come across professionally and liked. The Liberal Assembly at Harrogate approved negotiations for a merger, but rebelled against the perceived establishment by arrogating to itself the power to elect most of the negotiating team. I stood apart from this process, as I had already been approached to be that team's legal adviser.

The negotiating process left much to be desired. It was too leisurely, with weekly meetings. There was too much adversarialism, with separate team pre-meetings at which too many lines were drawn in the sand; for colleagues who were destined to work together, more openness would have been appropriate. And there was a minority on both sides that was merely judging the right moment to walk out with the intention of wrecking the process.

One of the key difficulties was finding a middle way between the SDP's excessive centralism (born of the previous Labour experience of their key figures) and the Liberal Party's fondness for anarchy (virtually anybody could attend the Liberal Party Assembly).

The blessing was that my counterpart as the SDP's legal adviser was Willie Goodhart, a QC who was subsequently to receive a knighthood and a peerage, with a mercifully wicked sense of humour and real courage. For example, after the miscarriage of justice relating to the Birmingham Four, he willingly co-proposed with me to party conference a motion calling for the resignation of the Lord Chief Justice! He and I were dedicated to finding practical solutions, and worked together with enthusiasm. We became life-long friends as a result. He sadly died in 2017 after a short, but deeply miserable, period of dementia.

But, towards the end, the negotiation process became very fraught.

There were silly arguments over the name, with no thought being given to the enormous reputational goodwill of the phrase "The Alliance", which had been the brand for the 1987 general election.

There was a partial Liberal walkout over inserting a commitment to the North Atlantic Treaty Organization (NATO) in the preamble to the constitution, into which it was spatchcocked to please the SDP's ideological purity. There was a partial SDP walkout by those who always intended to walk out. There was a mad expedition by Bob Maclennan to seek David Owen's blessing, which met with the predictable humiliating rebuff.

Finally, there was the disaster of a policy statement, which was drafted by two immature youngsters brought in by Bob with total insensitivity to the views of party members on both sides, in respect of which David displayed his all-too-frequent inattention to detail.

This caused a mega-crisis, which was only resolved by dumping the policy statement and asking three sensible people on both sides to start from scratch. Indeed, at a fraught Parliamentary meeting to address the crisis, the great battleaxe Nancy Seear turned to David Steel and uttered the memorable line, "David, you – as leader – have united the party in a way unprecedented in my long experience. Unfortunately, it's against you!"

The public damage was enormous.

Meanwhile, after each week's discussions, I had added to my working draft of what was to become the new party's constitution, and Willie and I kept the draft under continuing review. The resultant text was unchallenged when the negotiating process resumed after the policy mess had been sorted out.

The process then moved to the approval of the membership of each party. The Liberals convened a special conference in what felt like an enormous aircraft hangar at the back of a Blackpool hotel.

The day had been planned to achieve the right outcome. This was foreshadowed when Lynda (then three months' pregnant with our daughter Pippa, having announced her pregnancy after complaining that, because of the combination of my normal professional workload with the merger negotiations, she had not seen me for months!) and I arrived at the platform for the special train at Euston station, to find a hand-made sign saying "Those in favour: front 10 coaches. Those against: back two. NB: the two rear coaches will be detached at Crewe."

So, there was first to be a debate on the proposed constitution, which I was deputed to summate just before the leader's speech. The motion would then lie on the table for a general debate on the merger, after which the vote would be taken.

As Lynda and I (and perforce Pippa) sat through the opening debate, we could almost touch the fraught atmosphere. There was a swirl of emotion, not least because of the shambles of the policy statement. In short, there was a boil that needed lancing.

I rose to speak to an emotion-laden hall of over 2,000, including David Steel, who was on the platform waiting to speak after me. I addressed the constitutional issues that had been raised. I then said this:

"For four months, I have been involved in the technical issues of this process. Working together, Willie Goodhart and I, as lawyers, have drafted the constitution for the merged party; although I pause to reflect that – with the wisdom of hindsight – it might perhaps have been better if the constitution had been drafted by the leaders, and the lawyers had written the policy statement."

I had not realised in advance how effective this line would be as a boil-lancer. There followed what *Hansard* generally calls "prolonged laughter". In what seemed an age before it died down, I worried that David might feel hurt. I turned round to get a view of the platform. I need not have been concerned – to his credit, he was laughing his head off. We exchanged grins.

I resumed my speech about why the new party was desperately needed, quoting Andrew Marvel ("The grave's a fine and private place, but none methinks do there embrace"), but – as with the Oxford Union (see Chapter 1) – the speech would have flown whatever I'd said. As I walked through a still-applauding hall back to my seat, Tom McNally remarked, "And I thought you were a dull lawyer!" Shirley Williams, whom I had grown to love dearly during the negotiations, was similarly complimentary. Willie was sitting in the gallery next to Roy Jenkins, and he told me afterwards that they had both joined in the laughter. I walked on air for the rest of the weekend.

One of the features of the new constitution was the establishment of a trustee company to hold the party's premises and other key assets. Willie and I jointly formed this, and I became its secretary from 1990–2006, effectively running it. Until his sad death in 2002, its chair was the admirable Sir Peter Parker, formerly the chair of British Rail. At a reception, Peter said to me, "Philip, let me tell you a story. When the USA entered the Second World War, it was necessary to set up a joint command structure. Allenby, as chief of the Imperial General Staff, came into see Churchill. He proposed a series of committees, which the Americans – as the larger power – would chair. Churchill was alarmed. 'But they'll take all the decisions!' he exclaimed. 'No, Prime Minister,' said Allenby. 'We'll have all the secretaries!'" Peter, in his politest way, was telling me that my cover as a humble servant had been blown! We both laughed. I got my own back when he received the rare accolade of a second knighthood, and I wrote to congratulate him, suggesting that, at his age, "once a (k)night was surely sufficient".

Coalitions (1)

There are two prequels to this section, relating to two key individual players.

Paddy Ashdown, who sadly died as I was in the later stages of writing this book, was one of the most remarkable people to have come into contemporary politics. Too many MPs follow the modern path of being political researchers, then special advisers and – finally – get safe seats. Rather like the previous generation of High Court judges, with a sequence of public school, Oxbridge and the Inns of Court, they have little or no experience of real life.

Paddy was different. His service as an officer in the Special Boat Service had given him leadership abilities almost unique in the modern House of Commons. He had then honed his mind as a diplomat (OK, in MI6), which gave him the attribute possessed by the best civil servants of being able to analyse any problem from first principles. Finally, he had been a youth worker while he nursed his Yeovil seat, which he won in 1983.

At the annual October meeting of MPs and PPCs in 1985, I was leaving early to get to a borough council meeting when I heard heavy footsteps behind me, followed by a hand on my shoulder. It was Paddy himself, who then said, "Philip, I'm now trade and industry spokesman and I'll be on the committee dealing with the Financial Services Bill. I know SFA [sweet f*** all] about it. Please advise me on it." I did, which was not only interesting as a subject, but also gave me an insight into Paddy's powerfully clear mind.

I then supported Paddy during the post-merger leadership election (having written a lengthy personal letter to David Steel urging him not to stand, as it was clearly time for Moses (ie David) to give way to Joshua – and I actually wrote to Paddy before the special conference urging him to take a back seat that day, starting the letter "Dear Joshua").

Paddy was, above all, a strategic thinker, as I learned at meetings of the party trustees when he shared his thoughts with them. And, in my two years on the party's Policy Committee, which he chaired, I saw at first hand the unusual combination of somebody with enormous charisma but who was absolutely willing to share enthusiastically in a joke at his expense.

On one occasion, there was a proposal before the Policy Committee for non-military community service by youngsters. What to call it? It had the working title of "The Citizen Corps", but that was too easily sabotaged by adding an "e" at the end. Various ideas were chucked around the room. "I've got it!" exclaimed David Howarth (later to be MP for Cambridge City), "'The Ashdown Youth'!" Much to his credit, Paddy laughed loudest.

And I also saw his incredible level of personal courtesy to anybody who helped him in any way. The funniest example of this was in Wells. When Margaret Thatcher took her revenge on the Church of England (C of E) by foisting George Carey on them as Archbishop of Canterbury, my friends Alan Butt Philip and Christina Baron hosted a dinner at their home (which was appropriately named The Old Vicarage) for the Ashdowns and the Careys.

"May I do anything to help?" enquired Paddy on arrival. He readily consented to saying goodnight to the children. Sitting at the end of Frances' bed, Paddy asked solemnly, "Do you know who I am?"

"Yes," came the prompt reply. "You're the Archbishop of Canterbury."

In the run-up to the 1992 general election, Paddy wanted to be prepared for a balanced (or "hung") Parliament. He set up a working group, and brought me in as legal adviser. I had no knowledge of the subject, but conveniently knew a man who did.

But first, some background.

In 1980, I had been asked by the Liberal Party to give evidence on its behalf to a House of Lords Select Committee examining a European Green Paper entitled *Employee Asset Formation*. It tied in neatly with my pioneering work on employee share ownership.

It should be explained that select committees were a new Parliamentary phenomenon, wished on Margaret Thatcher (who mercifully did not understand their near-revolutionary potential) by her first Leader of the House, Norman St John Stevas. They have enormously improved the work of both Houses of Parliament (Houses), not least in giving a non-ministerial career path to serious backbench MPs.

So, in the early 1980s, when I went to the annual informal meeting between the Liberal lawyers and the Law Commission, and found on the table where I put my briefcase a set of papers of the House of Lords Select Committee on Europe, I put them into my briefcase and took them home to read.

On looking at them, my jaw dropped with disbelief (I re-elevated it with the aid of a large Scotch). I had in my hands the minutes of a confidential meeting hearing Civil Service evidence on the issue of Britain's monetary contribution to the European Economic Community (EEC) budget. I asked myself if this was a matter of national security, in which case I would have shredded the papers in the office the next day. I concluded that it was not, although it was clearly politically sensitive given Thatcher's demand for "our money back".

Three aspects struck me as I read the documents. Firstly (and hardly surprisingly), the Foreign Office was *communautaire* (ie supportive of co-operation with the European institutions), and the Treasury was decidedly not. Secondly, civil servants, having opposed select committees, were now using them. And, thirdly, the documents revealed the contrast between the UK's public negotiating stance and its private fallback position.

As I commuted to work the next day, I decided on my course of action. I was then a *The Times* reader (before its acquisition by Murdoch, so it was still a newspaper). It had recently appointed Fleet Street's first-ever Civil Service special correspondent – Peter Hennessy.

I rang him, and told him about the documents then burning a hole in my Linklaters' desk, focussing on what I thought would interest him most, which was the use being made of select committees by civil servants. Peter was interested, and we agreed that *The Times*' messenger would pick up a brown envelope from Linklaters' reception desk.

Unbeknown to Peter or me, life was about to become a lot more interesting than we had foreseen.

Peter walked into *The Times*' 11:00 hours news conference to plot the next day's edition. On the table was an advance copy of a speech to be given that evening in The Hague by Geoffrey Howe as Chancellor of the Exchequer, setting out the UK's public negotiating stance on its monetary contribution to the EEC budget.

After some sub-editorial hesitation, *The Times* ran, alongside each other on the front page, Howe's speech and a Hennessy piece on the Select Committee evidence.

There were significant consequences.

Firstly, a panicked Treasury Private Office got Howe out of bed in The Hague at 23:45 hours to inform him of the disaster. Secondly, a furious Thatcher assumed that the culprit was a disloyal civil servant, and ordered a full MI5 investigation. Thirdly, the secretary to the Liberal peers rang me to ask if I'd seen anybody pick up the offending papers (I replied in the negative, having been careful to shut my eyes at the relevant time). Finally, and – not least for this section – most importantly, Peter and I became life-long friends. One of his books on my shelves is inscribed "To Philip – a super-mole"!

So, in the early 1990s, I sought Peter's advice – in his new incarnation as a professor of history with a speciality in constitutional matters – on the task that now confronted me. He was brilliantly helpful, not only in terms of his expertise on the structure of the national government from 1940–1945, but also in his inaugural lecture (which I attended, and which became his book *The Hidden Wiring*) in relation to the structure of the Cabinet as the Executive Committee of the Privy Council, and the history of other committees formed on a cross-party basis, such as the Imperial Defence Committee in the early 1900s and a similar Attlee creation in the late 1940s.

The working group settled into its allotted task, under the chairmanship of [Lord] Richard Holme, a key party strategist[17] and adviser to successive LibDem leaders. The meetings were convivial (as an SJB partner, I could command private lunches or dinners for "client" purposes, so determined upon a rather wide definition of the term!).

My work was legal and secretarial, and we ended up with a procedural manual and a draft coalition agreement. This was, thanks to Peter Hennessy, based on the Second World War model, with the fullest possible participation by the minority partner.

Behind the scenes, and on a deniable basis, lines of communication were established between Richard on Paddy's behalf and Charles Clarke as Neil Kinnock's chief of staff. Kinnock, however, contrived to lose the 1992 general election, so I produced and stored a documents file for the record. This co-operative approach was revived in the run-up to the subsequent 1997 general election, which Tony Blair was clearly going to win. He and Paddy had engaged in private discussions about what became known as "the Project", which — in its fullest version — would have involved a full merger of both parties; this was always a pipedream given the tribalism of the Labour Party, as shown by its subsequent rejection of Roy Jenkins' proposals for electoral reform. This was unbeknown to the revived working group that Paddy had convened — this time under the chairmanship of (Lord) Tom McNally, as Richard was chairing the general election campaign. I was in the same role as previously.

This was a much more serious and heavyweight operation, involving my old friends Bob Maclennan, and also [Lord] William Wallace, whom I had known since Oxford. We had a 90-minute

---

17 He sadly died young. His memorial service at St Margaret's, Westminster (the parish church of both Houses), was packed, and included David Steel and Paddy Ashdown. The address was given by Sir Menzies Campbell. "Richard," he said, "was a great strategist and a great judge of risk — both when to take risks and when not. Advising David, he had to work hard to persuade him to take any; with Paddy, his task was to stop him taking too many." Memorial services are not supposed to dissolve into helpless laughter, but the muffled giggles proved too infectious. As usual, David and Paddy saw the funny side as much as anybody else.

meeting with Robin Butler as Cabinet Secretary,[18] even getting down to the legal authority for postponing the State Opening of Parliament if need be (the 1837 Prorogation Act, since you ask), and a 45-minute meeting with the Queen's private secretary, at both of which all options and procedural points were discussed, with me pinching myself with disbelief that I was present as a full participant. The 1992 procedural manual and draft coalition agreement were redrafted with this additional input.

Paddy also treated the working group as a sounding board. He very carefully used Tom as an indirect way of putting up the proposition that a couple of LibDems should take seats in a Labour Cabinet without an actual coalition. I was horrified, and prepared myself for the breakfast meeting at which it would be discussed.

Paddy put forward the idea.

I waved a hand, saying, "Paddy, to adapt a well-known phrase, this would be 'responsibility without power' – what you might call 'the reverse harlot[19] position'."

"Do you have a better suggestion for getting our ideas into practice?" he enquired.

"Yes," I said, having remembered Peter Hennessy's inaugural lecture. "Establish a Cabinet Committee with LibDem participation to deal with a segregated area of government, but without having collective responsibility for everything else."

"Can you do that?"

"Yes, there are precedents," I responded, quoting the examples in Peter's lecture.

And so, to my intense surprise, it came to pass. The Labour victory was so overwhelming that a coalition was inappropriate, but

---

18 There was a gloriously funny moment for devotees of the *Yes Minister* series (often perceived as a sitcom, when it was actually a training manual), when Butler – courteously escorting us on our way out of the meeting – stopped opposite the green, baize-covered door leading from the Cabinet Office to 10 Downing Street, and said, in reference to a famous episode, "That's the door out of which Sir Humphrey was locked!"

19 In the 1930s, Prime Minister Baldwin had said of the press, "They have power without responsibility – the prerogative of the harlot throughout the ages."

three months later a Joint Cabinet Committee sprang into being – see the articles at the end of this chapter. Sadly, it was merely consultative, whereas my proposal had been for it to have executive authority in relation, for example, to constitutional reform as a key LibDem objective.

But there was another spin-off from my work. With the advent of Scottish and Welsh devolution, and with Paddy's permission, I produced re-tailored versions of my draft coalition agreement to conform with the related legislation, and sent them to our Scottish (Jim Wallace) and Welsh (Mike German) leaders.

When the first set of Scottish Parliamentary elections produced a balanced assembly, the Scottish Labour leader, Donald Dewar, rang his LibDem counterpart Jim Wallace to propose a coalition. His proposal was merely in relation to ministerial positions; Jim politely suggested that there was more to it than that.

At the meeting to discuss policy, Dewar produced one side of A4; led by David Laws, the LibDems produced over 20, and got most of their policy proposals through. On the sidelines, Jim had a quiet word with Dewar, saying, "Donald, have you thought how we should run this government as a coalition?"

"Er, no," Dewar replied.

"Well, we have. This is the draft we have prepared."

Dewar skim-read it, and expressed himself content.

Golly! My drafting! In effect at the heart of the government of Scotland! And, later, in Wales too. It would have been unhelpful to have publicised the fact that the structure of devolved government had emanated from a London lawyer, but I wrote an analysis for a legal periodical – see the article at the end of this chapter.

The Project, however, did not come to pass. Effectively, Blair left Ashdown sitting at the end of a branch that he then sawed off. It is a serious criticism of Blair – perhaps to be recorded in history as more serious than the decision-making process in relation to the ill-judged Iraq War – that he did not use his massive power and authority to reorder British politics in a progressive direction.

Party Leadership

I had supported John Pardoe as leader in 1976, and Paddy Ashdown when David stepped down post-merger. When Paddy retired in 1999, the obvious successor was Charles Kennedy. He was decidedly not Paddy's choice; the latter despaired of Charles' disorganised laziness. So Paddy deliberately opted for an elongated timeframe for his successor to emerge, in the hope that an alternative would appear. Unlike the Conservative leader Michael Howard, who adopted precisely the same strategy with the desired outcome of David Cameron succeeding him, Paddy failed.

As a communicator, Charles was superb, and his lead role in opposing the Iraq War was both courageous and right. On the back of that, the 2005 general election result was a modified success, but much less striking than might have been the case had Charles run a disciplined campaign.

In its aftermath, it became apparent that the party was without effective leadership. I dropped in on a senior MP. He was brutal: "The three senior spokesmen – Vince [Cable] at the Treasury, Ming [Menzies Campbell] on foreign affairs and Mark Oaten on the home side – simply cannot get a meeting with Charles to discuss policy or, indeed, anything." I extracted from him that there was a consensus around Ming as the obvious successor (as they say in the Vatican, young cardinals vote for old popes!), but that Mark fancied himself. I hopped round to Mark's office in an attempt at gentle dissuasion.

I spectacularly failed, but did at least help to unleash a hornet's nest of dissatisfaction, which partially led to the chaos at the end of the year when Charles at last went public on his alcoholism, resigned on the basis that he would seek a fresh mandate, and was then swiftly disillusioned by an explosion in the Parliamentary party. At a subsequent occasion, I met Ming. "I think you were the butterfly!" he elegantly observed, on the – correct – assumption that I was acquainted with chaos theory (a part of mathematics relating to sensitive systems, in which a very small change may make the system behave completely differently).

Coalitions (2)

Nick Clegg followed Ming as leader, and was again confronted with the possibility of a coalition government. I was not directly in his loop (one issue with Nick was that he was too exclusive in seeking advice from his contemporaries and younger), but ensured that Paul Burstow – as Chief Whip – had my 1997 package, and I also gave a full briefing to Danny Alexander as Nick's closest colleague. And Nick, following Jim Wallace's retirement from Scottish government, elevated him to the Lords so as to have his experience available at Westminster at the heart of coalition government, as a previous Scottish Deputy First Minister.

As the negotiations progressed following the outcome of the 2010 general election, I had the privilege of a ringside seat. The federal executive met on the Saturday after polling day, with Nick and Danny in attendance. It met again on the Monday for an interim report on progress, and then on the Tuesday as part of a wider meeting to approve the deal. Ros Scott, as LibDem Party President, asked me to attend all these meetings as her legal and (party) constitutional adviser.

As my homework for the Saturday meeting, I decided to find out about the Labour Party's constitution. Clearly, Gordon Brown had lost the election, but – although the Parliamentary arithmetic was decidedly dodgy – we might just about do a deal with a different Labour leader, and the possibility would keep the Tories on their toes anyway. I rang a senior source, who had Peter Mandelson on the other line. The source reverted after some research, saying, "Right, Philip, we're in government. If the leader resigns, the Cabinet makes the appointment in the first instance."

I wrote an appropriate note, and handed it to Nick and Danny before the meeting as useful ammunition. At the same time, I offered my two pennies' worth to Nick that a full coalition was infinitely preferable to a "supply and maintenance" agreement, which would inevitably lead (as soon as a half-decent excuse could be found) to an early general election, which the Tories could afford and we couldn't.

As part of the negotiations for the coalition government, Jim Wallace was deputed to negotiate its mechanics with David Cameron's *consiglière* (in its original meaning, a member of a Mafia family who served as an adviser to the leader and resolved disputes within the family, but now used more loosely) Oliver Letwin, and went in with my Scotland draft in his back pocket.

The result emerged on the Cabinet Office website as *The Coalition Agreement for Stability and Reform*, only moderately changed from my draft (and with some 60% verbatim). I had to pinch myself every time I read it.

One of my key proposals had been a "Coalition Committee", with equal representation, to resolve differences between the coalition partners. Effectively, it was a device for the LibDems, as the junior partner, to a take a decision out of a Cabinet structure where it was a minority into a structure where agreement had to be reached by compromise. It became a committee of four, known round Whitehall as "The Quad", with Cameron and George Osborne on one side of the table, and Clegg and Alexander on the other.

One of the best aspects of the coalition government was that it restored Cabinet government, which had been damaged by Thatcher and eviscerated by Blair. This was fundamental to its success, and sceptics were confounded when it lasted its full five-year term.

I had also put a provision in my draft that the power of dissolution should be shared, in order to protect the LibDems, as the junior partner, from a unilateral dissolution by the Conservatives at a time of their choosing. This was effected in a different way, by legislating for a fixed-term Parliament that could only be brought to a premature end by either a two-thirds majority vote or a no-confidence vote followed by the failure of an alternative government to secure a confidence vote within a fortnight. I summarised the impact of this in two articles, which appear at the end of this chapter: a 2015 one about government formation in the immediate aftermath of a general election, and the second in 2018 about government formation in mid-term.

Procedurally, the coalition government was a stunning success. Politically, however, it had a rather sad history. Although there were a number of policy successes for the LibDems, there were also two avoidable mega-blunders: Nick wanted seamless government to prove that coalitions worked, so the LibDems lost a year of the differentiation that is so essential to a junior partner in government; and the tuition-fees issue (and the bizarre decision, perhaps by carelessness, to give Vince Cable ministerial responsibility for it) blew our "Trust" brand out of the water, even though the outcome was good in policy terms. If only it could have been called a "Graduate Tax" – which is what it was.

Around Government

As the dust settled after the formation of the coalition government, it slowly dawned on me that I had an opportunity to use it to forward items of public policy on which I had been working for years, primarily through the RSA and Tomorrow's Company. For the first (and probably only) time in my life, I had direct access to ministers, a number of whose mobile phone numbers were stored on mine.

Nor did I always have to take the initiative. On my return from my 2010 holiday, I found an invitation to a ministerial round-table discussion with Ed Davey, now a junior minister in Vince Cable's Department of BIS.

Ed was consulting on how to make shareholder communications focus on key issues, which had long been a concern of mine. Indeed, when I acted for Jacob Rothschild in the 1980s (see Chapter 2), he had pioneered the technique, in circulars to shareholders seeking approval for major transactions, of splitting the introductory letter into two: one from the chair setting out the key concepts, and a second from the company secretary with the detail. This was a good application of the journalist's practice of writing an article so that the reader could stop when he/she wanted, and the sub-editor could cut it short, without losing any key points in either case. I gratefully adopted the technique when chairing Mission Capital (see Chapter 3).

Mark Goyder and I used the meeting to advance the Tomorrow's Company project entitled "Simpler, Shorter, Smarter", which had at its heart the proposition that annual company reports should separate out key strategic issues from the routine morass in which they too often drowned (or were deliberately buried!). This was satisfyingly at the heart of the resultant regulations.

My long-standing interest and involvement with corporate governance had also given me an interest in pensions policy. The RSA had asked me to join its working group, whose principal proposal was to permit the aggregation of defined contribution schemes established by individual companies. The working group also highlighted how Scandinavian pension providers had the twin virtue of charging much lower costs than their British counterparts and leading on corporate-governance issues as investors.

In the run-up to the 2010 general election, I had obtained an endorsement of the RSA's proposals from Vince Cable (I drafted it, and Vince delegated Steve Webb to settle the text).

Steve became Pensions Minister in the coalition government, and provided a classic demonstration of how much an individual minister can achieve when left in post long enough (five years in his case). He had been an alarmingly young and bright professor of social policy, and came into government with a total understanding of state pensions, which he significantly reformed for the better. He took longer to master private pension provision, but – having done so – was an even more admirable reformer here too. His work was beyond the intellectual capacity of his boss Iain Duncan Smith (for whom Steve was a second pair of hands and a first brain), so he was left to his own devices.

One of the issues he addressed was auto-enrolment, which was (and is) a first-rate policy that effectively compels all but the tiniest companies to contribute to pension pots for their employees. David Pitt-Watson, the Hermes lead on pensions issues, with whom I had enjoyed co-operating in the RSA working group, pointed out forcibly and publicly that there needed to be tight regulation of charges, and rightly drew the parallel with stakeholder pensions where a cap had been imposed – in both cases, the Government was asking for trouble if it did not prevent excessive charging, for which it would be blamed.

There was an inadequate response from the Civil Service, so I fixed a meeting for David to put his case direct to Steve. When we arrived for the meeting, Steve greeted us warmly, but the body language of his civil servants was at a significantly lower temperature. As the meeting progressed, it became clear that we were in classic *Yes Minister* territory:[20] the civil servants were there to represent the interests of the pensions providers, and were extremely hostile to David, whom they regarded as their trouble-maker in chief. We made no progress, although Steve was careful to reserve his position.

David and I were disappointed. I made it my business to find Steve at the next party conference. "That was a miserable meeting, Steve," I said, making the *Yes Minister* point.

"Don't worry," was the reply, "I've moved them to different jobs!"

Golly! And the charges were subsequently capped.

Through the RSA and Tomorrow's Company, I also became involved in an organisation called Fair Pensions (now called Share Action), which was concerned with the charging issue, but also more generally with the way in which company pension schemes were run; their principal issue was that trustees were too often cowed by the short-termist nature of the investment policies adopted by the managers to whom they delegated investment decisions.

Fair Pensions was proposing to seek amendments to a convenient bill to set down in statute law the obligation of pension scheme trustees to have regard for what were seen by most investment

---

20 In a memorable scene, Jim Hacker's private secretary Bernard Woolley explains that the FCO [Foreign and Commonwealth Office] represented the interest of foreigners; the Department of Employment, the TUC [Trade Union Council]; the Trade Department, employers; the Education Department, teachers; etc.

managers as "soft" issues: environmental, societal and governance (ESG) issues. I helped with the drafting, but doubted that the idea would get anywhere without a strong ministerial prod.

There was a rather rudderless discussion, so I took my chance and weighed in with a strong plea to Vince to accept the amendment (of which I conveniently had copies to hand). He was very supportive, and Steve confirmed on the way out that he liked the idea too.

Vince put the proposal to his civil servants, who – not unreasonably – said that the Government should properly consult on issues of this nature before proceeding. Whether in an effort to assist or (I suspect) block the concept, they proposed referring the matter to the Law Commission, as the Kay Review had proposed.

I decided to help the process along. I was pleased to find that the Law Commission operated in a very open way, so that I was able to secure a meeting with the responsible commissioner to explain the issues, to which I also invited Mark Goyder. The commissioner readily grasped these issues and was clearly receptive. We submitted written evidence, and awaited the interim report. This was much less strong than I wanted, so – on being invited to a round table to discuss it – I weighed in strongly. The reply was positive, if nebulous: the Law Commission had moved on in its thinking. This was subsequently confirmed in a telephone conversation with the responsible commissioner.

The final report (Law Commission, 2014) concluded that the existing law was fine, but widely misunderstood; the parallel with the duties of company directors (see Chapter 4) was overwhelming. It did not recommend changes to statute law, because that was too blunt an instrument, but it set out – in an appendix entitled, with surprising snappiness, "Is it always about the money?" – a blistering destruction of the proposition that ESG issues were peripheral. It stated that they are financial factors relevant to the risk assessment that should accompany any investment decision.

Wow!

My final project involving government arose out of another Tomorrow's Company project, "Tomorrow's Business Forms", which argued for making the right choices in relation to ownership, structure and governance to deliver business and societal success, and indeed for reviewing those choices as each company developed.

Towards the end of the project, it suddenly dawned on me that we had hit on a major issue of public policy – how the public sector should assess private sector organisations commissioned to provide services, not least against the recent scandals involving providers of social care. And that assessment should not be merely cost-driven (and, in any event, I had learned in local government that the cheapest price was not necessarily the best value), but should look at the provider's business model, values and sustainability.

I arranged for this to be publicised in the *Financial Times*.

For various reasons, this point did not come out as strongly as I would have wished in the project document, but Mark and I thought it worth pursuing. Norman Lamb (a highly intelligent and good guy, who would have been a far better LibDem leader after the 2010 general election than Tim Farron), as Care Minister in the coalition government, was strongly supportive and indeed spoke at the project launch. We talked, in and around government, about ways of taking it forward, and in the end lighted upon the British Standards Institute (BSI) as the best route; Tomorrow's Company is working with them even now on developing a BSI "Trust Test" for this purpose.

Public Commentary

As one of my friends once observed to my wife at my 70th birthday lunch, his abiding memory of me could be described as "There goes Philip again, sticking his nose into somebody else's business!" And Lynda had some time previously bought me a coffee mug for the office bearing the legend "Everybody's entitled to my opinion"!

So, from time to time, I have enjoyed giving others the benefit (or otherwise) of my views, either within the LibDems or on a wider stage. I append to this chapter some of the examples.

One recurrent theme related to Israel/Palestine. Back in 1967, in the aftermath of the Six-Day War, I had gathered five prominent Jewish Oxford undergraduates to write a letter to *The Jewish Chronicle* (reproduced at the end of this chapter) advocating what subsequently became known as "the single-state solution". This harked back to some of the early liberal Zionist thinking.

As the situation darkened 40 years later, with the failure of Arafat to implement the Oslo accords, and the simultaneous assassination of Rabin and the Israeli side of the peace process, I became increasingly frustrated by the short-sightedness of successive Israeli governments, not least in the long-term interests of Israel itself. This came out in some letters to *The Independent*, and also in a long article I wrote for the British group of Liberal International following my 2010 visit to Israel recounted in Chapter 1 – see at the end of this chapter.

Judging the judges

As the candidates' committee ends a not uncontroversial year, and the party prepares for a new round of internal elections, INSIDER takes a look at the team which has caused such a fuss. They haven't been nearly as tough on re-approval as they might have been but some moribund timber has been eliminated. And a sharp eye is apparently being kept on social democrats who don't know why they've become Liberals.

1976: Liberator,

Judging
the Judges

ALAN BEITH

He has not attended any meetings and so has avoided any taint of collective reponsibility. He redeemed himself by firing David Penwarden as deputy chairman and chief scapegoat, appointing (though not as first choice, and without consulting colleagues) David Evans.

DAVID EVANS

He has played himself in slowly but well. Unlike his predecessor he is competent at chairing meetings and keeps a close eye on correspondence, thus ensuring that even rejections are tactfully phrased. He has also overhauled procedures well, but his greatest advantage is being sufficiently liked to get away with being effective.

JOYCE ARRAM

Her most productive contribution is her knitting, which like her comments lacks any shape or coherence. Her article in Liberal News was much resented. The RSPCA is rumoured to have persuaded Beith against his better judgement to keep her on the list of approved candidates.

BETH GRAHAM

Put on by sister Claire Brookes to represent the self-styled radicals against the nasty elitist establishment her radicalism has mainly been evidenced by querying the approval of Gavin Grant because ' folks don't approve of a man living off his wife's income'. One redeeming feature is that she has attended less than half the meetings.

GORDON LISHMAN

Gordon has been the pivot of most sensible decisions - experience with the elderly mentally infirm perhaps coming in useful. He is a producer of endless memoranda, most of which improve on translation.

MARTIN BIERMANN

Some of his contributions are useful, even if they are made 15 minutes, or sometimes a whole meeting, after discussion of the relevant item has been concluded. Could do with being more forceful, rather than complaining that he was bullied into silence.

PHILIP GOLDENBERG

He is not over-endowed with patience, nor easily controlled by the chair, thus having a disruptive influence on proceedings. Usually on Lishman's side in taking sensible decisions.

Another way to run the country . . .

Lib-Lab liaison offers shift in political culture

The recent creation of a joint Labour-Liberal Democrat Cabinet committee is a significant constitutional innovation. It enables a smaller party to co-operate in government without being bound by the doctrine of collective Cabinet responsibility that is a fundamental feature of British constitutional practice.

Britain has an adversarial political culture. Unlike other European Union members that have proportional electoral systems, it is not culturally or institutionally accustomed to co-operation between parties. Indeed, collective Cabinet responsibility has meant that, other than full-blown coalitions in times of national emergency, it has been almost impossible to contemplate parties working together.

The first break in this tradition was the 1977-78 Lib-Lab pact. Under this, there was a *de facto* shared responsibility for keeping in office a Labour Government that had lost its majority in the House of Commons and depended on Liberal votes. The only institutional structure was a non-Cabinet consultative committee for parliamentary business. The Liberal numbers in the House would not have supported a full coalition structure, even if one had been offered.

The difficulties of that arrangement clearly showed the need to find a device to preserve the independence of the smaller party. It had, in effect, to safeguard its identity, or risk being elbowed aside in a subsequent non-proportional general election where the choice would be perceived as being for the Government (meaning the larger party) or against it (a party which had not been involved with government).

The device had to avoid the doctrine of collective Cabinet responsibility. And so, a little-known constitutional precedent came into play.

As Peter Hennessy pointed out in his 1994 inaugural lecture as Professor of Contemporary History at Queen Mary and Westfield College, London, the Cabinet is, by historical development and under Britain's unwritten constitution, the executive committee of the Privy Council. Professor Hennessy illustrated this by citing how, during the Attlee Labour Government of 1945-50, Winston Churchill had raised matters of defence policy he wished to discuss privately. Attlee set up a Cabinet committee of senior ministers and members of the Conservative Opposition for this purpose. The committee operated under the aegis of the Privy Council, of which all concerned were members.

That precedent obviously derived much from the wartime Coalition Government. In 1997, it had attractions for a smaller party, such as the Liberal Democrats, wondering how it should respond to an offer of co-operation from a party of government with an overall majority that would render a full-blown coalition inappropriate.

A joint Cabinet committee, working together solely on agreed topics (and above all the constitutional reform programme agreed to by Robin Cook and Robert Maclennan in the run-up to the 1997 general election), would leave the Liberal Democrats free to disagree with other policies of a Labour Government, and not surrender its distinct identity.

And so it was. The outcome is obviously uncertain, but the concept of a cross-party Cabinet committee has proved viable in terms of constitutional law and precedent, and is at least a stepping stone on the path to a less adversarial political culture.

PHILIP GOLDENBERG

● *The author, a partner with the City solicitors S.J. Berwin, has a long-standing interest in constitutional law, and was a Liberal Democrat parliamentary candidate in the last general election.*

1997: The Times, *Joint Cabinet Committee*

'INEXCUSABLE' POLICY

Sir,—We are all deeply concerned for the future well-being of the people of Israel. When war broke out this summer we—obviously—profoundly hoped that Israel would win and were deeply relieved when she did.

Our present concern is that there should not be another war in ten years' time, with no guarantee of who will win and with the very real possibility of the use of nuclear weapons, in which case nobody will win.

We believe that Israel is now in a unique position to lay the foundations for a just peace; for she has it in her power to wipe out, at a stroke, the underlying cause of the hatreds and tensions that have accumulated in the Middle East.

All of us have, in this country, supported extensions to the Race Relations Act and measures conducive to a multi-racial society; and we assert that to delineate the citizenship of a State on an ethnic or religious basis is morally unjustifiable and politically suicidal.

We condemn without reservation the governments of Egypt and Jordon for cruelly using the Palestinian refugees as political pawns for the past nineteen years; but we consider that the current Israeli failure to grant unconditional return to the refugees, now living in appalling conditions on the East Bank of the Jordan, is completely inexcusable.

We call upon the State of Israel to admit these refugees without delay; not only is this a humanitarian imperative, but also it could be a first step towards the creation of a bi-national State of Palestine, which is, in our view, the only long-term solution to the problems of the Middle East. We regard the current call by Israel for aliya from the West as a futile and losing race against time.

We believe that the unconditional admission of the refugees, coupled with a statement of Israel's intention to form a bi-national State within the former boundaries of Mandatory Palestine, is the only way to relieve the present tension.

ANTHEA BROWN, St. Hugh's College, ex-president, O.U. Liberal Club.

IAN GLICK, Balliol College, ex-secretary, Halifax Young Liberals.

PHILIP GOLDENBERG, Pembroke College, ex-secretary, O.U. Liberal Club, ex-treasurer, O.U. Israel Society.

STEPHEN HUTTER, Christ Church, ex-chairman, O.U. Israel Society.

STEPHEN MARKS, New College, ex-president, Oxford Union, ex-chairman, O.U. Labour Club.

Oxford Union Society,
Oxford.

1967: The Jewish Chronicle,
*Advocating a "Single State
Solution"*

Israel: "Fascinating and Frightening"

Philip Goldenberg

After a fortnight's holiday in Israel last autumn, I wrote a personal note, to try to collect my own thoughts. Since then, there have been two developments of interest. Firstly, the public discourse in Israel has worsened, with nationalist Parliamentarians setting in train McCarthyite investigations of Israeli human rights organizations. Secondly, some leaders of the Anglo-Jewish community have started voicing some thoughts similar to mine. So mine may perhaps be of interest.

A few introductory points:

I write as a Jew, a Zionist (more of that later) and a liberal. Of course I am a LibDem, but I do not write in that capacity.

I unconditionally support the right of the State of Israel to exist within secure and recognized boundaries, free from fear of attack. But that is very different from supporting successive Israeli governments, particularly where, as all too often is the case, their actions and policies are in my view contrary to Israel's long-term interests.

When in Israel, I listened to family, friends and others, but have not verified everything they said. They are not representative. But they all hold liberal values and, as Israelis, share a range of emotions ranging from depression/despair to real anger at the present state of Israeli politics. One – a former Parliamentary candidate – said bluntly that he was too ashamed to discuss the topic.

I also had the salutary experience of reading Israeli newspapers for two weeks. Their priorities are (a) Israeli news (b) an amazingly detailed focus on US politics as they affect Israel and (c) occasionally, the Middle East generally. Britain and Europe hardly feature at all.

I start with a passing thought. It is apparent from one of the exhibits in the archaeological section of the Israel Museum that in

Israel *homo sapiens* was a contemporary, rather than a successor, of Neanderthal man. Perhaps this is a paradigm for the present Israeli government.

Israeli Politics

Israel is a vibrant democracy, which has made enormous and deeply impressive progress in a whole range of fields. It is a fascinating place, and a fascinating society. But it is also very frightening, not least to Israelis – and others – with liberal values.

I deal first with the systemic structural problems of Israeli politics. Israel is the world's worst advertisement for proportional representation. With controlled Party lists and a single national constituency (and therefore no effective threshold – 0.83% of the national vote gives one Parliamentary seat), there is an inherent fissiparous tendency, and enormous difficulty in forming a stable government. Various religious Parties, too many of whom are mired in institutional corruption, are thereby given blackmail positions which they readily exploit. To take a recent example, there was a proposal to give student grants uniquely to ultra-Orthodox Jewish males engaged in religious studies, while the general body of students effectively have to work to finance their studies. Ultra-Orthodox Jewish males are not only exempt from military service but (unlike ultra-Orthodox Jewish females) do not have to give corresponding non-military service.

So in general terms most governments lack the strength to take difficult decisions.

Of more immediate concern are the deeply illiberal values now polluting the political process and public discourse generally – a sort of race to the pit of populism, as exemplified by: the pending collapse of the Labour Party; proposed loyalty oaths for non-Jewish cit-

izens; the recent banning by the Ministry of Education of a proposed school textbook which set out in parallel the Israeli and Palestinian narratives; powers to communities to exclude "newcomers who don't fit in" – translate "Arabs"; and the increasing intolerance by the ultra-Orthodox of both Arabs and more secular Jews (causing eg friends who are long-term residents of Jerusalem to move to Tel-Aviv).

All this is coupled with an increasing intolerance of dissent, eg the refusal of the present Israeli Government to recognize the existence of J-Street, let alone engage with it.

Zionist Values

It is important to recognize that the values under attack are not just liberal values in general. They are also the historic values of Zionism itself, which (as pointed out in a brilliant lecture by Shlomo Avineri, a former Director-General of the Israeli Foreign Ministry, and now Israel's leading political scientist) were expounded by Herzl and Weizmann. If one defines liberalism as openmindedness, tolerance and generosity of spirit (the last being the proper translation of the Latin *liberalis*), then liberalism was at the heart of Zionism, with an emphasis on learning, humanity, science, and an express recognition that the Arabs in the then Palestine had rights that would need protection.

Why are these values being trashed by so many current Israeli politicians? Partly of course it is a response to the legitimate fear of extinction which is an inevitable product of the way in which surrounding Arab régimes and groupings have put the State of Israel under threat since its foundation. Those existential pressures do not encourage liberalism. But it is also a product of changing demography, with the increasing number of ultra-Orthodox Jews whose main concern is to strengthen their own intolerant grip on the rest of society, and also the cultural change wrought by extensive immigration from Russia, whose citizens are inevitably unused to the checks and balances applicable to a democratic culture (which has never been a feature of Russian society which moved almost straight from one form of dictatorship to another). It is no surprise that the most extreme political party (at least at present) is Israel Beiteinu, which is largely Russian in composition and electoral support. Its Foreign Minister is a fascist; and several of its Parliamentarians would have fitted in well as Labour Home Secretaries!

The Peace Process

Where does all this leaves the peace process. In doing so, I recog-

nize, as all who are not involved directly in the process should, that I may well not know things which would cause me to change my views. But I doubt if this is significantly the case.

Netanyahu is a follower, not a leader. He has become Prime Minister (which he intends to remain!) by forming a coalition with extremists who are deeply opposed to a peace settlement (to put it another way, they are in favour of settlements rather than peace). If he were ever serious about peace, he would form a Grand Coalition with the former governing Party Kadimah to deliver it. The evidence is that such a Coalition advocating a reasonable and credible settlement would receive majority public support.

However, Israeli public opinion has no belief that such a settlement is on offer. Sane Israelis know that Abu Mazen and Fayyad are as good counterparts as they will get; but also know that they have no capacity to deliver a peace that extends to Gaza, nor even a peace that will necessarily outlast a change of régime on the West Bank. Public opinion will not force Netanyahu to act unless Hamas can be brought into a process in which it accepts Israel's right to exist. In addition, a convincing and permanent resolution of the Iran nuclear issue is a necessary pre-condition of such public acceptance.

It follows from all this that I simply do not believe that any direct peace negotiations will succeed. Indeed, they serve no useful purpose when the issue is not the nature of a peace settlement (which is pretty much known and agreed) but the political will and leadership on both sides to achieve it. What the international community needs to do – and urgently – is to put together a deal which creates the conditions for precisely that political will and leadership. If and when that happens Netanyahu would blow with the wind of change and either lead, or be led, into selling a credible peace to Israeli public opinion.

Inaction on the part of the international community is not a sensible option; it will simply mean that the present peace process falters then withers. And public opinion on both sides would then harden, increasing the miasma of mutual mistrust.

Philip Goldenberg is a long-standing Liberal Democrat who has been involved in much of the recent history of the LibDems and its predecessor Liberal Party – he was one of the two lawyers who effected their merger and co-authored the original LibDem Constitution. An adviser to Paddy Ashdown, he led the technical side of Paddy's contingency planning for a "hung Parliament" and a possible Coalition Government. His work on the machinery of a Coalition Government was formative in the structuring of both the 1999 Scottish Executive and the 2010 Westminster Coalition Government.

2011: Interlib, *Israel*

7

Local Government

Introductory

This chapter does not set out to provide a record of my terms of office. Rather, it extracts and examines some key themes: what being a councillor entails (or should entail), group dynamics and councillor/officer relationships.

Being a Councillor

The ideal councillor is intelligent, diligent, a team player and a competent public speaker.[21] They also need significant interpersonal skills, interacting as they do with local residents, their political colleagues and opponents, and the council's officers. Plus, they have to balance, with intelligence and sensitivity, the quadrilateral of forces to which they are subject: the residents who elected them, the wider area that they govern, their political colleagues and their consciences.

---

21 At one particular council meeting, the public gallery was packed (this was not normal, but a discussion about a proposed traveller site always gives rise to significant public interest). The preceding item gave rise to some very boring Tory speeches. A line from Ned Sherrin addressing the Oxford Union came to mind. "Mr Mayor," I began, "if the late Dr Spooner were present tonight, and had sat through the collection of whinges we have just heard from the Tory group, he would surely say of that group, 'What a collection of shining wits I see before me!'" My LibDem colleagues, council officers and the public gallery burst into satisfactory gales of laughter. The baffled Labour mayor turned to the chief executive sitting next to him for an explanation, who was too helpless to provide one. The Tories sat in stony and puzzled silence until, around 20 minutes later, the face of their sole Oxbridge graduate indicated that he had belatedly got the joke.

Unfortunately, local political parties find it difficult to attract suitable people, so the reality is significantly different from the ideal.

Any sensible party runs a candidate-approval process, but needs to make up the numbers, and too often rewards activism uncritically. I pointed out in Chapter 5 that those who come into voluntary organisations often do so with primary or secondary motivations that have nothing to do with that organisation. They can instead be using it for displacement activity to address emotional issues affecting their lives: the need to feel wanted and self-important is a frequent motivating factor. That may, in turn, give an emotional edge to their involvement, to the detriment of the organisation, because they are more motivated by their personal success within the organisation than by its success against its competitors. I also recorded that, in my experience as a regional party chair, almost all problems in local parties that required regional intervention arose from a lax approval system that had let loose on the unsuspecting public an aspirant councillor who was incompetent, illiberal or psychologically flawed (sometimes all three), and whom the trusting public had then unwisely elected.

Woking LibDems' approval system was fine on paper, as it listed all the qualities set out previously, plus the need for the applicant to not only be a Liberal in name but also be a liberal by values and behaviour. The outcome of the approval process was rather less than fine, as I gradually discovered after I was elected for the first time in 1984.

Two good councillors had been elected in May 1983, but three of the previously elected four were less than ideal in terms of competence and diligence. Four more joined in 1986 when the Tories lost control, and there was a noticeable feature in the council chamber of young, no-nonsense professionals on the LibDem side and elderly has-beens in the Tory group.

The first real disaster arrived in 1987, with the election of Rosemary Johnson. She was a classic case of the displacement activity syndrome. In 1983, a heavyweight approval panel had originally rejected her: her hard work was acknowledged, but her motivation was unascertainable, she was found devoid of political ideology and she had no concept of the role of a councillor. See the analysis of client politics in Chapter 9.

In my experience, there are broadly three categories of LibDem councillors. The first are "wired" LibDems: they are politically committed, form their views on the basis of LibDem values and behave as team players. The second are good community people: their hearts are in the right place and they will follow a political lead. The third have significant negative personality issues. So long as the first two together are in a significant majority, the group will operate successfully, but if the third category is too dominant and carries the second category in perverting the group's workings, then the group is in real trouble, as the Woking LibDem group was far too often.

Indeed, a few years after I was elected, I started to keep a personal (and inevitably subjective) analysis of my colleagues. "Knowledge" and "intelligence" were overwhelmingly rated as excellent, good or OK, with only one or two being poor. "Efficiency" was too often poor or abysmal. For the "personality" and "judgment" scores, up to a third were rated as variable or difficult or even neurotic or diabolical. On the LibDem scale, nearly a half could at best be described as "mainly", while a sixth were wholly negative.

But there were some splendid exceptions. Here is an extract from my obituary of my excellent colleague John Magid:

John Magid – an Exemplary Liberal Democrat
As Liberals should be, he was fair, open-minded, tolerant and generous of spirit (the last being the meaning of the original Latin word "liberalis").

These values governed his behaviour. He was always a team player: selfless rather than self-interested, accepting any group decision and unwaveringly speaking publicly in its support. His was always the quiet voice of reason and balance, tempered only by an impish sense of humour and never the self-serving neurotic rant. He always judged issues objectively on their merits rather than on the basis of personal prejudice. He offered wise advice, listening to others and then gently moving them towards the right answer.

The Borough of Woking

Unlike its Guildford neighbour, Woking is not a historic town; rather, it is a collection of villages. The original (now Old) Woking flourished at the end of the 15th century, when Woking Palace was a royal residence and the site of the 1490 Treaty of Woking between Henry VII (whose mother, Margaret Duchess of Beaufort, owned it) and Maximilian of Austria. But, as the road network became of increasing importance, Woking declined as a result of not being on a coaching route.

The fortunes of the area were transformed when the original London/Portsmouth railway (via Basingstoke, Winchester and Southampton) was opened in 1838. What had been heathland around the new Woking station became a town centre. The present Borough of Woking consists of this area, together with the historic villages of Knaphill, Brookwood, Horsell, Woodham, Byfleet, Pyrford, Old Woking, Kingfield and Westfield, and the later developments of Sheerwater (a 1950s London-overspill estate) and Goldsworth Park (a massive 1980s private estate); they now so sprawl into each other that the boundaries are unclear, apart from Byfleet, which has only three roads in or out.

Another significant factor in the development of Woking also relates to the advent of the railways. This was the establishment of Brookwood Cemetery by the London Necropolis Company (LNC) to provide burial facilities at a time when the capital was finding it difficult to accommodate its increasing population of both the living and the dead. At a time when companies could not be incorporated by registration, but required a private bill, LNC's good faith was challenged at its Examining Committee on the

In Slough with David Steel…

...and John Pardoe

In a seafront Poole pub with Paddy Ashdown

With Shirley Williams when she spoke at the National Liberal Club

In campaigning mode in Brookwood

With Charles Kennedy in Woking

The formal opening of the new monastery in Brookwood Cemetery

The LibDem group take control of Woking Borough Council

With Sir Ming [Menzies] Campbell in Woking

basis that its vast land-purchase target (the whole of what is now the centre of Woking) made it a property speculator rather than a cemetery company. To demonstrate its genuineness, LNC abjured the normal power to sell surplus land, and on that basis got its bill. The local Tory MP, who had opposed its second reading, supported its third, though whether he was convinced by the argument or by the traditional Tory brown envelope is uncertain.

Brookwood Cemetery was originally accessible by rail from a special station – the LNC railway station – next to Waterloo station. Trains, with some passenger carriages reserved for different classes and others for coffins (also for different classes), ran into the cemetery on a dedicated branch from the adjoining South Western main line – the junction was just next to Brookwood station. Two stations were in the cemetery itself: Cemetery South for Anglicans, and Cemetery North for everyone else. Their platforms still exist; one of them is incorporated into the grounds of the new monastery (see below).

Woking is accordingly the only town that owes the core of its central development to the fraudulent promotion of a private Act of Parliament by a cemetery company, as I explained to an astonished Jo Grimond when I walked him through the town centre in 1984 to a campaign rally for that year's European Parliamentary elections.

Since party politics had taken over much of local government in the 1930s, Woking had been governed by the Conservatives. "Governed" was perhaps an over-statement, as governance consisted of an annual meeting between the Conservative Committee chairs and the senior council officers, at which broad strategy was set; after that, officers were left to their own devices. We were about to initiate a profound cultural change.

Horsell West: 1984–92

Horsell West was a ward immediately to the north-west of the town centre. Richard Sanderson had won our first seat there in 1983 by a majority of around 100. It was agreed that, having fought the

1983 general election, I would try to gain a second seat there the following year.

I was lucky. The Tory group leader, who chaired the Planning Committee, was up for re-election. He was the leading proponent of routing the new road into the town centre from the north-west through the much-loved green area at the eastern end of Horsell West. I became the leading opponent of this mad idea, and made it the key issue in my campaign; I got Ron Hore (our second councillor for Knaphill, an architect by profession and a brilliant cartoonist) to draw a Wells-inspired cartoon of Martians landing on Horsell Common, but this time armed with maps and a bulldozer.

The election outcome was predictable, although not its scale: you could have heard the proverbial pin drop as the returning officer, Woking's new chief executive, Paul Russell, announced that the Tory group leader had received 772 votes to my 1,541.

And so I attended my first group meeting. We elected one of the 1983 intake – Tony Kremer – as leader. We allocated portfolios – I got highways, for which the borough then had agency powers on behalf of the county. We began to plot how to use council (and committee) meetings to obtain publicity.

We adopted group standing orders, which I drafted off the party's model. These were important because they delineated how LibDem councillors should deal with the quadrilateral of forces described previously: the residents who elected them, the wider area that they governed, their political colleagues and their consciences. They recognised two rights of dissent from a group decision: where there was a key ward-related issue and where there was a genuine issue of conscience (not merely judgment). But, in each case, they required a prior discussion with the group leader or deputy.

In short, the group for the first time began to acquire a professional tinge.

I used my first two years to familiarise myself with highways issues, to learn how to deal with casework, to promote myself indirectly as the PPC, and to play an active part in building the party's electoral strength, particularly in the highly successful 1985 county council elections, where we increased our numbers from one to four out of seven-and-a-half divisions in the constituency, with a further by-election success to follow in 1986.

Council officers used to keep a file of correspondence per councillor. Mine rapidly became the largest! Furthermore, I developed a useful technique, which was dividing residents into those who could look after themselves with a little help and those who couldn't. Those falling in the first category were advised to write to the relevant officer to set out the issue, adding a last paragraph of "Cllr Goldenberg, to whom I have sent a copy of this letter, has asked that you send him a copy of your reply." Mysteriously, these letters received a much swifter reply than others! With the second category, I wrote the letter myself, and the residents were very appreciative of a successful outcome: I got more thanks from an elderly lady for whom I extracted a £500 payment from the council's insurers (after threatening them with opposing the renewal of their contract!) than from professional clients for whom I had worked nights to complete a multimillion-pound deal.

The key borough election year was 1986. Could we deprive the Tories of overall control? We did, by gaining four seats. With our 12 to the Tories' 15, we also overtook Labour (7) to become the larger opposition group. But the Tories kept all the committee chairmanships, as Labour's terms for putting us in control included an overlarge share for themselves. Our gain rate slowed over the next two years, and it was not until we reached 14 in 1988 that we were able to obtain a share of power.

Meanwhile, by 1987, Tony Kremer had served three years as leader, and it was logically time for a change. Richard Sanderson was the natural successor, but Kremer selfishly insisted on clinging on until he retired in 1988, equally selfishly then failing to put in the work to ensure that he passed his seat to the next candidate.

With the Tories and ourselves being almost equally represented after the 1988 election, they and we agreed to share the committee chairs equally. We took the Planning Committee (Ron Hore), Housing Committee (Chris Edwards) and Highways Committee (me), and held them for two years (1989 was a county council election year).

We all had a steep learning curve, but were at least as good as our Tory predecessors. It was fun to watch the faces of Tory councillors of the "born to rule" brigade looking up at us from the well of the council chamber as if a LibDem chair was against the natural order. But chairing was a tough call: every non-LibDem councillor was waiting to pounce on any political advantage (which, in all fairness, we had been when in the same position). I later blessed the on-the-job training I had received when I subsequently chaired endless AGMs of Mission Capital (see Chapter 3) and the TSA board (see Chapter 4).

Chairing the Highways Committee brought me into a serious working relationship with senior officers of the council for the first time. They were not culturally accustomed to an interventionist chair, with a professionally trained mind, who was not prepared just to go with the flow. I started with a meeting at which I was given a helpful general overview. I asked a couple of fundamental questions: How were budgetary priorities dealt with between different committees? And what was the overall strategy of the Highways Committee? I concluded that the first was a mystery and the second non-existent.

I required to see draft papers in advance of each meeting and complex papers at an earlier draft stage; this was clearly a novel approach. I pointed out that I needed their professional skills, and they needed my political ones. I promised that I would give them a political steer, but would never seek to stop them giving their professional advice, so long as we had discussed any concerns I had in advance. I ended up by saying that, although we had different disciplines (I was a lawyer, and they were engineers), we both knew what an almighty shambles was (I may have used a more colourful expression), and I needed to know early on if one had occurred or was in prospect.

This dialogue made me appreciate that, as I observed later in Whitehall (see Chapter 6), *Yes Minister* was not just a brilliantly funny comedy show, it was also a training manual! One of the really helpful lessons I drew from it was that, when faced with an officer recommendation that was clearly the product of internal debate and was now a corporate consensus, it was quite useful to speak direct to the key – by definition, the junior – officer involved, and get a grip on the underlying issues. I took this technique with me into the RSA (see Chapter 4).

I gave myself two main tasks as chair of the Highways Committee.

The first was influencing the council's budget. I worked hard on the papers, and steered them through the committee. My good work was, however, nearly negated when – at their discussion by the full council – upon being asked to explain why the Highways Department was doing so well in its allocation, Ray Morgan (then finance director, subsequently chief executive) said that it was because it had such an effective chair! Glares of mixed fury and envy demonstrated the unhelpfulness of his comment!

The second was to develop a strategy. Officers were, at best, lukewarm at shouldering this extra burden. So, learning from *Yes Minister*, I simply announced – at the end of the last meeting before the summer recess – that when we came back in the autumn, there would be an initial paper to this end. Officer resistance promptly collapsed.

Chairing the Highways Committee, for some strange reason, carried with it chairing the Licensing Committee, which regulated the taxi and private-hire trades, and also entertainment licences in public houses.

The former task involved balancing public protection against the reality that clocking up large mileages inevitably meant that minor motoring offences would be committed. We took a pragmatic view on this, while cracking down hard on violence or dishonesty. So, it took three routine motoring offences in a year before we hauled an individual in.

On one memorable occasion, the miscreant pleaded poverty and begged us not to remove his livelihood. He took a sheaf of papers out of his pocket and almost threw them at the borough legal officer who was effectively the prosecutor. The latter asked me if he might read them; as he did so, I noticed his strained expression.

"Excuse me, Chairman," he said, "may I just have a word with Mr X?"

"Yes, of course," I replied.

"Mr X, do you want me to give details of *all* these papers to the committee?" asked the prosecutor.

"Yes, yes," confirmed Mr X.

"Well, Chairman, there are numerous unpaid bills amounting to £Y, and [I could see him struggling to keep a straight face] a demand from the local magistrates court for a fine and costs in relation to a motoring offence that has not yet been brought to your attention."

I, at least, kept a straight face, which was more than could be said for the two female clerks, who pretty much disappeared beneath the table in helpless fits of giggles.

On the entertainment side, we encountered a gay pub where the police opposed the application on the grounds that it might result in violence if homophobic intruders created mayhem. I led the committee into the retirement room, and pretty much exploded at this approach to the rule of law. I was supported by a right-wing but libertarian Tory, and we allowed the application. Incensed by what had happened, the following day I rang the police inspector for the town centre. I explained what had happened, and voiced my concern.

"I'm sorry, Philip," came the response. "We should have done with you what we do with the licensing justices."

"Yes?" I prompted.

"Well, before each session, we brief them privately on everything we don't want to say in public."

"You what?" I shrieked, followed by some fiercely expressed legal analysis of the principles of natural justice.

Our chairmanships came to an abrupt and unpleasant end when the 1990 elections saw small Tory gains. They made us a reduced offer of two chairs. The group decision was to re-nominate me for the Highways Committee, and nominate Rosemary Johnson (who had been my deputy chair) for the Housing Committee. Tory snobbery refused to accept Rosemary, and I refused to serve in the hopeless position as the only LibDem chair in a Tory administration.

If this was Tory unpleasantness, the LibDem group was sadly about to match it twice over.

The first episode concerned the mayoralty. The convention was that the political groups shared this in turn, on a ratio determined by their respective strengths, and the nominee of each of them was then elected unopposed. On this basis, the deputy mayoralty for 1991/2 – and consequently the 1992/3 mayoralty – was a LibDem choice. The longest-serving councillor who was willing to undertake the role was me, and the LibDem group accordingly resolved to nominate me in preference to Rosemary Johnson, who had three years' less service.

The Tories disliked me intensely, and not only on a political level. Their then leader – a bad-tempered bully called Alec Grayson – had given an early warning of his approach when, at a social event to welcome a new senior officer, he had contradicted me when I was explaining the system and said that the nominee had to be, "the right sort of person". It was clear that his definition of this excluded (shades of Linklaters – see Chapter 2) anybody who was a fierce political opponent, mouthy and Jewish to boot.

So, when Richard Sanderson informed Grayson of my nomination, the latter insisted – contrary to every custom and precedent – that there should be a secret ballot of all councillors, between me and their decent, if dim-witted, nominee.

To his eternal discredit, Richard meekly accepted this outrageous proposal instead of giving it the short shrift it manifestly deserved (as I was later to discover when his son James was local party chair

20 years later, it is a male Sanderson genetic feature to have jelly where the spine should be).

This opened the gates of hell. On the numbers, I should have won. In a contested open vote in full council, I would have. But a secret ballot, in which Tory loyalty would result in a full vote on their side, gave a private opportunity to other councillors to go against their own group decisions.

This opportunity was gratefully taken, not only by a couple of Labour councillors with personal agendas, but also – outrageously – by three LibDems: Rosemary Johnson (miffed at being passed over), supported by her devotee Chris Edwards, and Anne Cartwright for unfathomable personal reasons.

This was a group mega-crisis, requiring outside intervention. Paul Burstow (then PPC for Sutton and Cheam, subsequently its MP and a minister in the 2010–15 coalition government) kindly provided it. I made it clear that I would resign unless either the group censured the individuals concerned or they apologised. In the end, Rosemary Johnson reluctantly did so, with Chris Edwards yapping at her heels. Anne Cartwright didn't even have the guts to own up.

It took some time to restore working relationships within the group. As this began to happen, the second issue came into view.

Richard Sanderson was in his fourth year of leadership, so his successor was under contemplation. The council's committee structure had been updated, so that there was now to be a Policy and Resources Committee, which pulled together policy and finance. The Labour group had indicated that they were prepared to support a LibDem nominee for this key position.

LibDem councillors began to contemplate who should take this up as group leader, not least as there was a groundswell of opinion that Richard's leadership skills were so conspicuous by their absence that he was incapable of leading a dog around the block.

Chris Edwards invited Rosemary Johnson and me round to his house. Partly, this was a bridge-building exercise. But we all recognised that we were the three most plausible successors to

Richard. A good and open discussion led to both of the others offering to support me.

Richard, however, was less interested in the good of the group than in the personal status of the chairmanship that he coveted (not that he had any idea what he would do with it). So he enticed Rosemary to support his continuing "leadership" with the offer of a key role, and she rapidly changed sides. This led to an acrimonious group meeting with two tied votes, which left Richard in place.

My principal role in 1991–2 was to chair the Car Parking Sub-committee of the Highways Committee, whose major activity was to introduce a controlled parking zone (CPZ) around the town centre, which had become impossibly cluttered by day-long commuter parking. The policy was splendid, but introducing it just before polling day in the 1992 local elections was a serious political mistake. We sorted some of the inevitable teething problems (see the end of this chapter for some of the publicity), but change is never welcome in the short term.

The council elections in 1992 immediately followed a general election, which the Tories had won. This (and perhaps the CPZ) inevitably affected the outcome, and I lost Horsell West by 19 votes. Given the events of 1991, I was not entirely sorry.

Brookwood: 2003–8

I set out in Chapter 5 how I came to be the candidate for the ward of Brookwood. It was very different from Horsell West. Because it was a single-member ward, its electorate was 1,900 rather than 5,500.

Some 1,200 were in Brookwood village itself, on or off the spine formed by Connaught Road. Some 350, inserted to make up the numbers, were on the separate Percheron Drive estate. The rest were scattered throughout the rural area, and took up five Saturday afternoons to canvass (the urban bits took 14 evenings).

It was a very personal campaign. Jenny Fowler was hugely supportive, and her home became our local base. I did all the canvassing myself, including a call on the then Russian (now Greek) Orthodox monastery in the middle of Brookwood Cemetery.

"And why should we vote for you?" enquired the impressive Father Alexis.

"For two reasons," I responded. "First, I'm more Russian than any of you. [They were all English converts.] Second, I'm the only candidate you're ever likely to have who can read both the Old and New Testaments in their respective original languages!"

They voted for me en masse, and I then helped them get planning permission for their new monastic building.

We had a small team that I had put together for polling day (the local party was, as explained in Chapter 5, totally unsupportive). We worked our socks off, calling on all our supporters. We got to the count. I won by seven votes, including the five monks!

One of my electors was Ray Morgan. It would have been wrong to ask his voting intentions, but he had been so appalled by our lunatic 1996–2000 councillor that he confessed to having voted Conservative in 2000 to get rid of her. Her replacement was the incredibly arrogant Mark Pritchard, who caused the by-election by resigning on being selected to fight the Parliamentary constituency of The Wrekin, and whom Ray found equally difficult.

At a fraught meeting, Pritchard snapped, "Mr Morgan, do you ever admit that you are wrong?"

"Yes," said Ray promptly, "I voted for you!"

I was faced with three interlocking tasks. The first was to be an effective councillor for Brookwood – partially because it was an end-of-borough ward whose issues would never be addressed without loud and persistent advocacy, and partially because I faced a re-election challenge in a year's time and knew the Tories would play dirty to try to get rid of me (they did!). The second was to reintegrate myself into the council. The third, and the most difficult, was to reintegrate myself into the LibDem group, where it was clear to me that the newer members had been thoroughly poisoned against me by Rosemary Johnson (see Chapter 5).

The second happened swiftly. The first item at my first council meeting was to elect Richard Sanderson as mayor, and the LibDem group readily agreed that, as his former ward colleague, I should propose him. I started by saying that I was back after an 11-year interval, and the whole council looked better for my return; I noticed that the grimaces of pain were not confined to the Tory benches.

I thought a bit of Tory-baiting was then in order, not least with a packed public gallery, so I continued, "Madam Mayor, I am here to represent the ward of Brookwood, which has 1,900 live electors and 240,000 dead ones – a balance between the living and the dead that will serve me well in dealing with the Conservative group on this council." This time the grimaces were less evenly-balanced.

I sorted five key ward issues in my first year. The first was the messy aftermath of the county council's shambolic handling of the major roadworks at a key junction, which had run well over both budget and time, and had helped my election campaign ("The Make-you-very-cross Roads" had been the title of my critique). The tatty local play area was, at my instigation, prioritised for immediate action. I forced through a massive traffic-calming scheme along the main Connaught Road, with two zebra crossings and a myriad of speed bumps.

Furthermore, I helped the monks with their proposed new monastery, arguing for its approval at the Planning Committee and bringing Ron Hore in to help with its design; part of the deal was that they would mark out the adjoining site of one of the two historic cemetery railway stations. I came as near to sainthood as was possible for somebody who was not only alive but also Jewish!

I also resolved the curious problem of why the developers of Percheron Drive (whose residents included Ray Morgan) had mysteriously failed to finish off all the loose ends – a subject on which my ear had been bent all around the estate. I rang the finance director of the developers, who started by being unhelpful. I upped the ante: "Let me guess the real problem," I said. "If you don't finish off the estate, you can avoid putting the profit through your accounts, thereby delaying corporation tax."

Spluttering noises at the other end served to confirm my diagnosis, so I increased the squeeze: "I sit on the Planning Committee. You make planning applications. It is not in your interest for me to be in a bad mood every time I hear your name. Nor would your reputation be enhanced by putting the reason for this delay into the public domain." Strangely, the work was completed shortly after this dialogue.

In addition, I had to deal with a traveller incursion, steering a careful course between supporting strong local opposition on legitimate planning grounds without pandering to the occasional racist tinge.

Throughout the year, I was harried by the Tory machine. The defeated candidate put out leaflets falsely suggesting that he was responsible for all my good work, but he was basically a good guy. We had dinner together a couple of years later. He apologised for the lies, saying that he had been forced to use the material drafted for him by the press officer of Woking Conservatives.

The Tory MP suborned the (self-appointed) chair of the local Residents' Association into this pack of lies. Notwithstanding all this, I won the 2004 election by 42 votes, having squeezed both the Labour candidate and our previous lunatic (who had morphed into a Green Party candidate) into virtual oblivion. When I switched on my computer after returning home from the count, there was a message from Father Alexis, timed at 09:00 hours that morning, which read "Today, in church, we lit a candle for you. If you now lose, it's your fault!"

Ward issues still abounded. I negotiated a difficult deal between the council and the residents of Sheets Heath for the long-overdue repair of the road bridge connecting them to Brookwood village, and the signed diversion of lorries for which it was too narrow. I overcame officer resistance to installing a sign stating "Right Turn First" at the Brookwood crossroads when I proved that such signs were used in other areas.

I had worked myself slowly back into the LibDem group, whose new members I began to assess. Rosemary Johnson was no longer there – though her husband Ian (a thoroughly good person in himself, but too nice to deal with the hard-faced Tories) was leader, and she was the campaigns officer, so still a key player in the local party – but the poison she had left behind was deep-seated.

There were some good community people. However, one colleague believed that he had a right to dissent in public from any group decision if God had told him to (even though God was not a group member), and indeed thought he had the right to upbraid me in public when he disagreed with me. This was particularly the case in relation to the Tory plan to site the new County Hall on the Brewery Road site, which – in the end – resulted in enormous wasted expenditure by both councils when the county Tories abandoned the project.

Another was alcohol-dependent and had an anger management problem; he had the habit of turning up at public occasions with his shirt hanging out of his trousers and his stomach hanging out of his shirt, with his breath smelling strongly of alcohol.

The 2004 elections were favourable, and we had an opportunity to take the executive with Labour support. Ian Johnson had authorised me to talk to the Labour group leader, and I reported cheerfully to the group that their only requirements were consultation on key issues. As the whole purpose of a political party is to take power to implement its policies, I saw no problems with this.

My cheerfulness was short-lived. God's representative asked who had authorised me to have the conversation (this had been the group leader). Rosie Sharpley jumped up and down like a neurotic Jill-in-a-box forecasting disaster. Tony Kremer, now the local party chair, demonstrated yet again his leadership role in Woking LibDems masturbatory tendency.

What on earth was going on? I asked myself. The answer slowly dawned as Diana Landon joined the nay-sayers.

"Who would be the leader of the executive?" she asked.

I suddenly got the point, which I had not previously considered. Ian Johnson was deputy mayor, so – under the council's constitution – was ineligible to serve on the executive.

Almost nobody else had, or felt they had, the political experience and the time commitment to take on the leadership of the executive. The logical choice was therefore me, but the combination of negativity and the Rosemary Johnson poison rendered this unacceptable to too many people. What a betrayal of the interests of the party! And what weak non-leadership by Ian, who didn't even put the contrary argument.

The one good consequence of this shambles was that Sue Smith began to form the view that Ian should be replaced as leader. My personal interaction with Sue during and after the 1997 general election had been unfortunate. She had, nevertheless, begun to appreciate my contribution to the group. In particular, I had led a compromise in relation to the introduction of wheelie bins – between the group's environmental Stalinists (this is a good thing environmentally, so lump it), and Rosie and her colleagues (some residents don't like this; therefore, we shouldn't do it) – by drafting a united group motion to the council insisting on sufficient staffing to deal with the myriad of resultant individual problems. It went through with all-party support.

So, Sue asked me to join her for lunch. She apologised for some of her previous conduct, and that gave us the basis for a warm and open discussion. We rapidly agreed that one of us should become leader.

I indicated that I thought I was better qualified in terms of political experience; she agreed, but was not sure of my having sufficient support within the group. I entrusted her with the task of weighing this, and – when she returned with a negative assessment (there was still too much poison) – I readily agreed to support her bid, which succeeded when Ian decided not to contest it.

Although we had funked taking power, I ended up as chair of the Standards Committee, which was a fairly new development imposed on local government after a number of scandals, and with a couple of independent members appointed after public advertisement. The system was rapidly weaponised by Tory councillors, who tried in vain to damage me on numerous occasions (see the article at the end of this chapter), and I responded in good measure.

In addition, I particularly enjoyed – after I had ceased to be a councillor – forcing an apology through gritted teeth from the Tory leader, who had failed to declare an interest in his local property company, which was actually a criminal offence. Surrey being Surrey, he was not brought to book by either the council or, indeed, the police!

Furthermore, I also learned a new area of law, which led to my appearing as a *pro bono* lawyer for various LibDem colleagues.

One of these cases involved the nearby Borough of Spelthorne, where the ruling Tories saw a wonderful opportunity to rid themselves of the most awkward (i.e. effective) LibDem councillor by arraigning him for failing to declare a prejudicial interest and hopefully disqualifying him. In a day-long hearing, I sufficiently engaged the panel's sympathy to get him off with a reprimand, to the evident dismay of Spelthorne's legal team. At the next quarterly meeting of the Surrey local government lawyers, the Spelthorne team protested at this injustice, which was caused by the wretched defending lawyer, naming me. The Woking Borough Council solicitor, with barely suppressed mirth, outed me as his former Standards Committee chair.

The next case involved the London Borough of Southwark, which was run by a thoroughly nasty Labour clique. Incredibly, they spent over £50,000 of public money on outside solicitors in an attempt to disqualify the leader of the LibDem opposition. In addition, they tried to hold the hearing in secret, which did not endear them to the local press. In another day-long hearing, I won a battle for open justice, then obtained the dismissal of one charge and a sentence of mere censure on the other.

Firing and Hiring the Chief Executive: 2005–6

Our group leadership change happened in May 2005, after the general and county elections were held on the same day. The latter had a particular significance, because – for the first time – there was clearly electoral fraud and corruption among sections of the Borough's Asian community.

Nor could it be pursued, because the "marked" electoral register (showing who had voted) mysteriously vanished from the count, thus rendering unviable any investigations of personation. I learned much later, on good authority, that it had been deliberately stolen.

When this became apparent, an investigation was clearly needed. The ruling Tory executive were unsurprisingly unenthusiastic, as their candidate had been victorious. So I drafted a joint LibDem/Labour motion to the council insisting on an inquiry.

Paul Russell, as chief executive, was also the returning officer, so he saw this as a personal attack, and stormed into the council's press office shouting, "Bloody LibDems." Russell had been a welcome new broom when he had been appointed as the council's first-ever chief executive in the early 1980s (his predecessor had been designated the "town clerk"). Twenty years later and still in the same job, he was jaded and manifestly coasting towards retirement. And, in the case of his outburst, he didn't pick his audience very well. The junior on the press team was the daughter of a LibDem MP, so I was briefed!

At the council meeting, the Tories defended Russell and angrily denounced us for daring to criticise him. The motion was passed. What would happen next?

Probably nothing, had Ray Morgan not intervened. He recommended that the internal audit team should review what had happened on a "missing asset" basis, with the asset being the marked electoral register.

A panel was then convened, chaired by the council's (unelected) independent member, to receive and consider Ray's report. The other members were Sue Smith and me, the Tory leader and deputy, and the Labour leader. In attendance were Morgan and Russell.

"Right," said Ray to the first panel meeting, "I have the report here. I will give it to all of you on two conditions. First, that it is confidential to you until the next meeting. Second, that you view it as an exercise in learning lessons, not attributing blame." He looked round the room for assent.

In my 33 years as a lawyer, I had learned lessons too. I smelled a large rat, and said, "Ray, your first condition is utterly fair, but you've read the report, and we haven't. So, I'd like to form my own judgment, please, on your second."

Russell was silent, and generally looked as though he wished he were somewhere else. The meeting dispersed.

Half an hour after I got home, the phone rang. It was Sue. *"Have you read it?"* she shrieked.

"No, I'm tired and was going to read it tomorrow," I replied.

"Read it now!"

I did.

Wow!

The report left open what had happened to the marked electoral register, although it listed and assessed the various possibilities. However, it revealed that the council's administrative arrangements for conducting elections were an unmitigated shambles. In addition, they were the personal responsibility of the chief executive as the returning officer, for which – adding insult to injury – he received additional remuneration.

We trooped in to the next panel meeting. Clearly, we had to – and did – commission a full report and action plan to be provided to the council. But what would the chief executive do?

It was clear what he should have done then (and at the previous meeting, having read the report in advance), which was to express his horror at the revelations, apologise and undertake remedial action as a top personal priority.

He did none of these. Again, he looked as though he wished he was somewhere else. Moreover, his expression suggested that a red-hot poker had been rammed up his rear end.

What were we to do? Sue and I asked Ray to meet us. He tried to hold the fort, but – under cross-examination – he did not dissent from my assertion that Russell's refusal to accept responsibility made his position as chief executive untenable. Sue and I thanked him, and he departed. We decided that we should brief the other political members of the panel. They agreed with us.

So, next day, from the car park of a motorway service station on the way up to the LibDem party conference, I rang Ray and asked him to proceed accordingly.

He said that it was in the interests of the council to avoid a long and tortuous process, and that it would be more sensible and cost-effective – as well as far less disruptive – to have an agreed retirement and pay-off rather than a disciplinary process. I had dealt with enough "retirements" as a corporate lawyer to agree on the spot.

This happened in late 2005. All political groups were given a confidential briefing paper, and the public statements effectively disguised the underlying facts.

The panel's subsequent report to the council on the failings in electoral administration and the extent of electoral fraud pulled no punches, although the Conservative group suffered a peculiar collective amnesia when reminded of how fiercely they had denounced the original request for an inquiry!

The same panel was then (minus the independent member) convened to sort out the recruitment of a new chief executive. The process was bureaucratic and convoluted, eventually culminating in a two-day session, in which the first day was spent interviewing a long list of candidates in order to reduce it to a short list for the second day. As often happens, the psychometric tests threw up really useful information concealed by skilled presentations, and helped the elimination process.

It was clear that the overwhelmingly right choice was Ray Morgan, but the panel had been shocked by the facetious – if not downright flippant – tone of the statement accompanying his application. So I took a lonely decision on the first evening to break the rules, and I rang Ray. *"Are you trying to throw this job away?"* I screeched down the phone. "It's yours to lose, but at the moment you're losing by choice. You just have to adopt a different style tomorrow. Please!"

He did, and was – rightly – chosen.

Power: 2006–7

It had been a very heavy year, and we emerged from the chief-executive selection process in the run-up to the 2006 local elections, on which I had not had time to focus – except for helping Denzil Coulson (see Chapter 5) to be selected for the Goldsworth West vacancy, which Rosemary Johnson had been eyeing up for her lapdog Chris Edwards. The Tories were still in the doldrums nationally after the 2005 general election, whereas we were riding relatively high. With the aid of a casual vacancy – which gave us an extra seat in a marginal ward – and a brilliant, under-the-radar campaign by Norman Johns in the seemingly safe Tory ward where I lived, we found ourselves in control of the council, with 18 out of 35 seats.

So, we formed the executive, with Sue as leader and me as deputy, supported by Ray Morgan, as he took up the reins as incoming chief executive. We all needed L-plates.

Ray was one of the most extraordinary people I have ever met. Highly intelligent and incredibly hard-working, he was brimful of ideas. Indeed, he had about 20 ideas before breakfast each day, of which 16 were pedestrian, three were smart and one was genuinely brilliant. His problem was his inability to distinguish which were which.

He needed to spar with people of his own level of intellect, so the relationship between the three of us was fun and challenging in equal measure. He also possessed chameleon-like powers of persuasion; he made you feel that he was on your side, while he was actually advancing his own agenda in a way calculated deliberately to make you feel it was yours.

This later stood him in good stead, as he foisted a reasonably progressive agenda on subsequent Conservative administrations; this was helped by the fact that he was more intelligent than the whole of the Tory group put together, although it must be admitted that this was not a particularly high hurdle. He was by far the most competent politician in the council, and was strongly committed to both social cohesion and environmentalism.

Our first task was portfolio allocation. I ended up with all the hard wiring: planning policy, car parks, on-street parking and many more. Housing should have had the attention of a separate portfolio holder, but Sue was rightly not prepared to take it on as leader, we needed Richard Sanderson for finance, and Rosie – in many ways the obvious choice – made it one of her long list of demands for deigning to join the executive that I took it on too. It was not sensible, as I could not give it the time it deserved.

We had some successes. Sue, in particular, spent much productive time improving Serco's hitherto questionable street-cleaning service standards. I led the review of on-street parking, which produced significant improvements. Sue and I stopped a proposed housing development that was being imposed on local residents without proper consultation.

But all these were process issues, which were not eye-catching in the public domain. What we absolutely failed to do was ruthlessly prioritise a menu targeted at retaining control in 2007 from the start. Plus, I drowned in my portfolio burden, and lost my capacity for political warfare in the process.

Into this vacuum, the Tories gleefully and ruthlessly stepped, urged on by a hard-nosed propagandist imposed on them by a Tory central office that was appalled by their loss of control. From autumn 2006 onwards, we were consistently and falsely painted as spendthrift and incompetent. And we utterly failed to run a combined political operation between the council group and the campaigns officer to counter this insidious tide of falsehoods.

This was partly a consequence of the sheer workload on key councillors and partly because Rosemary Johnson was campaigns officer, and saw that post as a powerbase that would be diminished by being shared. This flared up dramatically later when she tried to dictate to us the level of council tax we should impose. But it was mainly a collective failure based on inexperience to run effective literature as a party of government rather than of opposition.

The consequence was that, in the 2007 local elections, the Tories gained overall control.

Opposition and Exit: 2007–8

The Tory group had possessed, in opposition, the time to prepare for their return to power. Their theme was to slash and burn what they alleged was wasteful expenditure, in order to achieve their promise of a nil increase in council tax for the indefinite future ("indefinite" lasted only a few years).

My year was spent chairing the Oversight and Scrutiny Committee (OSC), and exposing some of their worst aspects: in particular, the fact that the nil increase in council tax was funded by a staggering 12% increase in the fees charged by the council for various services, which they were as keen to conceal as we were to publicise.

But I also left a positive legacy on a key issue. At my request, the OSC appointed a task group to consider options for the future of Brookwood Cemetery. I held four evidence sessions, and we identified a clear way forward: the council should purchase the cemetery, then divide it into two sections – a working cemetery to be run efficiently in the public interest (which would be a pleasant change) and the historic cemetery, which – if in public hands or run by a charity – would be eligible for heritage funding on a grand scale. Unfortunately, the then owners of the cemetery showed no interest in this proposal, so it was indefinitely pigeonholed.

But that ownership was to change hands a few years later, in a dramatic and unforeseeable way. Its owner was a Turkish Cypriot called Ramadan Guney. His brother-in-law was the infamous Asil Nadir, and indeed Guney offered the cemetery as collateral for Nadir's bail application when he was charged with fraud in relation to a company called Polly Peck.

On his death, Ramadan Guney left a common-law wife called Diane Holliday, who had borne him a young son. He did not provide adequately for either her or their son, so Diane applied to the court for such provision.

Ramadan had left the shares in the cemetery company to his son Erkin, who was charged with soliciting Diane's murder! Although acquitted, he was refused costs. In the absence of any other available assets, the High Court gave her ownership of the cemetery company, and this was confirmed by the Court of Appeal.

The council dusted off my proposals, and Diane was delighted to sell the cemetery to the council for £5 million, while retaining the other property assets – the residual Woking land referred to earlier in this chapter.

It might have been courteous for the controlling Conservative group to acknowledge that they were implementing my thinking, but courtesy was never their strongest card. I felt obliged to repair their omission with a letter published in the local paper, which appears at the end of this chapter.

Our 2008 election campaign was better than its dreadful predecessor, not least because – in the aftermath of the former – the party had eventually summoned up enough collective courage to fire Rosemary Johnson as campaigns officer. But it was not enough to stem the national tide as Cameron detoxified the Tories, and Gordon Brown led the Labour Party down the primrose path to electoral oblivion.

I had taken the decision that I did not want to remain on the council in opposition. So (see Chapter 5), I found a good local candidate to succeed me in Brookwood, while I went off to the less-promising territory of the ward where I lived to try to take a seat off the Tories. Sadly, we both failed. I lost my place on the council, but regained control of my diary.

Have tickets will travel

Mon-Sat
8.30am-6pm
Voucher
parking
only
1 hour limit

40p per hour
Buy vouchers from
shops

WOKING'S beleaguered motorists, already plagued by the town's notorious traffic wardens, will face a new enemy next week.....the buzz bikes.

The Council has hired a crack team to tear around on scooters ensuring the smooth implementation of the controversial new Controlled Parking Zone which begins on Monday.

Roy Davy, pictured left, and his colleagues will roam the streets of Woking on their scooters looking for illegally parked vehicles. Pictured with Mr. Davy are Mr.Philip Goldenberg, Woking Council Car Parks Sub-committee chairman, and Mrs. Doreen Elliott, Highways chairman.

Turn to p3 for full report and Townsman, p6.

Turn to p3 for full report and Townsman, p6.

1992: Woking News & Mail,
"Publicising the Controlled Parking Zone"

CRITICISM: Cllr Philip Goldenberg stands by his comments

'Arrogant Tories will not gag me'

Lib Dem cleared by Standards Board

WOKING Liberal Democrat councillor Philip Goldenberg has been cleared by the Standards Board after a complaint by the Conservatives.

Cllr Goldenberg, who represents Brookwood, was reported for comments he made about a planning application for a sheltered housing complex on the run-down Loampits Farm, in Mayford.

The scheme for the land, owned by former Tory councillor Bill Bocking, was approved last month with the casting vote of the chairman, Conservative councillor Michael Smith.

But it still needs the approval of the Government Office for the South East as a departure from Green Belt policy.

After the meeting, Cllr Goldenberg criticised the removal of affordable housing in the scheme for the expensive 46 extra care sheltered housing, which he said was against the original principle of the proposal.

In his statement he said approving the application was a Tory decision, which coincidentally benefited a landowner who was a former Conservative councillor on the 'sham excuse' of providing affordable housing for the frail elderly.

Cllr Goldenberg said this week: "I will not be gagged by Woking's arrogant Tories and the Standards Board backs me.

"The Standards Board performs a serious role, enforcing the Local Government Code of Conduct.

"Its time should not be wasted by party-political point scoring, as Woking Tories have done on this occasion by submitting a spurious complaint."

Cllr Smith said: "I was very upset that political allegations had been made about the decision.

"I do allow everyone the opportunity to speak for or against, but I am disappointed that the discussion was continued outside the meeting.

"Decisions are not made on a party-political basis.

"The majority of the committee's Conservative members were unaware that Mr Bocking had ever been a councillor."

He said the allegations were unfair and cast doubt on the integrity of the committee's non-political decision.

2006: Woking Informer, *"I will not be gagged!"*

Commend buying of cemetery

IN 2005/6, I established and chaired a Woking Borough Council task group which looked at options for the future of Brookwood Cemetery.

I concluded that the best way forward was to divide it into a working cemetery and a publicly-funded heritage site, as significant funding was needed to preserve the historic cemetery, which is presently a designated Grade 1 Historic Park and Garden, but clearly has the potential to be a World Heritage Site; and that funding could not be provided by the current trading activities.

So my solution was for the council to acquire the historic cemetery, and then seek the funding which would become available once the site was in the ownership of a public body.

Sadly, the private approach the council made to the Guneys as the then-owners was rebuffed. Once the ownership changed hands two years ago, I urged the council, both publicly and privately, to pursue my original solution, and I am delighted that this has now been brought to a successful conclusion.

While I have enormous respect for all the work John Clarke (Letters, December 26) has done in connection with Brookwood Cemetery, his criticism of the council's purchase is misplaced; nor can he be reasonably regarded as impartial, as he worked so closely with the Guneys.

Brookwood Cemetery has an amazing history. In his *Woking Advertiser* article (January 2), Iain Wakeford recalls its origins, but does not discuss the relevant Parliamentary process. At that time, a company could not be incorporated by registration as nowadays:

there needed to be a Private Act of Parliament. When the Bill presented by the London Necropolis & National Mausoleum Company was examined in committee, the point was made that the scale of its proposed land acquisition was far more than was needed for its purpose.

The promoter of the Bill denied this, and offered to demonstrate the company's good faith by excluding from the legislation the normal power to sell land. On that basis the Bill was passed, and the local Conservative MP, who had opposed it at second reading, then supported it, either on its merits or after receipt of the usual brown envelope. A decade later, the company came back to Parliament for an amending Bill, as it had discovered that it did indeed have surplus land that it wished to sell.

It then made a fortune (sadly subsequently dissipated) by selling off a very large proportion of what is now the centre of Woking. So Woking's unique claim to fame is that it owes its core development to the fraudulent promotion of a Private Act of Parliament by a cemetery company.

One of the objectives I most wanted to achieve when I represented Brookwood on Woking Borough Council was to find a permanent solution which would enable Brookwood Cemetery to be preserved and enhanced as a valuable local, and indeed national, public asset.

The council's purchase of the historic cemetery now makes this possible, and I commend it accordingly.

PHILIP GOLDENBERG
Councillor for Brookwood,
2003/8

2015: Woking Advertiser, *Letter re Brookwood Cemetery*

8

The Jewish Dimension

My Journey

It's worth starting with an insight into Judaism for those who are of a different tribe.

Judaism is not solely – and, arguably, not even primarily – a religion. It's more a way of life. It's a mishmash of religion, ethical values, cultural heritage and ethnic origin. As Chaim Bermant said in his book on the Rothschilds, their religious worship was nine parts ancestral and only one part divine.

Furthermore, Judaism has many strands. Exactly how many is arguable, but I identify seven:

- atheist;
- agnostic;
- Liberal;
- Reform;
- Masorti/Conservative: Orthodox by tradition but non-fundamentalist by belief;
- Orthodox; and
- ultra-Orthodox.

The Masorti, Reform and Liberal strands are essentially liberal; as with the majority of Anglicans, they positively seek a balance between received wisdom and modern insight. John Robinson's *Honest to God* and Louis Jacobs' *We have Reason to Believe* are remarkably similar in this regard.

Within the mainstream British Orthodox community, many members are liberal, but the establishment is sadly not. Historically, Judaism was decentralist, if not anarchic; for example, any rabbi could create another one. However, the Victorian Jewish aristocracy decided, for reasons of social conformity, to model its religious structures on those of the hierarchical C of E (which is why the United Synagogue they created is sometimes referred to sarcastically as the "S of E"!). Two early Chief Rabbis – the Hertz father and son – were German, so Teutonic authoritarianism was sadly built into its genes.

This led to the United Synagogue's dreadful treatment of Louis Jacobs (outstanding both as a scholar and as a human being) in the 1960s to ensure he never became Chief Rabbi. Hence also the paradox that the recent Chief Rabbi (Jonathan Sacks) could – as a brilliant social commentator and ethicist – write *The Dignity of Difference* (Sacks, 2002), which argued for people of different faiths to found their relationships on mutual respect, but as (Orthodox) Chief Rabbi would kowtow to the ultra-Orthodox, and relegate the Masorti, Reform and Liberal strands to outer darkness.

I was brought up in the Orthodox tradition, but my parents were so outraged by the treatment meted out to Louis Jacobs that they became founder members of his New London Synagogue (I attended its first Saturday service on their behalf).

As rebellious youngsters do, I drifted away from religious Judaism, while remaining comfortable with my cultural identity. I only returned to a formal religious affiliation when I married Lynda and decided it was wrong to deny our children a Jewish experience as part of their childhood. Our nearest synagogue was in Guildford, and Lynda's parents were members there.

Guildford Synagogue

The community was small and in decline. It had come into existence primarily because there was a significant Jewish element in the academic community of Surrey University. It was then (and had for years been) run by a maths lecturer, Sid Cornbleet, who was firmly in the Hertz tradition; he ran everything and disliked anybody acting on their own initiative, although his was – in human terms – a decent and benevolent dictatorship.

On his death, there was a decision to spread the workload. The deputy chair, Ray Spier, became chair. He would have been a natural member of the awkward squad in Woking LibDems. Appointed impressively by Surrey University as a full professor in his 30s, he never moved elsewhere and was retired early. His mind was brilliant, but his personality deeply flawed; he played self-assertion games by advancing absurd propositions on the basis that nobody would dare to challenge him, and then acting mightily offended when anybody (all right, yours truly) did so.

A new prayer leader emerged in the slightly exotic character of Aryeh Nusbacher, who was one of the more interesting people I have met. A lecturer at Royal Military Academy (RMA) Sandhurst who also fronted a series of television programmes on key battles in military history, he had a feminine side to which he eventually gave expression by gender reassignment, thereby instantly and dramatically disqualifying himself as a prayer leader. He neatly chose the new name of Lynette ("*Aryeh*" is the Hebrew word for "lion", and "Lynette" is one of the female names used in the UK that is close to the Latin "*leaena*" meaning "lioness").

Aryeh had drawn up a list of posts, and asked me to become burials officer. This was an interesting new challenge. The community had a segregated burial area in the Guildford municipal cemetery in Stoughton, but only Sid knew how the system worked. I started from scratch, with the clear view that – in the emotional turmoil following a death – a bereaved family would like to have all the relevant information in an accessible form. So what was needed was a procedural guide. I produced a draft, consisting of the general English law and procedure (including the call-out mobile numbers of each Surrey registrar of deaths, who would respond to an urgent weekend request from Jews or Muslims to come in and sign a death certificate to facilitate the speedy burial required by both religions – I passed this information on to Woking Muslims), and the relevant Jewish practices. Aryeh edited and approved the latter section speedily; it then took ages to get it approved by the synagogue's anal-retentive committee (pompously referred to by Ray Spier as "my committee"), which persistently sought to disimprove my drafting, until I blew my stack and said that – unless anything was actually wrong – they could either "lump it" or get a new burials officer.

By then, I myself had lumped it, in the sense that I had resigned from the committee, which not only took 90 minutes to conduct 20 minutes' business but was also chaired by Spier as his plaything. It would have been worth staging a coup, had we not lost both Aryeh and Alex Goldberg (the Jewish chaplain at Surrey University) from the community, the former in the strange circumstances described above and the latter because he moved away. I simply gave up on any hopes of progress.

However, I remained as burials officer, and expanded the role into officiating at occasional funerals and tombstone consecrations, on the basis that the requirements were some liturgical knowledge, a large amount of humanity and an authoritative presence.

On one memorable occasion, we were asked – out of the blue, by his non-Jewish family – to bury a Holocaust victim whose parents, on being sent off to die at Auschwitz, handed over their baby son to their neighbours. There was a shedload of emotion, which needed an outlet. So, at the end of the funeral, I addressed the family:

There was, in the 19th century, an English Prime Minister called Rosebery, who set himself three goals in life: to be Prime Minister, which he did; to own a horse that won the

Derby, which he did; and to marry money, which he did in spades – his wife was a Rothschild. She sadly died young, and he buried her at Willesden Jewish cemetery, saying "I have returned her to her people." Today, you have returned Hans to his people, and it has been our privilege to receive him.

There were floods of tears, but it was an important catharsis.

Multifaith Work

It started like this. When the LibDems ran Woking Council from 2006–7 (see Chapter 7), I was sitting through a December meeting of its Overview and Scrutiny Committee. Its Tory chair allowed an item of alleged urgent business, which consisted of one of the most unpleasant performances I have ever seen in public life. A Tory councillor called Michael Smith held up the pre-Christmas issue of the council's magazine, which had on the front cover a lovely picture of the local celebration of Diwali, prominently featuring a Muslim lady (who it later transpired was a council employee). He demanded angrily that it be pulped, on the extraordinary basis that it was an insult to Christians. I was literally speechless with anger.

When the considerable amount of dust had settled, a local Anglican vicar called Richard Cook – who was also the diocesan lead on multifaith issues – was quietly prevailed upon to set up an organisation called Woking People of Faith, to promote the concept that religion was not some sort of zero-sum exercise, but that all religious faiths enriched each other.

Invited to become involved, I thought this worthwhile and potentially educative. I also intended to ensure that its work was a dialogue rather than, by default, a Christian/Muslim duologue.

But I grew to realise there was a mismatch between its worthy intentions and its operational prowess. Richard's chairmanship could best be described as "charismatic chaos"; meetings were too often unfocussed and tedious, albeit kept alive by the sheer force of his personality. Much relied on the organiser, and we were lucky to have an Anglican priest called Pippa Ross-McCabe to try to keep us on track. She was rightly infuriated by the C of E's General Synod's dithering on the issue of women bishops. After one particularly dreadful week, she turned up at a function clearly seething. I did my best to cheer her up by saying, "Just think, Pippa. If the scriptural literalists were right, C of E bishops would have to be not only male but also Jewish!" Peals of laughter showed that I had succeeded!

Woking People of Faith had the constitution from hell – a classic camel created by a committee that was set the task of designing a horse. Among its other defects was a "Buggins' turn" system for choosing its chair. So, when Richard retired, his successor had to be a Muslim. The Shia nominee was, by definition, unacceptable to the majority Sunni community, and the Sunni nominee wholly lacked the leadership skills required of a chair. Plus, towards the end of her term, the Management Committee ran away from the challenge of having me as an activist chair threatening to change the way it worked, so in 2015 I retired to the status of a trustee.

However, in 2016–7, I was lured back to help in a thorough overhaul of its wretched constitution, and then found myself back in the deep end as deputy chair to overhaul its governance too, including firing Pippa's successor as organiser, whose narcissistic personality was doing nearly as much damage to Woking People of Faith as Trump was (and is) to the USA.

Nonetheless, the problems of Woking People of Faith were not solely related to its governance. At its first awayday, I advanced the proposition that evangelism and mutual respect were incompatible. How was multifaith work possible if Christians (and, for that matter, Muslims) had the testosterone-laden mindset that "Mine's bigger than yours"?

But it did much good work. Public meetings were held with speakers from various faiths and multidenominational audiences, normally with a high standard of dialogue. However, at one multifaith discussion, an Anglican priest did ask a Muslim speaker for his Christian name! And, at another event, a Quaker lady walked from her seat to the lectern and announced somewhat pompously that the Quaker tradition was silence – at which point the mobile phone she had left on her seat inconveniently burst into life...

In addition, there was a brilliant event in the town centre to mark the tenth anniversary of 9/11, at which Richard – in the presence of the Bishop of Guildford and a large crowd, and to his enormous credit – unhesitatingly delivered a speech that I had drafted. It's worth quoting in full as a robust affirmation of tolerance in the present state of world affairs, and I do so at the end of this chapter, together with a press report of the event and a letter to *The Independent* on a similar topic.

One of the features of trustees' meetings was to start with a "thought for the day". In 2013, mine was based on my holiday trip that year along the Danube and Rhine from Budapest to Amsterdam, and focussed on the Judaica we had encountered, together with some thoughts on how prejudice is a product of groupthink, and may be countered by individual contact: I append it to this chapter too.

Anti-Semitism...
Not the pleasantest of subjects, but, as it has significantly impinged on my life, it is an essential part of this book. And, regarding England, it is well documented in Anthony Julius' magnum opus *Trials of the Diaspora* (2010), which goes through group libels in particular (see the speech at the end of this chapter). I went to listen to him talk about it after a dinner in April 2010, in the run-up to that year's general election. He was asked for whom he would be voting. He excluded the LibDems, on the basis that they were anti-Semitic. I yelped with outrage, then collected myself sufficiently to say, "Anthony, your book is a record of horror, including group libels relating to the Crucifixion, the Black Death, etc. Yet here you are perpetrating a similar group libel on all LibDems. Please reflect, withdraw and apologise." He shamefully refused and lost the audience (of whatever political persuasion) in the process.

English (and English is more accurate here than British) anti-Semitism could, before the Second World War, be divided into two categories. There was the upper-class version: down-the-nose, snooty and behind-your-back (still alive and well in some golf and bridge clubs). Then there was its working-class counterpart: direct and in-your-face. The two were brilliantly and terrifyingly married by Oswald Mosley in the 1930s, in the best Roman tradition of a *popularis* – an aristocrat appealing to the working classes.

Two more categories then came into being. They were both consequences of the establishment of the State of Israel in 1948. Brought into being by the United Nations, it was nevertheless viewed as a colonial implant by the ideological left, albeit that – as Weizmann pointed out to Churchill – Jerusalem was the capital of the Jewish people when London was but a marsh. And radical so-called Islam found it offensive, notwithstanding the long history of Jews and Muslims living happily together, not only in the Middle East but also elsewhere, most notably the brilliant period of the Spanish *Convivencia* for seven centuries from AD 800 to AD 1492.

Indeed, I was at a multifaith event in Woking, to commemorate the contribution of ethnic minorities to the Allied effort in the First World War, when I was discussing the Jewish contribution with a high-ranking army officer. A Tory Muslim councillor intervened by stating, "I thought Jews were interested in money, not soldiering." An apology was eventually extracted under threat of a reference to the local authority's Standards Committee.

There is no single feature of these overlapping four categories. I guess that the underlying condition is xenophobia, coupled with the long-standing prominent involvement of Jews in finance (significantly necessitated by their exclusion from mediaeval trade guilds).

I've always been personally hesitant to fling the adjective "anti-Semitic" around too freely. It's just too easy an explanation for a bad outcome to which one may have contributed by one's own actions.

Sadly, however, successive dreadful Israeli governments have deployed it ruthlessly to counter any criticism, however justified and legitimate. On one occasion, I encountered this technique personally. Declining an invitation to attend the annual Independence Day bash at the Israeli Embassy on the grounds of some recent ill-judged action by the Israeli government, I received a letter accusing me of supporting terrorism!

Incidentally, just as it is wrong to condemn all criticism of Israeli governments as anti-Semitic, so it is naïve in the extreme to argue that no such criticism is so founded, particularly when it moves beyond legitimate political argument into denying the right of the State of Israel to exist.

...and its Impact

As far as the legal profession is concerned, there is a small amount of anti-Semitism in the snootier barristers' chambers and longer-established firms of solicitors, but it is largely on the wane. This type of anti-Semitism was a contributory feature in my failure to obtain a partnership with Linklaters (see Chapter 2). I could also sense a bit of it around the RSA's board of trustees, particularly in connection with my departure (see Chapter 4).

The business world is too variegated to be capable of easy analysis, but anti-Semitism (and indeed any form of xenophobia) would certainly not now be tolerated in any large company or organisation. However, and paradoxically, there are individuals in the Jewish business community whose behaviours are unintentional recruiting sergeants for anti-Semitism; Philip Green comes immediately to mind. When I came out of the M&S AGM held under threat of a hostile takeover by him, I was stopped by the BBC's Rory Cellan-Jones, who was brandishing a microphone, with camera and lights in attendance. Did I mind? No.

He began by asking, "Mr Goldenberg, you are an M&S shareholder. I am Philip Green, and I am offering you £4 for each of your shares. Will you accept?"

"No," I replied.

"Why not?"

"Because you're Philip Green."

The clip went straight onto the *One O'clock News*, and M&S' new chair, Stuart Rose, much enjoyed it.

Politics is a different animal. In the 19th century, emancipation of – and full participation in public life by – Catholics, non-conformists and Jews was a Liberal cause, against fierce Conservative opposition. Traditional upper-class anti-Semitism still lurks in the Conservative Party, although less than it did. The anti-Semitism of anti-colonialism and so-called "radical Islam" is now a shameful feature of the Labour Party.

Even the LibDems are not exempt: some of its more extreme critics of Israel are tainted by it. It's an enormous pity that, within the LibDems, the LibDem Friends of Israel and LibDem Friends of Palestine spend their time promulgating one-sided narratives and skirmishing with each other, rather than reconstituting themselves as a single discussion forum on the Middle East.

It's difficult to avoid the conclusion that my defeat in the 1994 Dorset European election (see Chapter 5), by the narrow margin of 1.2%, might well not have happened to a candidate with a less obvious Jewish surname, and enough reports came back of elector-level anti-Semitism to substantiate this view. As I discovered, the West Country is not instinctively multicultural – its strong, historical LibDem Parliamentary representation was essentially an anti-London, anti-Tory vote. Once proportional representation arrived for European elections, its true United Kingdom Independence Party (UKIP) xenophobic streak came out.

And it's downright impossible to avoid the conclusion that the dreadful mayoral incident (see Chapter 7) was not based on anti-Semitism on the part of both the then Conservative group and a minority of my colleagues.

That I lost out on a Linklaters partnership, a seat in the European Parliament and the mayoralty of Woking, in whole or in part, by reason of anti-Semitism is a pretty significant demonstration of its continuing destructive effect.

Speech on the Tenth Anniversary of 9/11: Woking Town Centre

We meet together today, as servants of God, on the tenth anniversary of an event known simply as "9/11", when some 3,500 human beings died as a result of an act which defiled both God's and our shared humanity, but was shamefully enacted under the banner of religious belief.

As people of faith, we assert that the hallmarks of true faith are love for God and love for one another. This shows itself in justice, generosity, self-sacrifice, compassion, the valuing of all life and active seeking after the transcendent. These ethical values unite us.

We acknowledge that religions developed historically within societies which themselves changed over time and continue to do so. In the course of that process, events have been instigated in the name of religion which cause us all to feel shame.

The consequences of 9/11 are still with us today. Not the least of these consequences is an increased tension between communities of all kinds and creeds. But it can never be the case that all members of any particular community can be blamed for actions falsely undertaken in its name.

It is a falsehood that all Muslims are responsible for 9/11, just as it is a falsehood that all Jews are responsible for the death of Jesus. Dreadful events flowed from the latter, and our task is to ensure that they do not also flow from the former.

We, therefore, as people of faith, commit ourselves to work in harmony and mutual respect with each other, to bear witness to our shared values and to carry them into the wider communities of which we are part. May God bless us all in this endeavour, and may we glorify God's name in so doing.

2011: The Wey, The tenth anniversary of 9/11

Judaica by River

A year in advance, we booked a long river cruise for our 2013 holiday, from Budapest to Amsterdam. I didn't give it a further thought until we set off, though Lynda bought tickets in advance for both the Rijksmuseum and the Anne Frank House during our post-cruise stay.

So I was taken aback by the extent of the Judaica we encountered.

This started with an optional tour of the *enormous* (second largest in the world after Manhattan) synagogue in Budapest, an architectural extravaganza with strong Christian and Moorish features. Only in 1944 did the Hungarian deportations begin, in which 75% of the community (600,000) souls perished. Those left in Budapest were driven into a ghetto, and suffered the deprivations of a harsh winter. When the Red Army relieved it, there were 2,281 unburied corpses. Of necessity, and in a total breach of tradition, 24 mass graves were dug within the curtilage of the synagogue; the photos are heart-rending.

When we reached Bavaria, an interesting pattern began to emerge. In Passau, Bamberg and Würzburg we were told about small renascent Jewish communities being strengthened by newcomers who had taken advantage of the collapse of Soviet hegemony to move west. And, in Würzburg, we went off on our own to visit the new Shalom Europa museum, giving the history of a community that flourished in the early Middle Ages but was destroyed as a consequence of being blamed for the Black Death; its nineteenth century revival was obviously abruptly terminated.

In many places, we were told of churches built on the sites of former synagogues. In Cologne, however, there are major excavations of the old Jewish Quarter, with a Mikvah clearly visible. .

Perhaps the most significant Jewish Quarter is in Amsterdam, where there is an amazing "Portuguese" synagogue, which has no power supply and relies on candles. I say "Portuguese", because it was called this upon its foundation as at the time The Netherlands were at war with Spain, so the usual appellation would have been a bit tactless! From this and the associated Jewish Museum complex, we learned that the Sephardim were the rich merchants, who had the same qualms about the impoverished Ashkenazi arrivals from Eastern Europe as the Anglo-Jewish aristocracy 100 years ago.

So finally to the Anne Frank House, from which Lynda emerged in tears, as I'm sure I would have done had I been able to manage the stairs.

And that signifies an important truth. We can't relate to the 6,000,000 murdered in the Holocaust - but we can relate to smaller numbers. Humanity comes naturally in individual relationships; prejudice is the product of group-think. As Woking People of Faith said on the tenth anniversary of 9/11 (in a speech of which I was the principal draftsman, but was willingly approved by our Anglican chair), Christians historically demonised all Jews for the death of Jesus; but this broke down as individual Christians and Jews began to know each other as human beings; and we must not now similarly demonise all Muslims for that terrible crime. The multi-faith work we do is a small, but important, contribution to reducing prejudice by providing a space for dialogue.

Philip Goldenberg

2013: "Judaica by River"

9
Conclusions

Organisational

Human beings used to walk on four legs, so our bodies were originally structured with the spine horizontal, and the internal organs hanging down from it. Analogously, in this book, my life experience is the spine and the various organisations I have encountered hang similarly.

Of course, they are different. Different by sector: public sector, private sector and voluntary sector. And different by size and maturity: neophyte, growing, mature and overripe. The potential combinations are varied, but the themes are constant.

In Chapter 1, I quoted the late Dick Crossman, who pointed out in a speech to the Cambridge Union that "politics" was not confined to Westminster and Whitehall, but was part of the lifeblood of most organisations. However, the nature of the politics of an organisation depends on its culture.

That culture does not depend on, although it is influenced by, the sector to which it belongs. Furthermore, those who argue that the private sector is inherently virtuous and the public sector is inherently vitiated suffer from the tunnel vision that is the besetting sin of Britain's adversarial tradition and the inadequate perceptions which that tradition engenders. But that culture is also influenced by the history of each organisation, by its position in the maturity cycle and by the extent to which its leading people – particularly incomers – can be positively countercultural.

So let's start with the normative sectoral features:

Sector	Cultural Advantages	Cultural Disadvantages
Public	Service ethos Deliberative processes	Excess bureaucracy Indecision Lack of urgency
Private	Nimble Inventive	Unethical Greedy
Voluntary	Enthusiasm Empathy Shared values	Amateurism Lack of accountability Tribalism (politics) Wrong personal motivation

These suffer from over-simplification, not least because it is then necessary to incorporate the cyclical features:

Cyclical Location	Cultural Advantages	Cultural Disadvantages
Start-ups	Dynamic Inventive	Overmighty founder
Growing		Uncertain culture Changing roles
Mature	Defined culture Agreed roles Sustainable	Defined culture Too comfortable Excessive cloning
Overripe		Stale Lacks purpose Complacent

The defined culture can, of course, have good and/or bad features!

All the law firms discussed in this book were, by definition, in the private sector, but that was not their key defining feature. Linklaters was a mature organisation, which was slower and less responsive than it should have been in terms of client service, but which had a largely decent (if somewhat patrician) set of values. However, it was too complacent and certainly had a cloning problem. SJB was a start-up that would not have happened without Stanley Berwin, but was equally over-dominated by him. It then, following his death, became a collection of warring satrapies, and the culture that evolved as it became an institution was fundamentally flawed by its greed and concomitant behaviour patterns – see the following textboxes. MCG was in the overripe category, lacking purpose and seriously flawed by gross managerial incompetence.

Here are three textboxes exemplifying cultural issues at SJB:

The Staff

The staff were paid at top rates, but too often were treated like dirt. This worked at the top of the business cycle, but not at the bottom, where staff loyalty would have been a useful resource; so redundancies were needed more (and more frequently) than would have been the case with a more sensible business model. Plus, too many of the greedy fat cats just thought that normal societal rules did not apply to them. At one partners' weekend, a departmental head, in a discussion about the role of trainees, observed that one of them provided him with sex and the other with drugs. There followed hearty laughter and lip-smacking from the chaps, in which the chapesses felt obliged to join.

Playing Power Games

I was made partner in charge of moving the Corporate Finance Department to a different floor. As I did not wish to be a lightning conductor for all complaints, I tasked all group heads with planning their own areas and explained I would determine any boundary disputes. One head ignored all requests for his group's plan. His deputy produced a very sensible plan. The head, on principle, countermanded it, then disappeared off to Argentina for a "marketing trip". The deputy came to see me and pointed out that the head's plan ignored all the interpersonal sensitivities of which the deputy had taken account. "It's your choice," I said. "If you so instruct me, I'll revert to your plan, but it's your responsibility." He did. However, the head had left his secretary with a watching brief, and I received a phone call from Argentina (the telephone was not needed!).

"Why the f****** hell have you changed my plan?" the head screeched.

I explained.

"I don't give a f*** about my deputy. F****** change it back."

I did.

When the head returned, he found a vast building hoist outside the window of his selected office, blocking all his light. He upbraided me angrily. "Why the f*** have I got the only office with no f****** light?" he demanded to know.

My patience snapped. Adopting his (non-) literary style, I responded: "Because you rang up from f****** Argentina, and insisted that this was the f****** office you f****** wanted, so you got it. You seem to have been hoist by your own hoist."

Louche Behaviour

More than one Partner engaged in a wholly improper relationship with a female member of staff (normally noisily in the shower room, since you ask!). The lady concerned in the end moved to a different law firm, where her habits suffered from the advent of modern technology. Invited to lunch by an email from a partner, she declined on the somewhat louche basis "she was having her legs plucked". The persistent partner asked if she would not rather engage in an activity which rhymed with this, and she duly accepted. The partner then sought to delete the incriminating dialogue; he had, however, not entirely mastered the system, and pressed what he thought was the 'Delete" button only to discover that he had given instructions for the email chaing to be printed at all terminals, identifying the sender and recipient. Ouch!

In the world of business, the CBI was also a classically overripe institution, but an incoming DG with a clear eye could see its problems, and remedied them with staggering efficacy; this demonstrated the merits of bringing in an outsider every five years. Mission Capital, by contrast, had become the plaything of an executive team.

The RSA was another overripe and complacent institution. In this case, the new entrant was a negative rather than a positive feature: Judge tore apart the inefficient, albeit pleasant, collegiality of the existing board, imposing himself as a brutal quasi-CEO. Key trustees embarked upon a course of damage limitation, until Gerry Acher (as incoming chair) and Matthew Taylor (as incoming CEO) could take the organisation forward. But not enough was done to embed this positive double change on a sustainable basis, and the next chair – Luke Johnson – undid much of the good work.

The TSA took me a long time to understand. Effectively, it – like SJB – was beset by a founder culture, but in a radically different way. Because of how it had developed (and all credit to the founders, without whom it would not have existed), it was run by its senior staff, with the board as a fig leaf in terms of corporate governance.

That worked in operational terms as long as the three original senior staff were in post, but was unsustainable thereafter. By the time I became chair, it was run – if at all – by a staff non-collective; i.e. there were departmental silos to whom joint working was an unknown concept. In addition, the board was utterly failing in its duty to provide effective corporate governance, including setting and monitoring priorities. The whole structure had to be torn apart and reassembled, while maintaining a favourable outside image. Effectively, my task in sorting it was akin to what Adair Turner had done at the CBI – I never made this comparison at the time, but – in retrospect – I owed him much as a role model.

The TSA had effectively moved from start-up to overripe, and omitted the intervening stages. As Michael Foot quipped of David Steel, "He has moved from the boy David to elder statesman with no intervening period whatsoever."

I set out my general observations on local political organisations at the beginning of Chapter 5, in which I pointed out that – in the case of some members – "emotional displacement" may give an emotional edge to their involvement that is to the detriment of the organisation, because they are more motivated by their personal success within the organisation than by its success against its competitors. The sad saga of Woking LibDems (by far the most dysfunctional LibDem local party I have ever encountered, so not to be taken as a general exemplar) dramatically illustrates this.

The first key analysis is this. If, in an organisation (particularly a voluntary one), a new person arrives on the scene with (as in my case) a significant skillset and what might be termed tactfully an assertive personality, strong and self-confident colleagues say, "Oh good. This is an asset," while those who are wrongly motivated as previously described say, "Oh dear. This is a threat." Of course, the perceived threat is not to the organisation, but to their place within it. And the inevitable consequence is to damage the organisation's potential for success, as any form of leadership (without which an organisation cannot succeed) is also seen as a threat.

There is another relevant issue, and it is called "client politics". It's most dramatic demonstration was in the London borough of Tower Hamlets in 2015, where the re-elected mayor was disqualified by the election court for having misused council resources to favour his Bangladeshi community with a view to gaining re-election by what was tantamount to bribery, as well as having committed a slew of election offences.

But client politics doesn't only operate at the level of the voting public; it can also occur within a local political party. I came eventually to the analysis that this was the Rosemary Johnson modus operandi; her prime motivation was to secure her own power base, so she created a cadre of people she helped to advance and who, in turn, were expected to give her unfailing loyal support, while doing down everybody who didn't go along with this behaviour pattern. In retrospect, everything she had done fell neatly into place.

The real sadness of all this is, of course, the thoroughly good and decent people in the Woking LibDems who were enveloped in this miasma, and were too good and decent to fight it.

At national level, there are additional issues that flow from the interaction of political tribalism, with the more general issue of the culture of adversarialism, which runs interactively through British politics, law and employee relations. This is a negative theme that flows through Chapter 6. The positive is the good that can be done through government, and this positivity also appears in Chapter 7, where I think the key lesson is how the councillor/officer relationship can be harnessed for good purposes – provided that councillors are clear-sighted in their objectives, and officers are compliant without being subservient; in other words, where there is good collegiate working. After 13 years on Woking Borough Council, I ended up with more respect for the officers than the councillors, albeit with exceptions on both sides!

Guildford Synagogue had the strange and unfortunate combination of being overripe, if not actually dying as an organisation, and then having superimposed upon it an over-dominant chair. By contrast, Woking People of Faith was a start-up with an initial chair whose dominant personality was a plus, but which – at the time I left the Management Committee – had significantly failed to mature into a pattern of sustainable governance success. Its achievements were too often in spite of its governance rather than because of it. However – after the constitutional changes outlined in Chapter 8 had been implemented, and I had successfully insisted that we fire our second organiser – the trustees (led by their admirable third chair, Simon Trick, with me supporting him as deputy) began to assume their responsibilities rather than abdicating them, and the organisation is pleasingly – albeit gradually – going from strength to strength. Here is the lesson: *delegate, don't abdicate!*

Finally, some thoughts on the role of a chair. My TSA experience has led me to the conclusion that there are two types of chair (or, indeed, any leadership role): a warrior and a healer. The former has a very clear view of what needs to be done, knows that it will not endear him/her to everybody but is essential for the organisation, and is prepared to lose some (but not all!) goodwill in forcing it through. The second is in general terms a status quo person but, where action is needed, is a gentle persuader administering dollops of soothing syrup to achieve his/her objectives.

Some organisations (above all, a political party) need a warrior leader at all times. Some (like Woking People of Faith) are the reverse. Some (like the TSA) need different leaders at different times: I was, out of necessity, a warrior; and Martin was the ideal healer to follow me, with Sanjay to follow him as the next warrior in due course. In the corporate world, the right balance is a deliberate duality, with the CEO as the warrior and the chair as the healer (not, as in the case of the RSA in the Judge era, the other way round – see Chapter 4).

Personal

This is my – as objective as possible – attempt at a personal balance sheet!

I've had my share of both good and bad luck.

I was lucky to have come into the world at all; lucky to have had good and caring parents, who shaped me and pushed me (not least into law and Linklaters); and lucky to have been involved with interesting people and organisations.

I was unlucky not to have been a Parliamentarian in either Westminster House or in the European Parliament, and deeply unlucky to have selected Woking LibDems as my local political home.

I was also unlucky to have suffered three negative outcomes as the result – wholly or partially – of anti-Semitism, thereby missing out on a partnership at Linklaters, the mayoralty of Woking and election to the European Parliament.

But I hope I've made something of my luck and of my opportunities. I'm proudest of three achievements:

- my public policy contributions in and around employee share ownership, company law and corporate governance;
- my groundwork in facilitating a coalition government; and
- helping to save the TSA for its beneficiary community.

Furthermore, I've done everything I could, with Lynda, to give the best possible start in life to our surviving children.

And that, m'lud, is the case for the defence!

Appendix

Towards the end of the production process for this book, it became apparent to my publishers (whom I thank most warmly for their professionalism and support) and me that it would make life easier for the reader to limit the number of articles appearing at the end of any particular chapter, and to transfer most of the longer pieces to this Appendix.

So, as the reader, you can choose whether to delve into them or not. But I hope you will at least skim-read them, and then enjoy the ones that interest you.

PG

Takeovers – will they ever be the same again?

by Philip Goldenberg

Philip Goldenberg

With the Company Law Review and the Human Rights Act, Philip Goldenberg, a senior corporate finance partner at City solicitors S J Berwin & Co, asks whether takeovers will ever be the same again. The answer, he says, is 'no'...

The Takeover Panel (the panel) is a remarkable institution. A voluntary unincorporated association exercising public functions, and indeed creating a system of quasi-law in competition with the general framework of company law. A body which originally claimed not to be amenable to judicial review, and in whose affairs the Courts, while rejecting this claim, have nevertheless hitherto been reluctant to interfere. An organisation which, given its voluntary nature, would be exposed to attack under art. 86 of the Treaty of Rome if it were to abuse its dominant position as a regulator; and yet, which, given the public functions it exercises, is subject to the obligations that arise in relation to public authorities under the *Human Rights Act 1998* (HRA 1998).

None of this, of course, is to decry the merits of the panel. Its rules are sensible, and indeed form the basis of the current draft EU Takeover Directive. Its operations are speedy and flexible; and its officials are helpful and courteous. But the House of Commons was on the side of historical inevitability when, in considering the Financial Services and Markets Bill, it allocated the ultimate control of market abuse in a takeover context not to the Panel, but to the statutory Financial Services Authority.

HUMAN RIGHTS

The HRA 1998 is relevant to the operations of the panel in two ways: the first general, the second specific.

The general issue arises under art. 6(1) of the 'convention rights', which provides that, in the determination of their civil rights and obligations, everyone is entitled to a fair and public hearing within a reasonable time by an independent and impartial tribunal established by law. It is probable (but not certain) that the panel (for this purpose including its internal appeals procedure) would be regarded as pronouncing a determinative judgment; but it is certain that the Panel is

not 'established by law'. Further, while it may well be 'impartial', it is difficult, given its composition, to argue that it is 'independent'.

This leads to the point of specificity. The traditional rigid distinction between 'public' and 'private' equity (companies whose shares are publicly traded and those whose shares are not) is now unsustainable, as the multitude of 'public to private' transactions shows; and the composition of the panel is very much on the public equity side. How can it therefore be seen to be an 'independent tribunal' in terms of art. 6?

A CHANGE IN ETHOS

Of great importance to the future of takeovers is a change in ethos which may be brought about by the Company Law Review. The process started in March 1998, with the publication by the Department of Trade and Industry (DTI) of a consultative document called 'Modern Company Law for a Competitive Economy'. This established a review process which, while managed by the DTI, is nevertheless independent and self-standing.

There is a further relevant convention right as regards takeovers. Article 1 of the First Protocol to the European Convention on Human Rights gives all natural or legal persons the entitlement to the peaceful enjoyment of their possessions except in the public interest and subject to the conditions provided for by law and the general principles of international law. There is a specific exception to this right (which might be better viewed as more specific wording in terms of the 'public interest exception') in relation to the State's right to control the use of property in accordance with the general interest.

This exception would presumably cover a compulsory purchase order (CPO) made in accordance with and for a purpose provided in statute law (although the Courts would clearly be open to argument that a particular CPO was inappropriate in terms of the applicable convention right). But the exception would not seem to apply to an expropriation of property other than for a public or general interest purpose. As is well-known, under the takeover provisions of the *Companies Act* 1985, an offeror obtaining more than 90 per cent of an offeree's shares may then expropriate the minority, subject only to the right of a dissenter to apply to the Court. There have not been many such applications, and the general wisdom has hitherto been that the Court would be reluctant to intervene (simply on the basis that, if over 90 per cent of shareholders have found an offer acceptable, why shouldn't everybody else). The application of art. 1 to the First Protocol, however, opens up the argument that dissenter minority shareholders could simply say that they wished to retain their shareholdings, and there was no public or general (as opposed to private) interest in favour of such shareholdings being expropriated. What view the Court would take, in terms of the balance between the dissenter's convention rights and a 'general interest' argument in favour of the traditional application of the present law, has yet to be ascertained. There is no doubt, though, that the balance has been tilted by the HRA 1998.

A CHANGE OF ETHOS

Of great importance to the future of takeovers is a change in ethos which may be brought about by the Company Law Review. The process started in March 1998, with the publication by the Department of Trade and Industry (DTI) of a consultative document called 'Modern Company Law for a Competitive Economy'. This established a review process which, while managed by the DTI, is nevertheless independent and self-standing.

A year later, the steering group of the review process published a strategic framework consultative document setting out the key issues as it perceived them, particularly the general framework of corporate governance. Various technical consultation papers followed.

In March 2000, the steering group published a much lengthier document called 'Developing the Framework'. While this was still in some senses consultative, it was nevertheless firmer on those issues already aired a year previously. So heavy (in all senses) is the document that it is known to cynical professionals as the 'Green Brick'!

One of the key proposals of 'Developing the Framework' is that listed companies should be obliged to publish annually an Operating and Financial Review (OFR), which would go beyond the traditional form of historic financial reporting to a much more broadly-based set of indicators.

An OFR would include:

• a developmental review of a company's business, including market changes, new products and services, and changes in market positioning;

• a company's purpose, strategy and principal drivers of performance;

• its key relationships with employees, customers, suppliers and others on which its success depends;

• a review of its corporate governance;

• the dynamics of a company's business, including a full SWOT analysis, which would go beyond the financial to market conditions, technological change, health and safety, environmental exposure, tangible and intellectual capital, brand development, research and development, and training;

• environmental policies and performance; and

• policies and performance on community, social and ethical issues and reputation.

It may be argued that any competent management would do all this anyway; but the effect of this change will be to compel less good management to improve their standards, and also to introduce a real measure of transparency.

SPECIFIC PROPOSAL

There is a specific related proposal in 'Developing the Framework' whose significance has so far been under-appreciated. In the event of a takeover bid, a revised OFR will need to be published; in the case of a recommended offer, this will presumably be a single OFR relating to the proposed enlarged group. This will significantly change the culture of takeovers, because offerors will no longer be able to get away with anodyne statements; for example, they will have to be much more specific about earnings enhancement or dilution.

The proposal will have a much greater impact on hostile takeovers. At the moment, the conventional wisdom is that the board of an offeree company which does not welcome a bid should limit its response to the fairness or otherwise of the consideration offered. Indeed, in some prominent cases, financial or legal advisers have cowed offeree boards into not robustly defending a bid on non-financial grounds.

For example, the directors of BOC could have chosen to contest the proposed takeover by Air Products. The eventual decision by the US competition authorities demonstrated after the event that there were good grounds for resisting the bid. Yet the board felt obliged to take the advice of lawyers who claimed that it was their duty to shareholders to recommend the bid. Likewise, the directors of Manchester United were advised that they were obliged to recommend without reservation the BSkyB bid for the Club. They (or at least some of them, including Mr Greg Dyke), would have preferred to warn of the undesirability of a football club becoming the cat's paw of a multinational media enterprise.

CONFLICT

Here is the point of conflict. The City Code on Takeovers and Mergers obligates directors of offeree companies to pronounce on the fairness and reasonableness (or otherwise) of a hostile bid. That is too often misinterpreted as being the totality of their duties in such a situation, and misstated as being such by financial and/or legal advisers.

The prospective new Companies Act will include a restatement of directors' duties – not by way of alteration, but by way of clarification and accessibility. These duties will make clear that directors are not obliged to think only of the short-term financial gains to shareholders when taking major decisions about the future. It should be perfectly legitimate for directors of an offeree company to say:

'This is a reasonable price. But the consequences of selling to this bidder at this price will be undesirable and we recommend against selling.'

Their reasons may include the impact upon the industry, its customers, its employees, its community or its future potential.

The shareholders can then decide whether or not to take this view into account. But neither the law, nor its interpretation by professionals, should drive directors to abdicate responsibility to financial or legal advisers, and claim that they are legally obliged to recommend a bid even if they think it will be bad for the company.

CRUCIAL

This is why the proposed OFR is crucial in the case of a hostile bid. The offeror and offeree will be bound to prepare separate OFRs, the offeror on the assumption of the bid's success and the offeree, if it resolves to oppose the bid, on the assumption of its failure. This process will at the very least force the directors of the offeror and offeree companies to set out their resultant plans and analyse their potential implications for customers, suppliers and employees, as well as for shareholders and the wider community. The result will, at the very least, be a more informed decision at the end of a more thorough process of examination.

I do not intend to argue against a market in corporate control, subject only to an appropriate framework of anti-trust legislation. But such a market works best on the basis of transparency. ❶

Philip Goldenberg

Senior Corporate Finance Partner, S J Berwin & Co

2002: Amicus Curiae, *Takeovers*

IALS Company Law Lecture— Shareholders v stakeholders: the bogus argument

Introduction

I should start by explaining the origins of this lecture. Earlier this year, I was invited, not only to deliver this lecture, but also, almost simultaneously, to participate in a seminar put together by the Centre for Socio-Legal Studies at Sheffield University on the general theme of the constitutional implications of participation, and to deliver a paper on precisely the topic on which I am now speaking.

At Sheffield, I did a double act with Professor John Parkinson of Bristol University. He talked generally about participation and company law; I talked specifically about the shareholder/ stakeholder debate, principally based upon the final report of the RSA's *Tomorrow's Company* inquiry, in which I had participated as its legal adviser. We each talked for half an hour. Accordingly, having been asked by the Institute for Advanced Legal Studies to lecture tonight for an hour on the same topic, one of the ways in which I have extended my Sheffield talk has been by selectively cannibalising into it a considerable amount of Parkinson (I should add, with his permission!). However, the responsibility for the result is solely mine.

Background

Fifty of the world's 100 largest economies are companies. The 500 biggest corporations control 25 per cent of the world's economic output. These and other large businesses have power, in the sense that their managers make choices that affect others significantly. The scope of this power is wide-ranging. As one commentator has observed:

'By making ordinary business decisions managers now have more power than most sovereign governments to determine where people will live; what work they will do, if any; what they will eat, drink, and wear; what sorts of knowledge they will encourage; and what kinds of society their children will inherit.'

In making decisions companies do not merely respond passively to market signals. It is true that their freedom of action is constrained by the operation of product, capital and labour markets, but within these constraints managers retain a large core of discretion. Nor is corporate discretion being eliminated by the trend towards globalisation. Domestic companies that operate in internationally traded sectors can no longer shelter from the forces of competition behind national boundaries; but globalisation has, if anything, increased rather than diminished the power of large multinationals—at any rate, until the politicians catch up by empowering matching supranational organisations (what might be exemplified as 'the Murdoch problem'). Economies of scale and scope, and the judicious use of strategic alliances and other forms of networking, have ensured that these organisations operate in conditions in which competition is highly attenuated.

The sheer economic clout of large public companies, and the international mobility of their activities, increase the ability of these organisations to resist attempts by national governments and broader political groupings to regulate

their operations in the public interest. Nevertheless, the image of the truly transnational enterprise, lacking a natural home base and willing to move any of its operations to wherever costs are lowest, has little basis in reality. Moreover, differences between national and regional economies— in terms of workforce skills, levels of trust, the development of social capital and locational characteristics—mean that not all are forced to compete to attract and retain corporate patronage on the basis of crude cost conditions alone. Accordingly, while the scope for intervention to reorientate corporate behaviour is far from unlimited, the power of international companies and the demands of the capital market do not completely block a reformist agenda.

The recognition that large businesses have power to make decisions that have important consequences for a wide range of groups has led many theorists to classify them as political organisations, possessing a public, rather than a purely private, character. In accordance with the principle that those who are directly affected by decisions should have a right to participate in making them, many of these theorists have argued that the relevant groups or 'constituencies' should be represented in some way in the company's decision-making structures. In this way, conflicts between the company and its external environment might be resolved internally, by political processes. This might then bring into existence what has been called a 'version of the corporation as the republic in miniature'. The forum often suggested for constituency representation is the board of directors, on the assumption that it is here that the ultimate power of control of the company lies.

However, at the moment the only power external to directors to which they are formally accountable for their general conduct of the company's affairs is that of shareholders. To them we turn next.

Shareholder conduct

How do shareholders actually behave? It is well documented that, in practice, only a small percentage of shareholders in listed companies exercise their voting rights. With shares in the majority of companies being very widely dispersed, each shareholder usually controls only a tiny proportion of the votes. This being so, most shareholders are, as it were, 'rationally apathetic'. That is, because whether or not they vote will on its own make no difference to the outcome, and because the costs of co-operating with other shareholders to bring about a particular result are likely to outweigh the benefits, the best solution is to remain passive. The upshot is the 'separation of ownership and control' identified by Berle and Means over 60 years ago, implying a level of freedom on the part of management to pursue goals at variance with the maximisation of shareholder returns.

This separation has been significantly reduced in modern times by the trend towards the concentration of holdings in the hands of institutional investors; this has in turn increased

Analysis

the incentives for more active engagement and reduced the costs of collaboration. There is now plenty of evidence to show that institutional investors have regular contact with the management of investee companies, although it became apparent from the *Tomorrow's Company* inquiry process that such contact is too often a 'dialogue of the deaf', with analysts and management retrospectively criticising the other for focusing exclusively on short-term issues.

The concern that managements are insufficiently accountable to shareholders, and as a result have too much freedom to act in their own interests or otherwise inefficiently, has been the predominant issue in the recent corporate governance debate in this country. So far, continued exhortations to shareholders to exercise their voting rights and to become more actively involved in the affairs of the companies in which they invest, and the modest, though not insignificant, recommendations in the Cadbury and Greenbury Codes of Best Practice, have been the only outcome. It should, however, be noted that the exercise by shareholders of their rights need not be confined to protecting their own financial well-being. It is open to shareholders to use their position as such to further other causes. A recent example is the campaign by the corporate-governance pressure group PIRC, which put forward resolutions at the AGM of Shell calling for it to improve its environmental and human rights policies and reporting practices.

In addition, a growing (but still small) proportion of the stock market is under the control of ethical investment funds. In general, these bodies simply refuse to hold shares in companies involved in proscribed activities such as tobacco and arms manufacture, but there are also other organisations, notably charities and campaigning groups, which are prepared to engage more actively with management in their capacity as shareholders to bring about changes in company policy. Such groups invariably lack the support needed for their resolutions to be carried, but their primary aim is usually to influence company behaviour by putting pressure on management through adverse publicity; and in this they are sometimes successful.

Directors' duties

That background brings us back to the self-evident proposition that, in the end, a company's directors take its key decisions. Indeed, that is their role. So it would be useful briefly to review their duties.

The traditional view, based upon a 1925 case, was that the twin tests of 'absolute honesty' and 'reasonable skill' together constituted the totality of a director's duties. Clearly, over half a century later, life had moved on beyond this, but the case law had not. In 1986, however, the Insolvency Act laid down a specific test upon which directors of an insolvent company ought retrospectively to be judged in order to ascertain whether they had properly discharged their duties. It is worth setting out this test in full, as it appears at s 214(4):

'... the facts which a director of a company ought to know or ascertain, the conclusions which he ought to reach and the steps which he ought to take are those which would be known or ascertained, or reached or taken, by a reasonably diligent person having both:

(a) the general knowledge, skill and experience that may reasonably be expected of a person carrying out the same functions as are carried out by that director in relation to the company; and

(b) the general knowledge, skill and experience that that director has.'

In one of the better pieces of judicial law-making, Hoffman LJ, in the 1993 case of *Re D'Jan of London Ltd*, applied this section generally as giving a yardstick for the discharge of directors' duties. It is worth lingering on it for a moment. Limb (a) has a particular resonance for executive directors (in other words, a finance director is expected to be able to read a balance sheet) and limb (b) for non-executive directors, although neither of them is so expressed or should be regarded as exclusive. Limb (a) is also more objective in character; limb (b) more subjective.

The historic misconception ...

But if these are the duties of directors, to whom are they owed? Or, to put the question in another way, *cui bono*? For whose benefit should they be discharged?

The traditional view of the legal model of the company is a principal–agent model, the directors being the agents and the shareholders the principals. It is conceded that, technically, the directors are agents of the company rather than of the shareholders; but it is argued that the shareholder–director relationship is sufficiently close to one of agency to allow it to be analysed in those terms. According to this view, the shareholders appoint and are entitled to remove the directors from office; the directors' fiduciary duties allegedly require them to act exclusively in the shareholders' interests; and the directors are obliged to report annually to the shareholders on their stewardship of the business.

Now it is certainly true that the shareholders' rights of participation conferred by company law, which are exercised by voting in general meeting, conform with the principal–agent conception; and such rights can be divided into three categories.

First, while the corporate constitution invariably vests the power to manage the business in the board, to the exclusion of the shareholders, the latter have a range of rights that allow them to monitor the performance by the directors of the management function. In addition to the ability of the shareholders to remove the directors from office (or, by special resolution, to give them management directions), the directors must, for example, seek shareholder consent for a variety of transactions in which there is a possibility that they will advance their own interests to the detriment of shareholders.

Secondly, the Companies Act 1985 allocates to the shareholders various powers that define the boundaries of management authority. The approval of the shareholders must accordingly be obtained for such matters as altering the size and structure of the company's share capital and its constitution more generally. The provisions in the Companies Act 1985 are only minimum requirements and they may be supplemented in the company's own constitution. It is not uncommon, for instance, for a company's articles of association to lay down borrowing limits that can be exceeded only with shareholder consent.

Finally, decisions that affect the relationship of the shareholders between themselves, for example changing the rights attached to shares, form the third category of issues that must be resolved by the shareholders in general meeting.

... and why it is wrong

I do not regard this traditional view as an adequate statement of the modern position. To my mind, the better way is to start by separating out two different concepts: *duties* and *interests*.

It cannot be stated too often that the only *duty* owed by a director of a company is to that company. This is true, to give the most obvious example, even of the statutory obligation to

Shareholders v stakeholders

have regard to the interests of that company's employees. A director, under the general corpus of company law, owes no duties whatsoever directly to shareholders or creditors.

However, in discharging his or her duties to the company of which he or she is a director, the director must have regard (if the company is solvent) to the *interests* of shareholders, or, if the company is, or may be about to become, insolvent, then to the *interests* of creditors. It was amusing to observe, upon the publication of the *Tomorrow's Company* report, that Mr John Redwood complained that any attempt at long-termism constituted 'mugging investors', by depriving them of immediate high dividends. But there again, he was previously a merchant banker!

It is noteworthy in passing that the general body of European company law clearly views directors as in some sense 'holding the balance' between shareholders and employees. This was clear from the Second Directive on Company Law, which imposed the need to seek shareholder approval for the allotment of unissued capital, and gave equity shareholders a (waivable) pre-emption right upon the allotment of new equity shares. The Second Directive, however, specifically excluded from these requirements any shares issued pursuant to an employee share scheme, and ss 80 and 89 of the Companies Act 1985 faithfully reflect this; and this exclusion was based upon that view.

There is an interesting little secondary argument at this point. If directors have to have regard to the interests of shareholders, which are the shareholders concerned? There is a line of logic that it is the continuing body of shareholders, rather than merely the temporary incumbents: see Megarry J in the 1970 'Scientology' case of *Gaiman v National Association for Mental Health*, where he used the phrase 'the interests of both present and future members'. This line of logic is supported by the fact that, where shareholder ratification of an action taken by the directors is sought, the ratifying body consists of the shareholders at the time ratification is sought, rather than at the time of the relevant action. An alternative view may be, more simply, that the directors should have regard to the shareholders at any particular time, but act in their long-term interests; and exactly this point was made earlier in this lecture series by Marian Pell in the context of demutualisation.

The 'modern misconception'

If I have called the view that directors are responsible solely to shareholders the 'historic misconception', then there is equally a 'modern misconception'. This relates to the wretched word 'stakeholder'. I call it 'wretched', because it has now been used in so many senses by so many people that it is an obstacle, rather than an aid, to understanding.

This modern misconception derives from the discussion of a 'stakeholder society'—a worthwhile political and socio-economic concept of an *inclusive*, rather than an exclusive, society, which conforms with the general rule applicable to most modern political thinking, namely that 'Ashdown + 12 months = Blair'. However, the application of this concept to a company is a very different matter. And I must say that I am deeply unimpressed by some of the sloppy thinking on this evidenced in various recent articles in some legal periodicals (for example, in the May 1997 issue of *Business Law Review*). As Sir Samuel Brittan observed in a *Financial Times* article when this debate was raging (and I do not have the exact words): 'If directors are accountable to everybody for everything, they will end up being accountable to nobody for anything.'

Indeed, no system of corporate governance found in practice currently mandates multi-constituency board representation, though there are examples of systems which incorporate dual participations, of shareholders and employees. The absence of multiple representation no doubt reflects fears that increased complexity of decision-making, and confusion over corporate objectives, would seriously detract from the wealth-creating capacity of the company. But there is also considerable room for doubt about how effective such an arrangement would be in furthering the interests of the relevant groups. Ideally all groups on whom the company has a significant impact should be included if a defensible balancing of interests is to be achieved; but identifying and facilitating representation for all of them would be likely to prove impossible. There is in addition a real danger that outcomes would either be arbitrary, being determined by the bargaining strength of particular constituencies and the variable composition of coalitions between them; or else little different from current ones, given management's superior access to information, the ability of managerial insiders to set the agenda, and their greater expertise in the practicalities of running the business.

The bogus debate

In June 1995, the Royal Society for the Encouragement of Arts, Manufactures and Commerce launched the final report of its *Tomorrow's Company* inquiry. The theme of this is that the companies which will sustain competitive success in the future are those which focus less exclusively on present shareholders and on (inevitably historic) financial measures of success, but instead include all their relationships with stakeholders—employees, customers, suppliers, financiers and the community generally—and a broader range of measurements in the way they think and talk about their purpose and performance. This was called the *inclusive approach*.

My core argument in this lecture is that this *inclusive approach* should be seen as bringing an end to the sterile debate of 'shareholder versus stakeholder'. In my view, it is only by giving appropriate weight to *all* stakeholders that directors can maximise the sustainable growth in value of their companies for the benefit of shareholders, both present and future.

What consequences does this analysis have for directors' duties? We were struck, during the inquiry process, by the number of directors who thought that company law pushed them towards pleasing the current body of shareholders rather than securing the long-term health of the business, eg by investing in research and development or improving environmental standards. The inquiry team were pleasantly surprised when I advised them that, if anything, the opposite was the case.

Here is the basis of that advice:

- Directors' *duties* are owed to their company, not to any third-party group. This is true even of their statutory duty to have regard to the interests of employees.
- In discharging that duty, they must have regard to the *interests* of shareholders (if the company is solvent—if it is insolvent, then creditors take the place of shareholders for this purpose).
- This obligation to have regard to the interests of shareholders is *not* related to the actual shareholders at any particular moment in time, but to the general body of shareholders from time to time (one may alternatively, as I said earlier, express this that it *is* to the actual body of shareholders, but in their capacity as continuing share-

Analysis

holders). Accordingly, the duty of directors is to maximise the company's value on a *sustainable* basis.

- There is nothing in law to prevent directors from having regard to the interests of third parties with whom the company has a relationship (sometimes called 'stakeholders')—employees, customers, suppliers, financiers and the community generally—if they judge, reasonably and in good faith, that to do so is conducive to the success of the company.
- Indeed, for directors not to give appropriate weight to *all* their company's key relationships may well inhibit them in the proper discharge of their duty.

Now I am not arguing that company law prescribes *how* directors should balance all the factors that crowd in upon them when they make decisions. It does not, for example, tell them to work in partnership with their suppliers, rather than seeking to maintain short-term power-based adversarial relationships designed to minimise costs. It does not compel them to build up a good record of environmental practice so that, if anything does go wrong, they can pray that record in aid. It does not tell them to value human resources as the key element for their future rather than as a cost on the profit and loss account.

Indeed, in this regard, company law is not—and in my view should not become—prescriptive. Nor could it be, for different companies will rightly arrive at different decisions appropriate to themselves. Rather, company law is facultative. It allows directors to have regard to this wider canvas. And the contribution made by the *Tomorrow's Company* inquiry to clearing up this misconception, in my judgment, removed a significant barrier to change.

Practical examples

What does this mean in practical terms? Let us, briefly, take some examples.

- A company that skimps on environmental protection risks a disaster in which it loses not only money but also reputation, which is part of its intangible 'licence to operate' (a phrase to which I will return later).
- A company which pays out so much by way of dividend that it cannot invest adequately for the future risks losing out in an increasingly competitive global market (so much for 'mugging investors'!).
- A company which saves employee costs but thereby loses the loyalty of its staff will damage its relationships with customers and suppliers (British Gas, for example).

Almost the *locus classicus* for this proposition is the case of *Brent Spar*. Shell were perfectly right to conclude that, in environmental terms, the best course was to dispose of this rig by dumping it at sea. However, its sole advance consultee was the UK government. It ignored both the European dimension and the environmental movement. When it announced its decision, it incurred vast hostility from both, with consumer boycotts in Germany and elsewhere and an environmental debate in which it was manifestly the loser. In the result, Greenpeace honourably admitted that its initial reaction had been wrong, and that Shell had indeed reached the right decision in environmental terms. Shell will have wondered in retrospect how much damage to its reputation, and how much actual financial loss, could have been avoided if its scientists had gone to Greenpeace in advance, and convinced them of the correctness of its proposed course of action.

On a lighter note, and to demonstrate that the identity of key stakeholders will vary significantly from one company to another, one of the examples we discussed in the course of the *Tomorrow's Company* inquiry was a company whose business consisted of running a chain of public houses. In its particular case, a key set of stakeholders were the relevant licensing justices, without whose consent it simply could not operate, and of whose requirements (no doubt different in each relevant area) it had to be aware in formulating its business strategy.

Licence to operate

So far, we have dealt with the internalities of a company; how it makes decisions internally. Let us now turn to some externalities.

'No man is an island' wrote Donne. Nor is a company. Although the concept of a 'licence to operate', which was discussed in the *Tomorrow's Company* report, may sometimes seem intangible, it can on occasions become quite real. Let us take some examples.

Retail customers in their purchase behaviour, at least in aggregate, influence the nature of the goods and services that companies provide. More importantly for present purposes, they can have some effect on the wider social consequences of the company's conduct, for example in relation to its environmental or human rights record. By refusing to buy a particular company's products, consumers threaten its profits. The rational response of a company whose aim is to maximise profits will be to remedy the cause of consumers' concerns if the cost of so doing is less than the value of lost sales and ongoing reputational damage. Consumer action is likely to be most effective when it is part of an organised boycott. The assurance that many other consumers are also avoiding the company's products helps to reduce the 'collective action' problem associated with individual ethical purchase behaviour. That is, if I wish to register disapproval of a company's policies by buying substitute goods, there is no point in my doing so unless I am confident that a sufficiently large number of other customers will do likewise. The existence of an organised campaign can create this confidence. Even then, customer boycotts tend to be successful only where the issues are narrowly defined (*Brent Spar* again), and it is often difficult to sustain their momentum on a continuing basis.

Apart from consumers, other groups that have market relationships with a company (employees, business customers, suppliers and financiers) also have potential influence upon company policy-making. For example, banks lending on the security of properties now inevitably seek warranties and/or make investigations into potential exposures under environmental law.

In addition, some directors may also have a broader disposition to respond to public pressure. They may view the company's reputation, and their own, as valuable in themselves, for example, or simply be concerned to 'do the right thing'. Relationships with interest groups need not necessarily be adversarial, therefore, and there may be room for constructive dialogue. The DTI's Advisory Committee on Business and the Environment, for example, has recently suggested that companies should discuss business decisions that have major environmental implications with interested parties at an early stage, before key decisions are taken. The resulting dialogue could 'lead to better solutions, provide environmental gain', and at the same time satisfy business objectives.

The ability of those who wish to influence a company's policy effectively divides into two categories. Those who have key contractual relationships with it are obviously on

Shareholders v stakeholders

the inside track, and, either as part of a contractual negotiating process or generally within an ongoing relationship, have an inherent ability to make their voices felt. For anybody else, one of the first necessities is for adequate information about the company's activities and their impact.

In the absence of detailed and reliable information, it is almost impossible to identify those companies whose policies (or absence of policies) should be most severely challenged, and hence to ensure that consumer efforts are appropriately targeted. The social disclosure requirements currently contained in the Companies Act 1985 are very limited, comprising a duty to disclose the company's policy on the employment of disabled persons, information concerning arrangements for securing the health and safety of the company's employees, and action taken to inform and consult the workforce on matters of relevance to them as employees and to promote employee share schemes. It is now common, however, for companies to disclose information additional to that required by law.

The most popular subject for disclosure is the company's environmental performance. According to recent research, 79 of the FTSE 100 companies produced an environmental report in 1996. There are, however, significant drawbacks to voluntary disclosure, particularly where the information revealed is not independently audited. In an earlier survey of environmental disclosure in the UK it was observed that 'the majority of the information provided was selective and almost solely concentrated on the positive aspects of a company's environmental performance'. Most disclosures would appear to have been public relations driven, making it virtually impossible to derive a comprehensive picture of the company's environmental record. There is a clear case for imposing on companies that have a significant impact on the environment a duty to disclose information on a standardised basis and to have the information independently verified. This need not involve enormous expense, since most companies already collect and analyse the relevant information for internal management purposes: indeed, if they do not do so, they are running a considerable risk in terms of the requirements of environmental legislation, not least as regards personal exposure for the directors.

Indeed, I would make a more general point. It is a little-noticed point of company law that s 257 of the Companies Act 1985 permits the contents of directors' reports not only to be varied by statutory instrument, but also to be so varied in different ways as regards different categories of companies. There is to my mind a significant case for the DTI and the Stock Exchange together, with the benefit of a period of public consultation, considering whether it would not be wise to differentiate between companies whose shares are publicly traded on the one hand and the remainder of companies on the other in terms of their disclosure obligations, with more onerous and wide-ranging obligations on the former category. Let me note that, in this, we are to my mind dealing with a process rather than an event, and I would like best practice to emerge and be generally accepted under each heading before in the end prescription is applied; but, in terms of broadening reporting duties from merely the historic and the financial, this process seems to me essential.

The inclusive approach

This brings me neatly on to the key message of the RSA's *Tomorrow's Company* report. The inquiry noted that, while Britain had a few outstanding businesses, the average performance of UK companies was significantly worse than that

of its competitors; and more recent government material has confirmed this. The inquiry's central recommendation to improve this position was that companies adopt an 'inclusive' approach to business relationships. That is, each company should pay greater attention to cultivating long-term relationships with those who are key to its success—employees, customers, suppliers, financiers and the community in which it operates. While these relationships are the key to competitive strength, they are often subordinated in the drive to maximise short-term shareholder returns. The IPPR's Commission on Public Policy and British Business reached a similar conclusion.

It is also worth noting the point that, in the case of large listed companies—Marks & Spencer, say, or British Telecom—there will often be a 'category overlap' between employees, customers and shareholders; and that in itself reinforces the need for the inclusive approach.

This entails relationships which are co-operative rather than adversarial. The essence of a co-operative relationship is that it is beneficial to each party, but that the full benefits do not accrue immediately. Rather, they flow over an extended period. For either party to be willing to enter into such a relationship, it must have some confidence, therefore, that the relationship will endure, and that the value of its investment in the relationship will not be reduced by the opportunistic conduct of the other. As regards relationships with employees, it is increasingly recognised that in the modern economy the knowledge and skills of employees and effective team-working are of central importance to competitive strength. Companies that provide good training, and enhance the employability of their staff, put themselves in a favourable position to take full advantage of their employees' talents. Employees who are treated as partners in the organisation and not just dispensable factors of production are, furthermore, liable to respond constructively and innovatively to the challenges they face in carrying out their duties and, with a positive attitude to the firm, to need less supervision.

The advantages of co-operative relationships between a company and its customers and suppliers can be understood by contrasting relationships based on 'classical' contracts with those involving 'relational' contracts. In a classical contract in a common law jurisdiction and its concomitant tradition of adversarialism (but contrast Japan), the parties attempt to set out in exhaustive detail their respective rights and obligations in the various situations that might arise during the course of the agreement. Given the impossibility of anticipating all future contingencies, the contract is nevertheless likely to be incomplete or to contain provisions that are inappropriate in the circumstances that actually unfold. The parties do not regard themselves as owing any additional obligations extending beyond the letter of the agreement. As a result, the adjustment process is liable to be adversarial in character, with each side attempting to obtain the maximum advantage for itself. Renegotiations are thus often time-consuming and disruptive, and may involve the exploitation of its bargaining position by one side or the other.

In addition, there is no commitment to continue with the relationship beyond the date specified in the contract, and dealings are likely to be terminated where a third party can offer a better price. Often, it will be appropriate to transact in this way, for example when obtaining routine, standardised supplies. The company does not tie itself into a relationship that in changed circumstances may become disadvantageous to it, and in the absence of long-term commitments

Analysis

resources can quickly be moved out of unproductive uses.

In other situations, however, relational contracting may bring considerable advantages. In this case, while the relationship between the parties will be founded in a formal agreement, they will not view that agreement as capturing the totality of their mutual rights and obligations. Rather, they will regard each other as owing more extensive obligations of co-operation and good faith, to the point that each party will be expected to incorporate the interests of the other in its decision-making. In contrast with classical contracting, the non-adversarial character of the relationship promotes the free flow of information, in effect lowering the boundaries between the organisations to allow collaboration in such areas as product design and cost reduction, monitoring of quality, and delivery schedules.

This in turn flows through into the nature of legal drafting. In a common law jurisdiction with an adversarial culture, around 5 per cent of a commercial contract consists of a positive statement of the parties' intentions, with the remaining 95 per cent dealing with what happens if things go wrong. The emphasis is therefore 5 per cent on marriage and 95 per cent on divorce. This may of course have something to do with the fundamental mistake of whoever foolishly introduced American lawyers to word processors! It was interesting for me, sitting in New York for a week one hot summer on a deal which involved both American and Japanese lawyers, to see this cultural clash, with the Japanese lawyers being quite happy with a contract consisting solely of the 'marriage' element, relying on peer-group pressure to resolve any subsequent disagreements.

A further advantage of high-trust relationships is that they lessen the risks associated with transaction-specific investments. For example, a supplier of components will be reluctant to make costly investments in a production process tailored to the requirements of a particular customer, unless it is confident both that the relationship will be sufficiently long-lasting for the investment to be recouped, and that the customer will not opportunistically seek to alter the terms of trade once the supplier is locked into the relationship by virtue of having made the investment. For the same reasons a customer will not wish to become dependent on a particular supplier without credible assurances of fair dealing. Where a company's trading partners are prepared to make transaction-specific investments, it ought to be in a position to reap the advantages of flexibility and reliability which are normally associated with absorbing the relevant activity within the organisation itself. But, at the same time, because the trading partner remains an independent entity benefiting from 'high-powered' market incentives and avoiding the penalties associated with an overly complex organisation structure, the stimulus for innovation and cost-cutting, from which both enterprises should benefit, remains.

Conclusion

The real test, in my view, for the business community generally is whether it can move from adversarialism to partnership; from a zero-sum transactional approach to a win–win relationship approach.

In my view, and that of the *Tomorrow's Company* inquiry, the successful company of the future—Tomorrow's Company—will:

- clearly define its purpose and values, and communicate them in a consistent manner to all those important to the company's success, recognising that we live in the famous 'global village', and can no longer get away with giving different messages to different audiences;
- use its stated purpose and values, and its understanding of the importance (relative and absolute) of each relationship, to develop its own success model from which it can generate a meaningful framework for performance measurement;
- value reciprocal relationships, understanding that, by focusing on and learning from all those who contribute to the business, it will best be able to improve returns to shareholders;
- work actively to build reciprocal relationships with its identified key stakeholders through a partnership approach, expecting such relationships to overlap; and
- act, with others where appropriate, to maintain a strong licence to operate.

By doing so, Tomorrow's Company will demonstrate the bogus nature of the shareholder versus stakeholder debate, which it has been the purpose of this lecture to expose.

Philip Goldenberg MA (Oxon) FRSA AFSALS *Partner, S J Berwin & Co*

1998: IALS Lecture

THE WALL STREET JOURNAL.
WSJ.com

AGENDA | JANUARY 8, 2010

Cadbury: a testbed for stewardship

By MARK GOYDER
AND PHILIP GOLDENBERG

For the past six months the U.K. corporate-governance discussion has been all about stewardship. Sir David Walker—who conducted a review into governance of the U.K.'s banks—has called for major investors to exercise it. The Institutional Shareholders Committee has come up with its code. The Financial Reporting Council is taking this forward.

Yet at the same time we are witnessing a battle for control of Cadbury PLC, a company with a unique history, values and brand. The CEO has talked about the importance of the Cadbury heritage in choosing a new owner. The chairman tells us that the bid is all about price. And some of those long-term investors who are now talking about stewardship seem to have taken their profit and sold shares as the battle developed.

What is good stewardship in a takeover situation?

Major Study

In 2008, Tomorrow's Company completed a major study of ownership. It concluded that shareholders had four functions. The first is to provide finance. The second is to elect directors and hold them accountable. The third is to trade shares and through this to set the market price. And the fourth (too often neglected) function is stewardship.

In 2009, we talked to the owners and managers of many different businesses to understand the essence of stewardship.

Stewardship is a joint responsibility. Directors and investors should each play their part in doing four things well:

The first stewardship job of boards and investors is to provide a clear mandate within which directors and managers can then get on with the job. This covers purpose, values, strategy, relationships, roles, responsibilities. We call this "setting the course."

The second job is to ensure there is a proper focus on performance. Boards and investors need to be sure that management is operationally excellent and forever improving.

The third is to be able to read the risks and opportunities that lie beyond the immediate boundaries of the business: from changing tastes, technologies and trends in the marketplace to fresh demands from society and government. We call this "part of the landscape."

Finally there is planting for the future. Good stewards make sure the right investments are being made in innovation, plant, reputation and talent, so that they do indeed pass on the company to their successors in the strongest possible shape.

Not Price Alone

These stewardship principles are important to the long-term creation of shareholder value. So why should a board or a long-term investor turn its back on them as soon as a bidder looms in to view?

A focus on price alone is mistaken from the point of view of the interests of shareholders; and for directors it is based on a flawed understanding of the law.

The ultimate shareholders—the beneficiaries—have an income need that generally stretches over decades. Of course, if they believe current management isn't up to the job, they need to take action, and disposal to a better owner might be the right option. But if asset managers make a decision on price alone, they risk doing a disservice to those beneficiaries; and the pension trustees who are their clients can, if they wish, give them clear guidance on the need to prioritize the building of strong and enduring companies.

Fund managers may do very nicely out of accepting a bid. The short-term gain may help the "star" manager achieve a target and even obtain a bonus. But pension-fund trustees have to worry about the soundness of the machinery that will generate dividends over 30 years—and that means looking at much more than the price on offer.

What about the obligations of directors? Directors' fiduciary duties, are owed to their company, not directly to its shareholders. True, the City Takeover Code imposes a specific duty on offeree-company directors to advise shareholders whether an offer price is fair and reasonable. But—as almost no merchant bankers and far too few City lawyers understand— neither the Code, nor the general law, imposes a duty on directors to recommend a bid on price grounds alone where they feel that it isn't in the best interests of the company.

If Cadbury directors feel that a Kraft wrapper isn't the best packaging for the company they have built up, they have not only a right but also a duty to say so.

A Stewardship Culture

To build stewardship in the capital markets of tomorrow, we need to encourage the development of a class of committed stewardship investors. Here's how:

1) The investment industry should create a new Investment Council, which would be committed to the highest standards of stewardship, and which would build on the four stewardship principles to create a kite mark for stewardship investors.

2) This council would promote collaboration between investing institutions to lower the effective cost of stewardship.

3) Consumer bodies and regulators should start to rank different asset managers and different funds on their stewardship performance, including their effectiveness if fulfilling their stewardship responsibilities in a bid situation.

4) Government should require pension trustees to define their policy toward stewardship investment and at the same time require asset managers to set out precisely how far each of their funds follows stewardship principles. The trustees could then make clear in the mandates what criteria they want asset managers to apply when judging the appropriateness of a particular bid.

—*Mark Goyder is founder director of Tomorrow's Company and joint author of "Tomorrow's Owners—defining, differentiating and rewarding stewardship". www.tomorrowscompany.com. Philip Goldenberg gave legal advice to the 1995 RSA Tomorrow's Company inquiry, and the U.K. Company Law Review. He is a consultant to Michael Conn Goldsobel.*

2010: Wall Street Journal, "A testbed for stewardship"

How to form a government from a hung parliament

Government formation in a hung Parliament has hitherto been shaped by a mixture of convention and realpolitik. To this has been added the Fixed-term Parliaments Act. Philip Goldenberg (a long-standing adviser to the Liberal Democrats and the principal author of the Coalition's Machinery of Government Agreement, but who writes here in a personal capacity) guides 'Independent' readers through the jungle.

Duty of the Incumbent Prime Minister

Following an inconclusive general election, an incumbent Prime Minister should stay until he can give clear advice to the Queen. He is entitled to try to put together an arrangement under which he can obtain Commons approval for a legislative programme. If he concludes that he cannot do this, then he should resign and advise the Queen to send for somebody else who can [Heath March 1974; Brown 2010].

The 'One Shot Rule'

An incumbent PM who loses the vote on his legislative programme must resign, and advise the Queen to send for somebody else with the best chance of succeeding where he failed. This is because a legislative programme can only be put to the House by somebody invited by the Queen to form a Government. In this sequence the incumbent Prime Minister is by convention not entitled to another shot. But, if the incumbent has resigned before facing Parliament, and his successor then fails and resigns (as convention dictates), then the position is reversed and he would be invited by the Queen to have his shot.

'Don't give the Queen a problem!'

The Queen has the prerogative power to choose whom to invite to form a government. Indeed, before the Conservatives had a leadership election system, the Queen was used by that party to settle its internal rivalries [most recently, following the resignations of Eden and Macmillan]. But, in modern times, as the Palace told No 10 in 2010: "Please keep the cameras at your end of The Mall".

The Royal invitation

The Queen invites an individual to form a government. The invitee can accept on the spot (and kiss hands on appointment], decline or [Home 1963] say that he'll go away, try and then report back. Don't tell Nigel Farage, but the invitee then becomes a formateur in accordance with mainland European practice.

Motion of [No] Confidence

The Fixed-term Parliaments Act (whose core purpose was to stop the Prime Minister of a coalition government seeking an early dissolution without the consent of the smaller party] has inserted into statute law a definition of a [No] Confidence vote. This was designed to apply to a government losing the confidence of the House in mid-Parliament, and provides for an early dissolution if either two-thirds of all MPs so vote, or if a government suffers a No Confidence vote and a Confidence vote is not then passed within a fortnight. But it does not apply to the process of post-election government formation, when a vote on a legislative programme is effectively a confidence vote, but not in the specified statutory form.

No early dissolution

In the process of post-election government formation, therefore, the only route to an early dissolution is a two-thirds vote of the whole House. Realpolitik says this won't happen while either of the larger parties thinks that it can maintain a government, whether in coalition or not, and whether commanding an overall majority or not.

What to expect

As in 2010, a longer period than has traditionally been allowed, with the State Opening of Parliament delayed until 27 May (which the Queen can further postpone]. Unlike 2010, there is no financial crisis dictating that speed is of the essence; and the Commons is likely to be more kaleidoscopic. So expect a busy three weeks (or a bit longer] until it is apparent what will fly and what won't get off the runway.

2015: The Independent, *Forming a Government from a Hung Parliament*

A Big Crisis, a Bigger Opportunity

By Philip Goldenberg

Not unreasonably, everybody is presently focussing on the Parliamentary imbroglio around the BREXIT vote(s), and the Tory Leadership. But there's another elephant in the chamber, which could blow the present structure of British politics to smithereens.

Assume that the House of Commons throws out May's BREXIT deal, and that Labour then tables a no-confidence vote (both highly likely). Assume that the no-confidence vote succeeds (less likely, but possible, particularly after the recent *volte-face* by the DUP). What happens next?

Under the Fixed-term Parliaments Act of 2011, there has to be a General Election unless an alternative administration obtains a vote of confidence within a fortnight. Suppose Corbyn fails to obtain one (highly likely so long as it is understood that there is another option). The Palace then has to ask somebody else. But whom?

No single other Party could form a viable administration. But there is a hidden Party which could. This consists of the vast majority of MPs who would seek to avoid at all costs the economic disaster of a hard BREXIT, and would therefore support a second Referendum now that the facts are known, as David Davies and Jacob Rees-Mogg used to advocate when they found it convenient to do so.

Rôle of the Monarchy

The Queen has the prerogative power to choose whom to invite to form a Government. Indeed, before the Conservatives had a leadership election system, The Queen was used by that Party to settle its internal rivalries (most recently, following the resignations of Eden and Macmillan). But, in modern times, the Palace is deeply reluctant to intervene; as it told No 10 after the inconclusive 2010 General Election: "Please keep the cameras at your end of The Mall!".

However, in this situation, the Palace would have no alternative but to intervene, in order that The Queen's Government could be carried on. So it would summon potential leaders of a "Coalition of the Willing", or the famous GOAT (Government of all the Talents), consisting of the silent Commons majority which prefers a second Referendum to a hard BREXIT. Let's say Dominic Grieve, Keir Starmer, Vince Cable and Iain Blackford.

The Queen's would then invite them to select a potential Prime Minister, who could either accept on the spot (and kiss hands on appointment), or – more probably (Alec Home in 1963) – say that he'll go away, try and then report back. It is a beautiful irony that the invitee would then become a *formateur* in accordance with mainland European practice!

As I discovered in the run-up to the 1997 General Election, when I was Paddy Ashdown's lead technical/legal adviser on Coalitions and Hung Parliaments, and four of us met him for 45 minutes, the Queen's Private Secretary is (or was then) pretty cute at contingency planning. It would be surprising if the present incumbent were not doing just this as I write.

What happens next?

The fledgling administration would then seek to achieve a majority for a confidence vote. Its platform on BREXIT would be to pause Article 50, while it ran a second Referendum on the choice between REMAIN and a hard BREXIT. On the basis of previous statements, the EU would willingly grant a postponement for this purpose.

But resolving the BREXIT *imbroglio* in this way would not be the only prize. A coalition of the centre would have been created in government. It could then constitute itself as a new Party. Once the European issue had been sorted, it could seek the authority of a General Election to re-shape British politics for a generation, rejecting both extremes, and based on a free market economy but not a free market society, combining responsible capitalism with social justice. The electorate could then make a positive choice, rather than voting either Conservative or Labour because of the deficiencies of the other.

Crises beget opportunities. This is a big crisis, and an even bigger opportunity.

Philip Goldenberg was a long-standing adviser to the Liberal Democrats and the principal author of the Coalition's Machinery of Government Agreement.

2018: The Independent, *Big Crisis, Bigger Opportunity*

EXIT from BREXIT

By Philip Goldenberg

Theresa May's EU exit deal has been rejected by the House of Commons, and the European Union will not alter it in a way which will change the Parliamentary arithmetic. The House of Commons has also made it clear that it will effectively veto a no-deal crashout. The Tories will be supported by the DUP in rejecting a Corbyn No Confidence motion. The European Union will not grant anything more than a short extension to the two-year deadline of the end of March applicable to the UK's notice of intended departure from the EU under Article 50 of the Lisbon Treaty unless there is a significant intervening event, such as a General Election or a People's Vote.

A People's Vote is the right answer; a decision by referendum should not be reversed without the authority of the people. If the Prime Minister thinks her deal is so good, there is no logical reason why she should not put it to a popular vote against the option of remaining. Indeed, this concept of a second Referendum once the proposed exit terms had been negotiated was advocated by David Davies and Jacob Rees-Mogg before they found it inconvenient to do so.

But a People's Vote can only happen with the co-operation of the Government to put through the necessary legislation, and seek an appropriate extension to the Article 50 deadline. The House of Commons has no mechanism to impose it.

And the Prime Minister has set her face against a People's Vote, continuing to insist on the false binary choice of "Her Deal or No Deal" – a deeply flawed game of chicken on such a monumental issue.

So does the House of Commons have an escape route? Enter stage left Houdini, in the unlikely guise of a Humble Address.

The Humble Address

Not rediscovered until recently as a substantive assertion of Parliamentary sovereignty (as against its traditional ceremonial rôle), the Humble Address is a mechanism under which a House of Parliament can make its desires and opinions known to the Crown. It cannot, however, be moved in relation to any legislation.

Addresses have, in the words of *Erskine May* (the authoritative guide to Parliamentary procedure), historically comprised "every matter of foreign or domestic policy". The mechanism has recently been used with dramatic effect, first to compel the release of economic assessments relating to BREXIT and then to force the publication of the Attorney-General's full legal advice on the "Irish backstop". In the latter case the Speaker accepted the proposition that for the Government to refuse to comply with a Humble Address would be a contempt of Parliament, at which point the Government caved in.

The Escape Route

The European Court of Justice has recently ruled that a Member State which has given an Article 50 Notice may unilaterally withdraw it, so long as such withdrawal is irrevocable and unconditional, and is effected in a way which is compatible with that Member State's constitutional requirements. In the case of the UK which has no written constitution, the UK Supreme Court held that this means the authority of Parliament, which is why an Act of Parliament was needed to authorise the UK's Article 50 Notice.

So, given that the House of Commons cannot compel the better option of a People's Vote, its only available method of preventing a crashout is to compel the withdrawal of the UK's Article 50 Notice.

And, on the basis of *Erskine May,* it can do so by a Humble Address, and it would be a contempt of Parliament if the Government failed to implement it.

In the public interest, I provide a draft:

THAT an humble address be presented to Her Majesty, that she will be graciously pleased to procure that her Government irrevocably and unconditionally revokes the Notice it gave under Article 50(2) of the Treaty of the European Union pursuant to the authority conferred upon her Government by the European Union (Notice of Withdrawal) Act 2017.

Philip Goldenberg was a long-standing adviser to the Liberal Democrats and the principal author of the Coalition's Machinery of Government Agreement.

2019: The Independent, *Exit from Brexit*

I have divided the pieces at the end of this chapter into two categories: serious and fun.

The former category includes national political commentary – either general or specific – on privacy law, tax policy and the National Health Service (NHS) (including a "no-fault" claim system for medical injury claims). Those on "Mansion Tax v Council Tax" reflect my part in the internal LibDem argument needed for the gradual shift of the ill-considered former proposal into practical form. They are largely self-explanatory, but the quotation from Pericles' annual commemoration of the fallen during the Peloponnesian Wars relates to the death of Nelson Mandela. They culminate with the disaster of Brexit, which brought me back into political involvement, with three school debates.

The latter category are pithy single-point letters to The Independent, before it sadly went online. Some of them were so pithy as to need a contextual explanation, which I also provide.

The Serious Miscellany

Blair and Lib Dems

Sir: "What reasons," asks Donald MacIntyre, "would now justify the [Liberal Democrats'] stubborn refusal of [cabinet] office?" ("Why Blair will soon invite Ashdown into the Cabinet", 30 December). Let me give two.

First, the history of coalition governments under a first-past-the-post (FPTP) electoral system shows that, at the subsequent election, the perceived electoral choice is for the government (vote for the larger party) or against it (vote for the opposition). The smaller coalition partner suffers heavily from a loss of its distinct identity. So a coalition could only be based, so far as the Liberal Democrats are concerned, on a cast-iron commitment to a reformed electoral system being in place before the next general election.

Second, Mr MacIntyre answers his own question with his next words: "Blair is now impatient to gather together the collective anti-Tory forces while he is ahead". The worst way forward for British politics would be the combination of a single party containing "all the sensible people" on the one hand and the continuation of a FPTP electoral system on the other as, by definition, sooner or later some non-sensible party would win.

The better way is to embrace the pluralism inherent in a reformed electoral system, and recognise that there is at present, within British politics, a spectrum of five parties (six in Scotland and Wales), with the Conservatives fundamentally split between the English Nationalists on the one hand and a Christian Democrat-type strand on the other, and the Labour Party divided between "New Labour" and the "Tyrannosaurus Tendency". "Gathering together the anti-Tory forces" under a FPTP electoral system is precisely the opposite of that pluralism.

PHILIP GOLDENBERG
Woking, Surrey

Privacy law

YOUR report "PM against privacy law" (12 February) reveals some very confused thinking on this topic at the heart of government.

Upon the incorporation into British domestic law of the European Convention on Human Rights (ECHR), there will be both a right of privacy and a right to freedom of expression. UK judges will have no choice but to balance these rights in any particular decision, effectively creating a tort of breach of privacy with a defence of legitimate public interest; in so doing, they will have regard to the existing body of case law under the ECHR.

In extreme cases, where damages would be an insufficient remedy, the court could prevent publication by injunction; but all the experience of defamation law suggests that such cases would be rare.

It would be wholly wrong for such an extreme power of prior restraint to be exercisable by a voluntary body such as the Press Complaints Commission (PCC). Indeed, following the incorporation of the ECHR into UK domestic law, the usefulness of the PCC may well be called into question generally; as Sir Louis Blom-Cooper rightly observed, "Self-regulation will always protect the self."

PHILIP GOLDENBERG
Woking, Surrey

Supporter of Israel, but not all its policies

Sir: If proof were needed of why Independent Jewish Voices ("IJV", with which I have no present involvement) came into being, it lies with the description of them, by your correspondent Geoffrey Charin (letter, 16 February), as "anti-Israel".

I support the existence of the State of Israel, and wish to see it survive and prosper in peace and security. I just despair of various policies adopted from time to time by Israeli governments inimical to the prospects of such survival and prosperity.

That seems to me to be the position also held by IJV. To call it "anti-Israel" is a perversion of language. It fails to distinguish between State and Government; by Mr Charin's logic, it would mean all of us who disagree from with policies adopted by the UK Government are "anti-British".

I intend to continue to subject the policies of both governments to what I hope is a coherent, rational, consistent and constructive critique.

PHILIP GOLDENBERG
WOKING, SURREY

Ivor Morgan objects to electoral reform on the basis that minority parties could make or break governments by "wheeling and dealing in smoke-filled rooms".

But this can equally well happen at present; in the run-up to the 1992 general election, the parliamentary arithmetic was such that deals were made between the Tories and the Ulster Unionists. And is it not better for deals between political parties to be open and transparent, with published coalition agreements (as has happened in Scotland and Wales), rather than the present system?

PHILIP GOLDENBERG
WOKING, SURREY

We did vote for the Coalition

I have no problem with the Archbishop of Canterbury saying what he did, and indeed, as a Liberal Democrat, I have some sympathy with his critique of the way in which the Health and Education Secretaries have launched policy initiatives significantly beyond the Coalition Agreement.

But I do have a problem with some of your correspondents who have sought to delegitimise the Coalition Government on the basis that "nobody voted for it".

Under the British constitution, we elect a parliament, not a government, let alone a prime minister. If for once a general election under our woeful electoral system produces a genuinely representative parliament, in that no party has an overall majority, then the Queen's government has to be carried on, and a parliamentary majority created to support it, whether by formal coalition or a different relationship. So a coalition between two different parties, with a coalition agreement as to policy which synthesises their two manifestos, is beyond peradventure constitutionally legitimate.

Where those two parties between them received nearly 60 per cent of the votes cast, it's rather more legitimate than a single-party government with 35 per cent of the votes cast.

PHILIP GOLDENBERG
WOKING, SURREY

Perspectives on the tax people

Helpful staff, terrible laws

I don't doubt Sean O'Grady's account of his unfortunate personal dealings with HM Revenue and Customs, but his article (8 September) is unfair in extrapolating those dealings into a generalised cheap shot at HMRC staff.

First, my personal experiences are very different. Once I have got through to the right person (and the call system is indeed a nightmare), I have nearly always been dealt with courteously, professionally and – on occasions – in an exceptionally helpful and constructive way.

Second, it should be recognised that HMRC staff are operating a tax system of Byzantine complexity, which politicians have never got round to reforming in the fundamental way that is needed.

This is because, historically, tax law has grown up under a common law system, with rules of strict interpretation, often leading to the elevation of form over substance and giving vast scope for armies of professional advisers to promote ever-more inventive avoidance methods. This was eventually countered by a couple of House of Lords decisions, and some new laws, but this has been mere tinkering.

What is needed is to tax substance over form; to eviscerate much of the detailed legislation; to adopt a general anti-avoidance principle; and to provide a full advance clearance mechanism.

PHILIP GOLDENBERG
WOKING, SURREY

Value cap beats 'mansion tax'

Your correspondent David Watson (letters, 30 March) is exactly right in his critique of a "mansion tax". It would require an entirely new collection system, with consequential disproportionate costs, and would give rise to all sorts of avoidance mechanisms, including splitting large properties into separate units.

But he is less perspicacious in his proposed alternative of higher stamp duty, which is a charge on a purchaser, not a vendor.

At present, a principal private residence is exempt from capital gains tax, an exemption limited to a specified land area. This dates from when top-range properties were country estates, and was, in effect, a mechanism to prevent the wealthy avoiding capital gains tax by over-investing in property.

Nobody conceived at the time that there would be £20m properties in London standing on very small areas of land.

So it would be logical to extend this mechanism accordingly, so that the principal private residence exemption applies only up to a specified valuation ceiling, with the excess being within the capital gains tax net.

PHILIP GOLDENBERG
WOKING, SURREY

For David Cameron to say, as you reported yesterday, that there will be "no more concessions" to Tory eurosceptics is patently risible. Like Oliver Twist, they will always be back for more until they force us into the status of an island with no say in our natural regional

market, and without a special relationship with the US, which is founded in its eyes in being its gateway to the EU.

PHILIP GOLDENBERG
Woking, Surrey

I welcome the fact that the Government is considering imposing on the NHS and its staff a "duty of candour". But this will not work in isolation.

It needs to be part of a more fundamental reform in relation to claims for damages. So long as there is a right to sue for the consequences of medical mistakes, this will inevitably engender a defensive mindset. What is needed is a "no fault" claim system, as recommended over the years by Royal Commissions. This would promote an open culture (as in the airline industry), and save the vast sums that are spent by both sides on litigation.

PHILIP GOLDENBERG
Woking, Surrey

"The whole earth is the tomb of famous men."
            – Pericles.
Philip Goldenberg
Woking, Surrey

In his parliamentary sketch (17 July), Donald Macintyre describes as "a bit rich" Jack Straw's condemnation of the sacking of the former Attorney General Dominic Grieve for "speaking legal truth to power".

In the run-up to the Iraq war, and in contravention of the Cabinet Manual Questions of Procedure for Ministers, Straw is said to have advised the then Attorney General, Peter Goldsmith, not to circulate to the Cabinet the latter's full and balanced opinion on the legality of that war.

Had it been circulated, the Cabinet might have taken a different decision, or more ministers would have resigned. Had Goldsmith himself resigned on the point, with a public explanation, Parliament almost certainly would have withheld its consent.

So "blatant hypocrisy" might have been a more apt phrase.
Philip Goldenberg
Woking, Surrey

**FIGHTING FOR ISIS
COULD BE TREASON**
British citizens who, in the
words of the 1351 statute
law, adhere to the Queen's
enemies in her realm,
giving them aid and comfort
in her realm or elsewhere,
are guilty of treason. And
the 1916 trial of Roger
Casement established that
the wording included acts
committed abroad.

If the UK takes hostile
action against the self-
styled "Islamic State", then
any British citizens who
actively support that entity
are guilty accordingly.
They could also be deemed
to have adopted a dual
nationality, and hence
could lawfully be deprived
of UK citizenship without
breaching international law.
Philip Goldenberg
*Woking,
Surrey*

I am surprised that you
quote a retail expert (6
December) as saying that
the conduct of Premier
Foods in requiring supplier
payments to retain their
status is lawful. I thought
that the abuse of a
dominant market position
was a fundamental breach
of EU anti-trust law.
Philip Goldenberg
Woking, Surrey

**FORGET MANSION TAX
- FIX COUNCIL TAX**
You say (Editorial, 23
December) that the Lib
Dems invented the concept
of a mansion tax, so cannot
now easily disown it.

Actually, the Lib Dems
have kept the name but
changed the substance. They
realised that establishing
a new tax base, with a
whole potential new set of
avoidance mechanisms (like
dividing a house into two),
and the need for individual
valuations which could all be
the subject of appeals, broke
a fundamental principle
of tax reform, in that the
costs of administration
and collection would be
a disproportionately high
percentage of the receipts.
So their mansion tax is now
a label for higher council
tax bands, which avoids all
these problems.

No doubt Labour, and Ed

Balls, will again catch up in
due course.
Philip Goldenberg
Woking, Surrey

Your editorial (12 February) rightly says that cultural change is needed in the NHS to create a climate of transparency, but misses a fundamental prerequisite for achieving it.

That is to change the law to bar claims for medical negligence, and substitute a statutory compensation scheme. This would also have the advantage of saving the wholly unproductive costs of the present litigation-based method of dealing with these issues.

Philip Goldenberg
Woking, Surrey

Daniel Feingold (letter, 1 April) poses a false antithesis by distinguishing between Zionists and anti-Zionists.

Many Jews are "Liberal Zionists". As one of them, I support the nobility of the original principled idealism of Herzl and Weizmann, and regret that it is being trashed by current Israeli right-wing politicians, such as Netanyahu and Lieberman, who are a danger to Israel's long-term survival.

Philip Goldenberg
Woking, Surrey

Brexiteers getting what they wanted

Dear Editor

IN DESCRIBING the UK's membership of the European Union as merely 'an international treaty' Jonathan Lord MP has clearly not read, or not understood, the recent High Court judgment.

As citizens of the EU, British residents currently enjoy rights enshrined in UK law, such as the freedom to work, or live, elsewhere in Europe.

The court held that these rights can only be removed by UK legislation, which is a matter for Parliament rather than the Government. And, as the triggering of Article 50 may in itself lead to the removal of those rights, such a decision needs Parliamentary approval.

All the court has done is uphold Parliamentary sovereignty, which is precisely what Brexiteers campaigned for.

Philip Goldenberg
Woking

In his opposition to the proposal for the devolution to Greater Manchester of health services, Andy Burnham betrays an alarming ignorance of Labour history.

When the NHS was in the process of formulation, there was a lively disagreement between the statists (led by Aneurin Bevan), who wanted a national system, and the localists (led by Herbert Morrison) who wanted it run by local councils, with the potential for integration with social services. Sadly, Bevan won; and it is only now, 70 years later, that common sense and localism have reasserted themselves.

Philip Goldenberg
Woking, Surrey

The Fun Miscellany

In 1996, Sir Richard Scott delivered a robust report into Government connivance in the unlawful sale of arms to Iraq. Atypically, I went into plagiaristic poetical mode:

Lines on the Scott Report

I come to praise Sir Richard, not to bury him.
The good that Ministers do they bruit abroad,
The evil by spin doctors is interred.
Sir Nick knew not the law, but well he meant
And Lyell is an honourable man!
Alas, poor William! He misled the House
But in deceiving meant not to deceive,
And Waldegrave's an honourable man,
A Fellow of All Souls — no sophist he!
So are they all — all honourable men!
So shouldst a citizen be ever found
Standing above a corpse laid on the ground
In hand a knife which streameth forth with gore
The plea will win "He knew not what he did,
But well he meant, t'was but an accident".

(With apologies to William Shakespeare)

Philip Goldenberg, Prospective Liberal Democrat
Parliamentary Candidate for Woking.

When the Referendum Party came into being, I signed up our hamster Percy as a member so that I would receive their mailings. She sadly died, so I informed the party:

People

THERE was considerable delight in the household of **Woking's** Liberal Democrat candidate in May, **Philip Goldenberg,** when a circular dropped through the letter box from the Referendum Party – now, to be more accurate, known as the Referendum Movement.

Why the delight? Because it was addressed to **Percy,** Philip's family hamster – who unfortunately died in the summer.

But so as not to disappoint, Philip wrote back to Referendum Movement chairman **Lord McAlpine** explaining the problem.

"I have asked Percy's successor **Patsy** whether she is prepared to join, but I am afraid that her limited financial resources do not permit such extravagances on her part," he wrote.

But there was a sting in the tail, so to speak. Patsy is apparently worried about the Movement's internal democracy which is – according to Philip – "manifestly designed for a self-perpetuating oligarchy".

At the 175th anniversary dinner of the Oxford Union, I ran into William Hague:

A rose by any other name ...

PERHAPS William Hague is more Shakespearean in character than Pandora had previously believed. The *Liberal Democrat News* has just published an account of the recent 175th anniversary dinner of the Oxford Union which casts a new, possibly darker light on Young William.

An informant overheard the solicitor Philip Goldenberg asking another returning Union member if he recalled a tribunal of inquiry into possible misdeeds during a long-ago Union election. "Oh hell, yes I do," said William Hague, who had appeared as an "alleged miscreant" before the other man. "When you were running for public office last year," continued Goldenberg, "I very nearly wrote to *The Independent* pointing out that, while you appeared before me, you did not feature in my judgment; and that I was forced into concluding either that you were as pure as the driven snow, or that you had a pretty good capacity to work through a heap of shit and come out smelling of roses." Hague reportedly found this very funny. Still, Richard III he's not.

I couldn't resist a dig at David Owen:

Sir: Following the formation of the Axis pact in the late 1930s, some politically incorrect wit observed: "Serve Hitler right – we had the Italians last time!" This quotation springs to mind following the announcement that Lord Owen is to have a leading role in the anti-EMU campaign.
PHILIP GOLDENBERG
Liberal Democrats
Woking, Surrey

One on pub names:

Pub brothel

Sir: In "The 50 best Village Pubs", you said that the "unusual name" of a pub called The Case Is Altered stemmed from a dispute between its first landlord and the licensing authorities (17 August).

The name occurs elsewhere, however. It is generally believed to originate from British soldiers who had served in Italy, where the words Casa Altera

(literally "the other house") meant a brothel.
PHILIP GOLDENBERG
Studland, Dorset

A couple on Royal Bank of Scotland (RBS), which was the bank that had to be rescued by the Government after being spectacularly mismanaged:

RBS "insiders" have put into the public domain legal advice to the effect that, should the Government block the board's proposed bonus payments, the board would "have no alternative but to quit". While it would obviously easier to comment if this advice were published in full, it seems nevertheless ill-founded.

Most articles of association incorporate a provision that the directors have full powers of management, subject to the right of shareholders, by a special resolution (requiring a 75 per cent majority of those voting), to give them an over-riding direction.

The Government will, if RBS shareholders approve the bank's participation in the asset protection scheme, have an 84 per cent interest in RBS, and could therefore give precisely such an over-riding direction.

While the RBS board might not like this, and might choose to resign out of protest (or perhaps pique), it is difficult to see that the directors would be legally obliged to do so, as complying with such an over-riding direction could hardly constitute a breach of directors' duties..

PHILIP GOLDENBERG
WOKING, SURREY

Sir Fred open to legal action

Thomas Wiggins (letters, 4 March) is unduly pessimistic about the rights of RBS shareholders to sue Sir Fred Goodwin.

Here is the way, assuming that RBS itself (either of its own motion or kicked by the Government as its majority shareholder) is not willing to do so.

A group of shareholders (it would be good to see at least some financial institutions breaking from the City club to join in) formally request the board of RBS to institute proceedings against Sir Fred for misfeasance. If RBS refuses, the shareholders apply to the High Court to commence a "derivative action" under the 2006 Companies Act – suing on behalf and in the name of RBS and entitled to use its money to pursue the action. Any takers?

PHILIP GOLDENBERG
WOKING, SURREY

In the context of the row over MPs' expenses, particularly in relation to second homes, I made an imaginative suggestion:

Keith Farman (letters, 28 April) suggests buying a hotel near the House of Commons to provide accommodation for MPs. But there is a simpler and less costly option. After 2012, there will be an entire athletes' village, with spartan accommodation, looking for new occupants.

PHILIP GOLDENBERG
WOKING, SURREY

The elderly lothario, Italy's ghastly Prime Minister Silvio Berlusconi, was investigated for misconduct with a minor:

Too old

Should not Berlusconi have been charged with over-age sex?

PHILIP GOLDENBERG
WOKING, SURREY

The equally dreadful Rupert Murdoch closes the News of the World in a failed attempt to save its editor, Rebekah Wade:

> Greater love hath no Murdoch than this, that he lays down his title for his friend.
> **PHILIP GOLDENBERG**
> WOKING, SURREY

Another dig at David Owen:

> ## Cross reaction
> Please correct your front-page howler in describing the cross-bencher Lord Owen as a "Liberal Democrat peer" (13 October) before the Party suffers mass resignations.
> **PHILIP GOLDENBERG**
> Woking Surrey

One of my late father's favourite stories came in useful:

> The horseburger scandal recalls the story of the New York deli which advertised sausages as being "50 per cent chicken". On examination by the relevant authorities, the chicken content was found to be 2 per cent. In court, the proprietor's defence was that the sausage mixture consisted of an equal number of horses and chickens.
> **PHILIP GOLDENBERG**
> Woking,
> Surrey

A good quote from Cicero:

Pleasures of age?

Terence Blacker writes about
late-flowering lust (31 July).
Cicero had it right in his treatise
on old age: *Summmam voluptatem
nullis egere* – the greatest pleas-
ure is not to feel the want of any.
PHILIP GOLDENBERG
Woking, Surrey

I went to the theatre to see the wonderful Helen Mirren in The
Audience. A subsequent performance suffered interference from
external noise. In the interval, she went out in full theatrical fig
and gave the noisemakers some unladylike words of disapproval. I
couldn't resist this thought:

After her recent "performance",
will Helen Mirren next play the
Duke of Edinburgh?
PHILIP GOLDENBERG
Woking, Surrey

Both the Mayor of Toronto, and the – woefully inadequate – chair
of the Co-operative Bank had been forced out as a result of drug
addictions.

**MAN WITH THE
PERFECT CV**
Should not the Mayor of
Toronto become the next
chair of the Co-op Bank?
Philip Goldenberg
Woking, Surrey

An ultra-left-wing political commentator for The Independent suggested a link between socialism and nationalism. I helped to clarify his thinking:

> **SINISTER PRECEDENT**
> Political scientists have a label for the overlap Owen Jones (16 January) suggests between socialism and Ukippery. They call it National Socialism.
> **Philip Goldenberg**
> *Woking, Surrey*

And another dig I couldn't resist, this time at David Cameron:

> You report (27 June) an EU diplomat as saying that Jean-Claude Juncker's alcohol consumption "has been raised by a number of EU leaders". If I'd been in his position dealing with Mr Cameron over the past month, mine would have been too.
> **Philip Goldenberg**
> *Woking, Surrey*

Boris Johnson, on a mayoral trip to Japan, had joined in a game of rugby with some waif-like children and had flattened one of them. He said he hadn't seen the victim. At the same time, there was public concern about fatal accidents suffered by cyclists at the hands of careless lorry drivers. I loved the chosen headline:

> **DANGER OF BULKY OBJECTS IN MOTION**
> The Mayor of London is working on proposals for ensuring that lorries have all-round visibility to protect vulnerable cyclists.
> Perhaps these proposals should be extended to tubby, middle-aged politicians playing rugby with vulnerable children.
> **Philip Goldenberg**
> *Woking*

And then there's Brexit:

> **Who is on which side in EU debate?**
>
> IN the run-up to the EU Referendum, campaigners on both sides will at best present complicated facts in simplistic ways, and at worst deliberately distort them.
> So it is also helpful to look at who is on which side.
> Those who advocate the UK leaving the European Union include:
> ■ The self-seeking self-publicist Boris Johnson;
> ■ The charlatan Nigel Farage;
> ■ The extreme left-winger George Galloway;
> ■ The French fascist leader Marine le Pen;
> ■ The Russian communist leader Vladimir Putin; and
> ■ The Bonkers Brigade of the Conservative Party.
> So it's not a difficult decision for sane people, is it?
> **PHILIP GOLDENBERG**
> **White Rose Lane**
> **Woking**